DAILY TEXTS

Bible Texts with Hymn Verses and Prayers
for Every Day in the Year

2008

Two Hundred Seventy-Eighth Year

The Moravian Church in North America
1021 Center St., Bethlehem, PA 18018
459 S. Church St., Winston-Salem, NC 27101
www.moravian.org

Moravian Daily Texts 2008

Book design: Sandy Fay, Laughing Horse Graphics, Inc., Doylestown, PA

Printed by McNaughton & Gunn, Inc., Saline, MI

Printed in the United States of America

ISBN: 978-1-933571-05-8 large print edition
ISBN: 978-1-933571-04-1 paperback edition
ISBN: 978-1-933571-01-0 hardcover edition

ISBN 978-193357104-1
51000
9 781933 571041

NEW EVERY MORNING

"The steadfast love of the Lord never ceases, his mercies never come to an end; they are new every morning."
Lamentations 3:22,23

The first printed edition of the *Daily Texts (Losungen)* was published in Herrnhut, Saxony, in 1731. The title page of that edition quoted the passage from Lamentations and promised a daily message from God that would be new every morning. It was an outgrowth of a spiritual renewal of the Moravian Church (Unitas Fratrum) that dated from August 13, 1727.

In 1722 refugees from Bohemia and Moravia began arriving at the estate of Count Nicholas Ludwig von Zinzendorf (1700-1760), where he gave them a welcome and land on which to establish the settlement of Herrnhut ("Watch of the Lord").

Each day the settlers came together for morning and evening devotions, consciously placing their lives in the context of God's Word. On May 3, 1728, during the evening service, Count Zinzendorf gave the congregation a "watchword" for the next day. It was to be a "Losung" (watchword) to accompany them through the whole day.

Thereafter one or more persons of the congregation went daily to each of the 32 houses in Herrnhut to bring them the watchword for the day, and engage the families in pastoral conversations about the text.

From this oral tradition, the *Daily Texts* soon became fixed in printed form. Zinzendorf compiled 365 watchwords for the year and the first edition of the Losungen was published for 1731.

Even in the first editions there appeared the characteristic coupling of a Bible verse and hymn stanza. Zinzendorf called the hymns "collects" and considered them to be the answer of the congregation to the Word of God. *The Daily Texts* would be a great deal poorer without the mixture of God's Word and our human response.

The watchword soon became accompanied by a "doctrinal" text. The idea of an additional text grew out of a number of collections of texts from the Bible that were put together by Zinzendorf. Such additional lists (some of them for children) were used for special study within the groups in the community, and they came to be referred to as doctrinal texts.

For the *Daily Texts*, as for the whole Moravian Church, Count Zinzendorf's death (May 9, 1760), was a turning point. His co-workers sensed the uniqueness of Zinzendorf's watchwords, textbooks, and lessons and had them published at Barby-on-the-Elbe in a four-volume collection 1762.

From then on the watchwords and doctrinal texts are distinguished by the way they are selected each year. The watchwords are chosen from various verse collections and, since 1788, they have been drawn by lot from a collection of around 2,000 suitable Old Testament texts. The doctrinal texts are not chosen by lot but are selected. The difference between the watchwords and doctrinal texts was explained in 1801 as follows: "The watchword is either a promise, an encouragement, an admonition or word of comfort; the doctrinal text contains a point of revealed doctrine."

By 1812 it was established that all watchwords would be drawn by lot from a selection of Old Testament texts, and the doctrinal texts would be selected from the New Testament. No doctrinal text is used more than once in a given year. By the end of the nineteenth century, the custom was established to relate the two texts in theme or thought.

Into all the world

Another characteristic of the *Daily Texts* that was already apparent in the early years of its publication was its worldwide distribution. Missionaries who went as "messengers" from Herrnhut after 1732 had a *Daily Texts (Losungen)* in their luggage. They felt united with their home congregation through the daily contemplation of the same Scripture passages.

The *Daily Texts* of 1739 lists a multitude of places around the globe where messengers were witnessing for the Savior. The introduction read:

> "The Good Word of the Lord, 1739, From all the Prophets for His congregations, and servants at Herrnhut, Herrnhaag, Herrendijk [Holland], Pilgerruh [Denmark], Ebersdof, Jena, Amsterdam, Rotterdam, London, Oxford, Berlin, Greenland, St. Croix, St. John and St. Thomas [Virgin Islands], Berbice [Guyana], Palestine, Surinam, Savannah in Georgia, among the Moors in Carolina, with

> the wild Indians in Irene [an island in the Savannah River in Georgia], in Pennsylvania, among the Hottentots [South Africa], in Guinea, in Latvia, Estonia and Lithuania, Russia, on the White Sea, in Lappland, Norway, in Switzerland, [Isle of] Man, Hittland [Scotland], in prison, on pilgrimage, to Ceylon, Ethiopia, Persia, on visitation to the missionaries among the heathen, and elsewhere on land and sea."

This distribution of the Moravians into every continent in the known world seems all the more amazing when you consider that the settlement at Herrnhut was only 17 years old, and the first missionaries had gone out only seven years earlier in 1732.

Present membership of the worldwide Moravian Church is over 700,000 in 19 provinces. The *Daily Texts* has a press run of over 1,000,000 copies in the German language alone. This far surpasses the 30,000 members of the Moravian Church in all of Europe. Other language editions bring the total circulation of this small devotional book to over 1.5 million copies. The *Daily Texts* is now published in 51 languages and dialects, including some of the following:

Afrikaans, Batak, Chichewa, Chinese (Hong Kong), Czech, Danish, Dutch, English, Estonian, Finnish, French, German, Hindi, Hmong, Hungarian, Indonesian, Inuktut (Labrador), Japanese, Kiswahili (Tanzania), Latvian, Miskito (Nicaragua, Honduras), Naga, Odiya, Ovambo (Nambia), Polish, Portuguese (Brazil), Rongmei, Russian, Swedish, Sepedi (South Africa), Setswana (South Africa), Simalungan (Indonesia), Slovak, Spanish (Argentina), Sranang (Surinam), Thai, Tibetan, Venda (South Africa), Xhosa (South Africa), Zulu (South Africa).

The physical form of the Daily Texts varies considerably from country to country. Some, like this North American edition, have a separate page for the verses, hymns, and prayers of each day. Others have several days' texts printed on one page, which makes a thin, pocket-size volume. Some are beautiful examples of the printing and bookbinding arts. Others are simply mimeographed and stapled together.

These external nonessentials pale beside the fact that this little book is probably the most widely read devotional guide in the world, next to the Bible. It forms an invisible bond between Christians on all continents, transcending barriers of confession, race, language, and politics. In its quiet way it performs a truly ecumenical service for the whole of Christendom.

North American editions

The printing of the *Daily Texts* in North America dates back at least to 1767, when the Losungen was printed "at Bethlehem on the Forks of the Delaware by Johan Brandmuller." The printer's imprint bears the date of 1767 as well and may have been an extra printing for the German version done at Barby-on-the-Elbe in Germany, where most of the printing was done for the Moravian Church those days.

During the crucial days of the Revolution, the German-language edition was printed in Philadelphia by Heinrich Miller, who had worked for Benjamin Franklin when he first came to America. The daily text for July 4, 1776, was from Isaiah 55:5 — "Behold, you shall call nations that you know not, and nations that knew you not shall run to you" (RSV).

English versions were printed in London as early as 1746, and the title page bears the imprint of "James Hutton near the Golden Lion in Fetter Lane." Hutton was the well-known London printer associated with the Moravian Church who was a friend of John and Charles Wesley in the formative years of their ministry.

The 1850s were crucial years for the Moravian Church in North America as the congregations established in the United States broke away from direct control from the Moravian headquarters in Europe. Both German and English editions of the *Daily Texts* were regularly printed in Philadelphia or Bethlehem, Pennsylvania, and in a few years the custom was established to include the statistics of the provinces and districts of the Moravian Church in North America.

The biblical texts for each day are chosen in Herrnhut, Germany, and then sent around the world to those who prepare the different language editions. Since 1959 the edition published in the United States has included a prayer for each day. For this North American edition, the hymns are chosen or written, and the prayers are written by Moravian clergy and laypersons from the United States and Canada. Each month is prepared by a different individual or couple, of a variety of ages, so that the prayers reflect the great diversity of devotion in the Moravian Church.

DAILY TOPICS FOR PRAYER

On August 27, 1727, certain members of the Moravian Church in Herrnhut, Saxony, formed a remarkable prayer union known as the "Hourly Intercession." This provided that, for every hour of the day and night, one of the volunteer intercessors would, for one hour in private, bear on his or her heart and mind the interests and hopes of the Kingdom of God in the world. This wonderful intercession continued for over 100 years.

On August 27, 1872, a Moravian Prayer union was formed in England as a form of resuscitation of the Hourly Intercession, and today its members are found in all areas of the Moravian world. You are invited to join in this prayer covenant. The following prayer suggestions may be helpful:

SUNDAY — THE CHURCH AT WORSHIP. For her purity and peace, unity and power. For the congregation to which we belong or with which we worship. For the ministry of the word of God. For the winning of people into fellowship with Christ. For all church schools, youth ministries, and other church groups at work.

MONDAY — THE CHURCH AT WORK. For the church in its mission next door and in other lands. For new congregations and specialized ministries. For the workers and leaders in these endeavors. For the worker volunteers to carry out the mission of the church.

TUESDAY — HOME AND SCHOOL. For households. For the Christian education of the young, and that our children may be led to give themselves to Christ. For all schools and teachers. For young people enrolled in colleges and universities. For the training of ministers in theological seminaries.

WEDNESDAY — FOR THOSE IN NEED. For all in special need, whether as aged, sick, poor, or homeless. For those in prison. For all victims of famine, oppression, aggression, and war.

THURSDAY — OUR NATION AND OUR WORLD. For those who govern and for those who are governed. For the guidance of God to all who are in authority. For unity of nations and all agencies for peace. For the whole human family and equal rights for all. For the guidance and blessing of God as humanity has entered the space age.

FRIDAY — OUR OWN CHURCH FELLOWSHIP. For the purity, zeal, and practice of the church as a witnessing fellowship of the love of God. That the church may be a light to the world wherever its congregations are found, and that it may be active in redeeming mission in these communities.

SATURDAY — THE WITNESS OF CHRISTIANS. That all who confess the name of Christ may grow in the grace and knowledge of Jesus Christ as Lord and Savior.

"O thou King of kings and Lord of lords, who desirest that all people should dwell together in unity, let thy will be known and done among the nations; guide their feet into the way of peace. Remember us and all humanity in thy mercy. Deliver us from the sins which give rise to war and conflict, and strengthen within our hearts the will to establish righteousness and justice in the earth. Give unto us and to all who worship thee the sincere desire to live in peaceful and loving fellowship with all people. Fix our minds and hearts upon thine eternal purposes for your children on earth."

— *A Prayer for Peace*

THE DAILY TEXTS IN FAMILY WORSHIP

Almost from the very beginning the *Daily Texts* has been used as a guide for family worship as well as for private and personal devotions. The use of the *Daily Texts* in family worship will vary from family to family and will be dependent upon a number of conditions such as the time available and the age of the children. One of the values of the *Daily Texts* is that it is adaptable to numerous patterns of use.

One pattern that is followed by many families is to begin the meal (usually breakfast or the evening meal) with the reading of the texts of the day and the accompanying hymn stanzas. After this, the family joins in the blessing or table grace. A suitable blessing may be chosen from among the following:

Come, Lord Jesus, our Guest to be,
and bless these gifts bestowed by thee.
Bless thy dear ones everywhere,
and keep them in thy loving care.

Be present at our table, Lord;
be here and everywhere adored;
from thine all-bounteous hand our food
may we receive with gratitude.

The worship of the family can then close with a prayer offered in the leader's own words or in those of the printed prayer offered in the *Daily Texts*. As a part of free prayer by the leader or in connection with the printed prayer, use can be made from day to day of the subjects of the Daily Topics for Prayer as given in the preceding pages.

ACKNOWLEDGMENTS

Bible texts in this publication are quoted from the *New Revised Standard Version Bible*, copyright © 1989 by the Division of Christian Education of the National Council of the Churches of Christ in the United States of America, and are used by permission. Verses marked NIV are taken from *The Holy Bible New International Version*, copyright © 1973, 1978, 1984 by International Bible Society. Used by permission of Zondervan Publishing House. Verses marked KJV are taken from the King James Version, copyright © 1607. Verses marked NASB are taken from the New American Standard, copyright © 1997 by Thomas Nelson Publishers.

Sunday readings are taken from the *Revised Common Lectionary*, copyright © 1992 by the Consultation on Common Texts (CCT).

Unless otherwise noted, hymn stanzas found in the *Daily Texts* are taken from the *Moravian Book of Worship*, 1995. The number found at the right of each stanza designates the source of the stanza in that hymnal. If the number is preceded by a p the hymn used is from one of the liturgies and the p designates the page number. The letter OW after a number denotes the *Liturgy and the Offices of Worship and Hymns*, 1908. The letters br after a number denotes the *British Moravian Hymn Book with Services*, 1960. The letter r after a number denotes the *Hymnal of the Moravian Church*, 1969. When hymns are copyrighted, information is given at the bottom of the page; we gratefully acknowledge permission to use copyrighted material.

Hymn stanzas are broken down by meter except when space would not allow.

The Scripture readings for Monday through Saturday are part of a plan to read through the Old and New Testaments in two years and the Psalms in one year.

Tuesday, January 1 — Psalm 1
Genesis 1:1-2:3; Matthew 1:1-17

Woe to the foolish prophets who follow their own spirit and have seen nothing! Ezekiel 13:3 (NIV)

Be thou my vision, O Lord of my heart; 719
nought be all else to me save that thou art —
thou my best thought, by day or by night,
waking or sleeping, thy presence my light.

Test everything; hold fast to what is good. 1 Thessalonians 5:21

In loving service may our lives be spent, 587
in other's gladness finding sweet content,
striving to show God's fellowship to all.
To show God's loving work-the servants' call.
In loving service may our lives be spent.

Precious Lord, grant us this new year a greater mindfulness of your presence. Having seen the light, may we resolve together to walk in it. Amen.

Wednesday, January 2 — Psalm 2
Genesis 2:4-25; Matthew 1:18-25

You have made human beings a little lower than God, and crowned them with glory and honor. Psalm 8:5

Fairest Lord Jesus! 470
King of creation!
Son of God and Son of man!
Truly I'd love thee,
truly I'd serve thee,
light of my soul, my joy, my crown.

In this is love, not that we loved God but that he loved us. 1 John 4:10

Jesus' love unbounded 770
none can e'er explain,
yet we, his disciples,
often cause him pain;
even they forget him
who have seen his face;
even they still grieve him
who enjoy his grace.

Alpha and Omega, though we bear your holy image, we are often the first to blame and the last to forgive. Teach us instead to be the first to love and the last to condemn. Amen.

Thursday, January 3 — Psalm 3
Genesis 3,4; Matthew 2:1-12

From the rising of the sun to its setting the name of the Lord is to be praised. Psalm 113:3

Let earth's wide circle round 552
in joyful notes resound:
may Jesus Christ be praised!
Let air and sea and sky
from depth to height reply:
may Jesus Christ be praised!

The night is almost gone, the day is near. Let us then lay aside the works of darkness and put on the armor of light. Romans 13:12

Long my imprisoned spirit lay 773
fast bound in sin and nature's night.
Your sunrise turned that night to day;
I woke — the dungeon flamed with light!
My chains fell off, your voice I knew;
was freed, I rose, and followed you.

You deliver us, Lord, from many things so that we can belong to Christ alone. May our lives which are freely lived, freely shared, and freely given bring honor, praise, and glory to your name. Amen.

Friday, January 4 — Psalm 4
Genesis 5; Matthew 2:13-23

Do not be afraid, Abram. I am your shield, your very great reward. Genesis 15:1 (NIV)

Tenderly he shields and spares us, 529
well our feeble frame he knows,
in his hands he gently bears us,
rescues us from all our foes.
Alleluia! Alleluia! Widely as his mercy flows.

Those who believe are blessed with Abraham who believed. Galatians 3:9

O let that faith which you have taught 703
be treasured in our breast,
the evidence of unseen joys,
the substance of our rest.

Faithful and heavenly Father, forgive us the things we love more than you. You are the source of every good thing, each tender mercy and all blessing. May we love you even more than these gifts. Amen.

Saturday, January 5 — Psalm 5
Genesis 6:1-7:10; Matthew 3

You shall eat in plenty and be satisfied, and praise the name of the Lord your God. Joel 2:26

I love to tell the story, 625
for those who know it best
seem hungering and thirsting
to hear it, like the rest.
And when, in scenes of glory,
I sing the new, new song,
I'll sing the old, old story
that I have loved so long.
I love to tell the story;
I'll sing this theme in glory
and tell the old, old story
of Jesus and his love.

Taking the five loaves and the two fish, Jesus looked up to heaven, and blessed and broke the loaves, and gave them to his disciples to set before the people; and he divided the two fish among them all. And all ate and were filled. Mark 6:41,42

As you, Lord, have lived for others, 648
so may we for others live;
freely have your gifts been granted;
freely may your servants give.
Yours the gold and yours the silver,
yours the wealth of land and sea;
we but stewards of your bounty
held in solemn trust will be.

Your generosity, Lord, humbles and inspires us. Make us more giving of all that we are. Make us more trusting in all that you are. Humbled and inspired, send us to all who hunger and thirst. Amen.

Second Sunday after Christmas
Epiphany of the Lord

Watchword for the Week — Praise the name of the Lord, for his name alone is exalted; his glory is above earth and heaven. Psalm 148:13

Watchword for the Day — Arise, shine; for your light has come, and the glory of the Lord has risen upon you. Isaiah 60:1

Sunday, January 6 — Jeremiah 31:7-14; Psalm 147:12-20
Ephesians 1:3-14; John 1(1-9),10-18

Epiphany of the Lord — Isaiah 60:1-6; Psalm 72:1-7,10-14
Ephesians 3:1-12; Matthew 2:1-12

You shall not make for yourself an idol in the form of anything. Deuteronomy 5:8 (NIV)

Jesus calls us from the worship 600
of the vain world's golden store,
from each idol that would keep us,
saying, "Christian, love me more."

Jesus said, "Whoever has seen me has seen the Father." John 14:9

Where is the blessedness I knew, 467r
when first I saw the Lord?
Where is the soul-refreshing view
of Jesus and his word?

The way, the truth, and the life, help us to follow you, to know you, and to live for you. Make us wise in our seeking and grateful for all we find in you. Amen.

Monday, January 7 — Psalm 6
Genesis 7:11-8:22; Matthew 4:1-11

Then once more you shall see the difference between one who serves God and one who does not serve him. Malachi 3:18

Jesus calls us; by your mercies, 600
Savior, may we hear your call,
give our hearts to your obedience,
serve and love you best of all.

Pay close attention to yourself and to your teaching; continue in these things, for in doing this you will save both yourself and your hearers. 1 Timothy 4:16

Your blessed people, trusting in your merit, 400
on the earth's extended face
from each other far, but one in spirit,
sound with one accord your praise.
May we never cease to make confession
that your death's the cause of our salvation;
we to you, our Head and King,
joyful hallelujahs sing.

Christ, the good Shepherd and Lamb of God, grant us this day the willingness and the strength to follow both your lead and your example. Amen.

Tuesday, January 8 — Psalm 7:1-9
Genesis 9; Matthew 4:12-25

Reuben said to his brothers, "Shed no blood." Genesis 37:22

O come, Desire of Nations, bind 274
all people in one heart and mind;
bid envy, strife and quarrels cease;
fill the whole world with heaven's peace.
Rejoice! Rejoice! Immanuel
shall come to you, O Israel!

Now that you have purified your souls by your obedience to the truth so that you have genuine mutual love, love one another deeply from the heart. 1 Peter 1:22

They who Jesus' mercy know 416
are from wrath and envy freed;
love unto our neighbor shows
that we are his flock indeed;
thus we may in all our ways
show forth our Redeemer's praise.

Purge from us, Prince of peace, all indifference or resignation to the devaluing and destruction of human life. Create in us hearts that are broken and filled with your love for this world. Amen.

Wednesday, January 9 — Psalm 7:10-17
Genesis 10:1-11:9; Matthew 5:1-16

There is forgiveness with you, so that you may be revered. Psalm 130:4

Then bless his holy name, 546
whose grace has made us whole,
whose loving kindness crowns our days!
O bless the Lord, my soul!

Therefore, knowing the fear of the Lord, we try to persuade others. 2 Corinthians 5:11

O Holy Spirit, stir us now, 299
inspire our hearts to make this vow:
we will go forth into the night
and share with all your gift of light.

Spirit of the living God, embolden us to preach and to proclaim, to speak, to sing, and to share the good news that is ours to tell! Amen.

Thursday, January 10 — Psalm 8
Genesis 11:10-12:9; Matthew 5:17-26

Your steadfast love, O Lord, extends to the heavens, your faithfulness to the clouds. Psalm 36:5

Lamb of God, you shall remain forever 346
of our songs the only theme;
for your boundless love, your grace and favor,
we will praise your saving name;
that for our transgressions you were wounded
shall by us in nobler strains be sounded,
when we, perfected in love,
once shall join the church above.

God is faithful; by him you were called into the fellowship of his Son, Jesus Christ our Lord. 1 Corinthians 1:9

You're our strength and motivation, 622*
Christ, you send us out to serve.
We hold back, but your salvation
gives us energy and nerve.
You still fill us with your Spirit;
lift us up on eagle's wings.
Give your call, we gladly hear it;
in your work our spirit sings.

You who are love and faithfulness, let each of us hear, respond, and give thanks for your call in our lives. Call us beyond ourselves. Call us to our neighbors. Call us to you. Amen.

Friday, January 11 — Psalm 9:1-10
Genesis 12:10-13:18; Matthew 5:27-42

Out of the depths I cry to you, O Lord. Lord, hear my voice! Psalm 130:1,2

When we seem in vain to pray 352
and our hope seems far away,
in the darkness be our stay:
hear us, holy Jesus.

The woman came up behind Jesus and touched his cloak, for she said, "If I but touch his clothes, I will be made well." Mark 5:27,28

May we in our guilt and shame 352
still your love and mercy claim,
calling humbly on your name:
hear us, holy Jesus.

Light of the world, reveal your glory. Drive away the darkness that hides you from us, and cast from our hearts the shadows in which we hide from you. Amen.

Saturday, January 12 — Psalm 9:11-20
Genesis 14,15; Matthew 5:43-6:4

Shall we receive the good at the hand of God, and not receive the bad? Job 2:10

Give patience as we watch and weep, 750
though mercy long delay;
give courage our faint souls to keep,
and trust you though you slay.

God is faithful, and he will not let you be tested beyond your strength, but with the testing he will also provide the way out so that you may be able to endure it.
1 Corinthians 10:13

I need thee ev'ry hour; 740
stay thou near by;
temptations lose their pow'r
when thou art nigh.
I need thee, O I need thee,
ev'ry hour I need thee!
O bless me now, my Savior —
I come to thee!

Your ways are high, almighty God, bringing us beyond understanding, to the limits of endurance, and to the very end of ourselves. Help us to find in these places, Lord, a deeper faith in you. Amen.

First Sunday after the Epiphany

Watchword for the Week — A bruised reed he will not break, and a dimly burning wick he will not quench; he will faithfully bring forth justice. Isaiah 42:3

Sunday, January 13 — Isaiah 42:1-9; Psalm 29
Acts 10:34-43; Matthew 3:13-17

And all the people responded with a great shout when they praised the Lord, because the foundation of the house of the Lord was laid. Ezra 3:11

Glorious things of you are spoken, 522
Zion, city of our God;
he whose word cannot be broken
formed you for his own abode;
on the rock of ages founded,
what can shake your sure repose?
With salvation's walls surrounded
you may smile at all your foes.

Do you not know that you are God's temple and that God's Spirit dwells in you? 1 Corinthians 3:16

We are God's house of living stones, 512
built for his own habitation;
he fills our hearts, his humble thrones,
granting us life and salvation.
Yet to this place, an earthly frame,
we come with thanks to praise his name;
God grants his people true blessing.

Build us, O God, into holy places from which you reach out to bless and to heal. Awaken in us a deeper commitment to the greater works Christ entrusted to our hands. In Jesus' name. Amen.

Monday, January 14 — Psalm 10:1-11
Genesis 16,17; Matthew 6:5-18

The Lord guards the lives of his faithful. Psalm 97:10

What God's almighty pow'r has made, 537
in mercy he is keeping;
by morning glow or evening shade
his eye is never sleeping.
And where he rules in kingly might,
there all is just and all is right:
to God all praise and glory!

And after you have suffered for a little while, the God of all grace, who has called you to his eternal glory in Christ, will himself restore, support, strengthen, and establish you. 1 Peter 5:10

Let ev'ry tongue and ev'ry tribe 403
responsive to his call,
to him all majesty ascribe
and crown him Lord of all.

How truly full of wonder it is, Lord, that you mind and care for us. You, who alone are holy; before whom the earth trembles and mountains melt. You, who alone gave yourself for the sake of the world. Thank you. Amen.

Tuesday, January 15 — Psalm 10:12-18
Genesis 18; Matthew 6:19-34

Obey me, and I will be your God and you will be my people. Jeremiah 7:23 (NIV)

As it was without beginning, 458
so it lasts without end;
to their children's children ever
shall God's righteousness extend.

They who have my commandments and keep them are those who love me. John 14:21

Unto such as keep God's cov'nant 458
and are steadfast in his way,
unto those who still remember
the commandments and obey.

Christ our teacher, gentle and humble in heart, help us relate trusting obedience to loving service. May we truly find rest for our souls under the yoke that is easy and the burden that is light. Amen.

Wednesday, January 16 — Psalm 11
Genesis 19:1-29; Matthew 7:1-12

The Lord your God is gracious and merciful, and will not turn away his face from you, if you return to him. 2 Chronicles 30:9

With grateful joy and holy fear, 785*
God's charity we learn;
let us with heart and mind and soul
now love God in return.

Jesus said, "The time is fulfilled, and the kingdom of God has come near; repent, and believe in the good news." Mark 1:15

Straight shall be what long was crooked, 264
and the rougher places plain!
Let your hearts be true and humble,
as befits his holy reign!
For the glory of the Lord
now on earth is shed abroad,
and all flesh shall see the token
that God's word is never broken.

The turning you ask of us, righteous Judge, is away from sin, evil, and selfishness toward the source of goodness and light. Let it also be through us a returning and a sharing of the love you give. Amen.

Thursday, January 17 — Psalm 12
Genesis 19:30-20:18; Matthew 7:13-23

How long, O Lord? Will you forget me forever? How long will you hide your face from me? Psalm 13:1

Pass me not, O gentle Savior, 772
hear my humble cry;
while on others thou art smiling,
do not pass me by.
Savior, Savior, hear my humble cry;
while on others thou art calling;
do not pass me by.

And even the hairs of your head are all counted. Matthew 10:30

O Jesus, you have promised 603
to all who follow you
that where you are in glory
your servants shall be too.
And Jesus, I have promised
to serve you to the end;
O give me grace to follow,
my master and my friend.

Lord, whenever doubt or fear gets the better of us, remind us gently but firmly that we are yours and belong to you. May we then be rest assured in your care and claim on our lives. Amen.

Friday, January 18 — Psalm 13
Genesis 21; Matthew 7:24-8:4

All that the Lord has spoken we will do, and we will be obedient. Exodus 24:7

O blessed Lord, teach me your law, 510
your righteous judgments I declare;
your testimonies make me glad,
for they are wealth beyond compare.

Jesus said, "Do not think that I have come to abolish the law or the prophets; I have come not to abolish but to fulfill." Matthew 5:17

You are the way, the truth, the life; 661
grant us that way to know;
that truth to keep, that life to win,
whose joys eternal flow.

Author and finisher of our faith and salvation, grant us the strength to love and keep your law. Grant us also the humility to accept our need for your help to do this. Amen.

Saturday, January 19 — Psalm 14
Genesis 22; Matthew 8:5-22

What god in heaven or on earth can perform deeds and mighty acts like yours! Deuteronomy 3:24

I have no help but yours, nor do I need 421
another arm but yours to lean upon;
it is enough, O Lord, enough indeed;
my strength is in your might, your might alone.

There are varieties of activities, but it is the same God who activates all of them in everyone. 1 Corinthians 12:6

Then forth they went, with tongues of flame 396
in one blessed theme delighting;
the love of Jesus, and his name,
God's children all uniting.
That love our theme and watchword still;
the law of love may we fulfill —
give love as love we're given.

I Am, reveal the power of this name! Ever present; ever living; ever active in loving kindness — you are. Gift us with a vision of your all-sufficiency to deliver us, make us one, and redeem all things to yourself. Amen.

Second Sunday after the Epiphany

Watchword for the Week — God is faithful; by him you were called into the fellowship of his Son, Jesus Christ our Lord.
1 Corinthians 1:9

Sunday, January 20 — Isaiah 49:1-7; Psalm 40:1-11
1 Corinthians 1:1-9; John 1:29-42

You gave me room when I was in distress. Be gracious to me, and hear my prayer. Psalm 4:1

For God, in grace and tenderness, 519
regarded us in our distress;
yea, to our aid himself he came;
let all adore God's holy name.

**God consoles us in all our affliction, so that we may be able to console those who are in any affliction with the consolation with which we ourselves are consoled by God.
2 Corinthians 1:4**

Christ bids each afflicted soul 416
"Come that I may soothe your grief.
No one who is strong and whole
needs a doctor for relief;
therefore have no fear, draw nigh,
that your want I may supply."

Release us, Lord, from the fear and shame of brokenness. Assure us that we can always cry out to you; that we can run to you and hide with all the innocence and intensity of a childlike faith. Amen.

Monday, January 21 — Psalm 15
Genesis 23:1-24:25; Matthew 8:23-34

Let us test and examine our ways, and return to the Lord. Lamentations 3:40

While we, deeply humbled, 746
own we're oft to blame,
this remains our comfort,
you are still the same.
In you all the needy
have a friend most dear,
whose love and forbearance
unexampled are.

Be careful then how you live, not as unwise people but as wise. Ephesians 5:15

'Twas grace that taught my heart to fear 783
and grace my fears relieved;
how precious did that grace appear
the hour I first believed.

What does it mean to "fear" you, Lord? Just as you show us how to love; grant us also a righteous perspective, a heavenly point of view, a godly fear that leads from death to life. Amen.

Tuesday, January 22 — Psalm 16:1-6
Genesis 24:26-66; Matthew 9:1-13

I will seek the lost, and I will bring back the strayed. Ezekiel 34:16

Know that the Lord is God indeed; 539
he formed us all without our aid.
We are the flock he comes to feed,
the sheep who by his hand were made.

Jesus said, "If a shepherd has a hundred sheep, and one of them has gone astray, does he not leave the ninety-nine on the mountains and go in search of the one that went astray?" Matthew 18:12

O Christians, haste, your mission high fulfilling, 618
to tell to all the world that God is light,
that he who made all nations is not willing
one life should perish, lost in shades of night.
Publish glad tidings, tidings of peace,
tidings of Jesus, redemption, and release.

Thank you, God of the sparrow, for loving each of us as if there were only one of us to love! Amen.

Wednesday, January 23 — Psalm 16:7-11
Genesis 25; Matthew 9:14-26

O Lord, you brought up my soul from Sheol, restored me to life. Psalm 30:3

As a mother looks with favor 659
on the new life in her arms,
searching ev'ry small expression,
sav'ring moments filled with charm,
so God smiles on ev'ry person,
so God takes such keen delight
in the praises that we offer;
we are precious in God's sight.

Jesus spoke to the disciples, "Take heart, it is I; do not be afraid." Then he got into the boat with them and the wind ceased. Mark 6:50,51

Perfect submission, all is at rest, 714
I in my Savior am happy and blessed,
watching and waiting, looking above,
filled with his goodness, lost in his love.
This is my story, this is my song,
praising my Savior all the day long.
This is my story, this is my song,
praising my Savior all the day long.

Your love, Jesus, is truly majestic, soaring higher than poetry or melody. It is the world's brightest hope and deepest dream, but also the path we walk together and the very air we breathe. Loving God, we praise you! Amen.

Thursday, January 24 — Psalm 17:1-7
Genesis 26; Matthew 9:27-38

I call upon God, and the Lord will save me. Psalm 55:16

My soul before you prostrate lies; 721
to you, its Source, my spirit flies;
O turn to me your cheering face;
I'm poor, enrich me with your grace.

When they bring you to trial and hand you over, do not worry beforehand about what you are to say; but say whatever is given you at that time. Mark 13:11

If dangers gather round, 615
still keep me calm and fearless;
help me to bear the cross
when life is bleak and cheerless,
to overcome my foes
with words and actions kind;
O God, your will disclose,
your counsel let me find.

Having you as our advocate, in whose favor we have our being, open our eyes to the needs of others. Make us, by your Spirit, defenders and upholders, allies of all who suffer. In Jesus' name. Amen.

Friday, January 25 — Psalm 17:8-15
Genesis 27:1-29; Matthew 10:1-16

The Lord said to Cain, "What have you done? Listen; your brother's blood is crying out to me from the ground!" Genesis 4:10

Savior, now with contrite hearts 741
we approach your throne of love,
asking pardon for our sins,
peace and comfort from above.
You once suffered on the cross
to atone for sinners' guilt;
may we never, Lord, forget
that for us your blood was spilled.

Whoever hates his brother is in the darkness and walks around in the darkness; he does not know where he is going, because the darkness has blinded him. 1 John 2:11 (NIV)

What splendid rays of truth and grace, 596
all other light excelling!
This I know when he in love
makes my heart his dwelling!

How easily we distance ourselves from the hateful, dear God! Has such a mark as Cain's ever fallen on us? Are we blind also? Even so, draw us from darkness into the light and cleanse the sin it reveals. Amen.

Saturday, January 26 — Psalm 18:1-6
Genesis 27:30-28:9; Matthew 10:17-25

Consider that this nation is your people. Exodus 33:13

Come, O long-expected Jesus, 262
born to set your people free;
From our fears and sins release us;
O, in you our rest shall be.
Israel's strength and consolation,
hope to all the earth impart,
Dear desire of ev'ry nation,
joy of ev'ry longing heart.

God has not rejected his people whom he foreknew. Romans 11:2

He by his name has sworn, 468
on this we shall depend,
and as on eagles' wings upborne
to heav'n ascend.
There we shall see his face,
his pow'r we shall adore
and sing the wonders of his grace
forevermore.

Eternal God, we share a long history and living witness with many who are like us and more who are not. Help us to recognize our brothers and sisters and the countless ways you bless us all. Amen.

Third Sunday after the Epiphany

Watchword for the Week — The Lord is my light and my salvation; whom shall I fear? The Lord is the stronghold of my life; of whom shall I be afraid? Psalm 27:1

Sunday, January 27 — Isaiah 9:1-4; Psalm 27:1,4-9
1 Corinthians 1:10-18; Matthew 4:12-23

The Lord said to Moses, "Who gives speech to mortals? Is it not I, the Lord? Now go, and I will be with your mouth and teach you what you are to speak." Exodus 4:11,12

"When through the deep waters I call you to go, 709
the rivers of sorrow shall not overflow;
for I will be with you in trouble to bless,
and sanctify to you your deepest distress."

Peter and the apostles answered, "We must obey God rather than any human authority." Acts 5:29

"The soul that on Jesus still leans for repose, 709
I will not, I will not desert to its foes;
that soul, though all hell should endeavor to shake,
I'll never, no, never, no, never forsake!"

Master and Friend, your holy word clarifies our loyalties. Purify our hearts to will one thing — that your will be done. In us and through us, on earth as it is in heaven. Amen.

Monday, January 28 — Psalm 18:7-15
Genesis 28:10-29:14; Matthew 10:26-42

My times are in your hand. Psalm 31:15

Other refuge have I none; 724
hangs my helpless soul on thee;
leave, ah, leave me not alone,
still support and comfort me.
All my trust on thee is stayed,
all my help from thee I bring;
cover my defenseless head
with the shadow of thy wing.

If we live, we live to the Lord, and if we die, we die to the Lord; so then, whether we live or whether we die, we are the Lord's. Romans 14:8

Then shall we in ev'ry state 586
soul and body dedicate
unto him who for us died,
till with him we're glorified.

Word of life and truth, guard and guide us away from all vain striving for the world's acceptance and approval. May we seek first and most diligently your kingdom and righteousness. Amen.

Tuesday, January 29 — Psalm 18:16-24
Genesis 29:15-30:24; Matthew 11:1-10

Turn my heart to your decrees, and not to selfish gain. Psalm 119:36

My heart is weak and poor 604
until it master find;
it has no spring of action sure,
it varies with the wind.
It cannot freely move
till you have wrought its chain;
enslave it with your matchless love,
and deathless it shall reign.

The love of money is a root of all kinds of evil. But as for you, man of God, shun all this; pursue righteousness, godliness, faith, love, endurance, gentleness. 1 Timothy 6:10,11

Grant us grace to see you, Lord, 313
mirrored in your holy word;
may we imitate you now,
and on us your grace endow;
that we like to you may be
at your great epiphany,
and may praise you ever blessed,
God in flesh made manifest.

How recklessly we spend and break ourselves, Bread of life, serving wealth, pleasure, and ourselves. Despite our best efforts and good intentions, our deepest hunger is for you. Feed us, Jesus. Amen.

Wednesday, January 30 — Psalm 18:25-29
Genesis 30:25-31:21; Matthew 11:11-24

Take your position, stand still, and see the victory of the Lord on your behalf. 2 Chronicles 20:17

To the hills I lift my eyes, 729
the everlasting hills.
Streaming forth in fresh supplies,
my soul the Spirit feels;
will he not his help afford?
Help, while yet I ask, is giv'n;
God comes down, the God and Lord
who made both earth and heav'n.

Do not worry about tomorrow, for tomorrow will bring worries of its own. Matthew 6:34

Teach me your patience; share with me 735
a closer, dearer company.
In work that keeps faith sweet and strong,
in trust that triumphs over wrong.

Christ, triumphant! Grant us a claim in your victory over fear, doubt, sin, and death. Accept our surrender to your claim on our lives as we cast our cares and our pride upon your mercy, love, and grace. Amen.

Thursday, January 31 — Psalm 18:30-36
Genesis 31:22-55; Matthew 11:25-12:8

They went to their tents, joyful and in good spirits because of all the goodness that the Lord had shown to his servant David and to his people Israel. 1 Kings 8:66

The church is God's abiding place, 439
his altar is within,
and here by faith we see God's face,
are cleansed from stain of sin.
A sanctuary for the soul,
where love can cast out fear,
where broken spirits are made whole,
for God himself is here.

To him who by the power at work within us is able to accomplish abundantly far more than all we can ask or imagine, to him be glory in the church and in Christ Jesus to all generations, forever and ever. Amen. Ephesians 3:20,21

All glory to our Lord and God 485
for love so deep, so high, so broad —
the Trinity, whom we adore
forever and forevermore.

Your overwhelming power is at work within us, God of dreams and wonders, and yet our asking and imagining is too small. Flood our hearts and minds, Holy Spirit, that we might dream impossibly and envision eternity — today! Amen.

Friday, February 1 — Psalm 18:37-45
Genesis 32:1-21; Matthew 12:9-21

In the Lord I take refuge. Psalm 11:1

Plenteous grace with thee is found, 724
grace to cover all my sin;
let the healing streams abound;
make and keep me pure within.
Thou of life the fountain art,
freely let me take of thee;
spring thou up within my heart,
rise to all eternity.

Such is the confidence that we have through Christ toward God. 2 Corinthians 3:4

Jesus, great High Priest of our profession, 400
we in confidence draw near;
grant us, then, in mercy, the confession
of our grateful hearts to hear;
you we gladly own in ev'ry nation,
Head and Master of your congregation,
conscious that in ev'ry place
you are giving life and grace.

O Lord of the heavens and the earth, you alone are our refuge and strength. May our witness be rooted not in our capacity for doing, but in our confidence of knowing Christ Jesus as Lord. Amen.

Saturday, February 2 — Psalm 18:46-50
Genesis 32:22-33:20; Matthew 12:22-32

Before I was humbled I went astray, but now I keep your word. Psalm 119:67

Give deep humility; 750
the sense of godly sorrow give,
a strong desiring confidence
to hear your voice and live.

The Lord answered Paul, "I am Jesus whom you are persecuting. But get up and stand on your feet; for I have appeared to you for this purpose, to appoint you to serve and testify to the things in which you have seen me and to those in which I will appear to you." Acts 26:15,16

Lord, speak to me that I may speak 646
in living echoes of your tone.
As you have sought, so let me seek
your erring children lost and lone.

Almighty God, your majesty renders humble both the great and the small. In humility, we ask you to open our eyes and raise us up to testify to your awesome power and love. Amen.

Last Sunday after the Epiphany
Transfiguration of our Lord

Watchword for the Week — God said, "This is my Son, the Beloved; with him I am well pleased; listen to him!" Matthew 17:5

Sunday, February 3 — Exodus 24:12-18; Psalm 2
2 Peter 1:16-21; Matthew 17:1-9

Speak the truth to one another. Zechariah 8:16

Keep me from saying words 615
that later need recalling;
guard me, lest idle speech
may from my lips be falling;
but when, within my place,
I must and ought to speak,
then to my words give grace,
lest I offend the weak.

Love does not rejoice in wrongdoing, but rejoices in the truth. 1 Corinthians 13:6

We covenant with hand and heart p209
to follow Christ our Lord;
with world, and sin, and self to part,
and to obey his word;
to love each other heartily,
in truth and with sincerity,
and under cross, reproach, and shame,
to glorify his name.

God of truth, teach us how to speak the truth as Jesus speaks: with unconditional love, grace, mercy, and peace. May his name be praised. Amen.

Monday, February 4 — Psalm 19:1-6
Genesis 34; Matthew 12:33-45

Unless the Lord builds the house, those who build it labor in vain. Psalm 127:1

There is a balm in Gilead 500
to make the wounded whole,
there is a balm in Gilead to heal the sin-sick soul.
Sometimes I feel discouraged,
and think my work's in vain
but then the Holy Spirit revives my soul again.

Paul wrote: We are God's fellow workers; you are God's field, God's building. 1 Corinthians 3:9 (NIV)

My hope is built on nothing less 771
than Jesus' blood and righteousness;
no merit of my own I claim
but wholly lean on Jesus' name.
On Christ the solid rock, I stand;
all other ground is sinking sand,
all other ground is sinking sand.

Redeemer God, you heal our underlying sin with the balm of Jesus' blood and prepare a new heart foundation. Thus restored, you invite us to labor together in the church built upon the rock of Christ. Amen.

Tuesday, February 5 — Psalm 19:7-14
Genesis 35:1-36:8; Matthew 12:46-13:9

The Lord God is a sun and shield. Psalm 84:11

Peace be to this congregation, 556
peace to ev'ry soul therein;
peace, which flows from Christ's salvation,
peace, the seal of cancelled sin,
peace that speaks its heav'nly Giver,
peace, to earthly minds unknown,
peace divine that lasts forever
here erect its glorious throne.

Jesus said to his disciples, "Why are you afraid? Have you still no faith?" Mark 4:40

Sometimes 'mid scenes of deepest gloom; 787
sometimes where Eden's bowers bloom,
by waters calm, o'er troubled sea,
still 'tis his hand that leadeth me.
He leadeth me, he leadeth me;
by his own hand he leadeth me,
his faithful foll'wer I would be,
for by his hand he leadeth me.

Blessing and honor and glory and power be unto you, O Ancient of days! To you who calm even the wind and the waves, we surrender our lives in faith. In the name of Jesus. Amen.

Ash Wednesday

Wednesday, February 6 — Psalm 20
Genesis 36:9-43; Matthew 13:10-23

Ash Wednesday — Joel 2:1-2,12-17; Psalm 51:1-17
2 Corinthians 5:20b-6:10; Matthew 6:1-6,16-21

**When you have eaten your fill,
take care that you do not forget the Lord.
Deuteronomy 6:11,12**

Praise God, who gives our daily bread 816
and has again our table spread.
May he with all his gifts impart
his crowning gift, a thankful heart.

**So, whether you eat or drink, or whatever you do, do everything for the glory of God.
1 Corinthians 10:31**

Break now the bread of life, 502
dear Lord, to me,
as when you broke the loaves
beside the sea.
Beyond the sacred page
I seek you, Lord;
my spirit waits for you, O living Word.

Lord God, in this season of Lent may we be reminded that you seek mercy rather than sacrifice. Instead of denying ourselves in the body, we resolve to share the spiritual food of Jesus with our neighbor. Amen.

Thursday, February 7 — Psalm 21
Genesis 37; Matthew 13:24-35

Have no dread or fear of them. The Lord your God, who goes before you, is the one who will fight for you. Deuteronomy 1:29,30

If dangers gather round, 615
still keep me calm and fearless;
help me to bear the cross
when life is bleak and cheerless,
to overcome my foes
with words and actions kind;
O God, your will disclose,
your counsel let me find.

Paul wrote: Therefore I am content with weaknesses, insults, hardships, persecutions, and calamities for the sake of Christ; for whenever I am weak, then I am strong. 2 Corinthians 12:10

Jesus loves me! This I know, 726
for the Bible tells me so.
Little ones to him belong;
they are weak but he is strong.
Yes, Jesus loves me,
yes, Jesus loves me,
yes, Jesus loves me,
the Bible tells me so.

Savior of humankind, you have overcome even death itself so that we might fear nothing, but go forth in strength and love to proclaim the gospel. Hallelujah! Amen.

Friday, February 8 — Psalm 22:1-8
Genesis 38; Matthew 13:36-46

Restore me, and I will return, because you are the Lord my God. Jeremiah 31:18 (NIV)

My soul he doth restore again, 720
and me to walk doth make
within the paths of righteousness,
e'en for his own name's sake;
within the paths of righteousness,
e'en for his own name's sake.

God says: Listen! I am standing at the door, knocking; if you hear my voice and open the door, I will come in to you and eat with you, and you with me. Revelation 3:20

Open the hearts of all who hear 225r
to make the Savior room;
now let us find redemption near,
let faith by hearing come.

Lord our God, we exile ourselves from your fellowship through sin and disobedience. In your mercy and grace, you invite us to be restored and refreshed by the bread of life. In the name of Jesus. Amen.

Saturday, February 9 — Psalm 22:9-21
Genesis 39; Matthew 13:47-58

Happy are those whose strength is in you, in whose heart are the highways to Zion. Psalm 84:5

He leadeth me: O blessed thought! 787
O words with heav'nly comfort fraught!
Whate'er I do, where'er I be,
still 'tis God's hand that leadeth me.
He leadeth me, he leadeth me;
by his own hand he leadeth me,
his faithful foll'wer I would be,
for by his hand he leadeth me.

Finally, be strong in the Lord and in the strength of his power. Ephesians 6:10

Stand up, stand up for Jesus, 752
stand in his strength alone;
the arm of flesh will fail you,
you dare not trust your own.
Put on the gospel armor,
each piece put on with prayer;
where duty calls, or danger,
be ever faithful there.

Lord God almighty, we confess our inclination to rely upon our own strengths and abilities in our walk through life. Help us to lay hold of the strength that comes only from a heart surrendered to you. Amen.

First Sunday in Lent

Watchword for the Week — Be glad in the Lord and rejoice, O righteous, and shout for joy, all you upright in heart. Psalm 32:11

Sunday, February 10 — Genesis 2:15-17,3:1-7; Psalm 32
Romans 5:12-19; Matthew 4:1-11

You show me the path of life. Psalm 16:11

Thus may we, as your anointed, 716
walk with you in truth and grace
in the path you have appointed,
till we reach your dwelling-place.

It is sown in dishonor, it is raised in glory. It is sown in weakness, it is raised in power. 1 Corinthians 15:43

Believing souls, rejoice and sing, 137r
your risen Savior see,
and say, "O death, where is thy sting!
O grave, thy victory!"
Rejoice, your conquering Savior lives,
he lives to die no more;
and life eternal freely gives,
since he our sorrows bore.

Risen Christ, through Calvary you have shown us the path to eternal life. We fear neither death nor the grave, for we know we will rise in immortality to join you. Until then, we wait and serve in your name. Amen.

Monday, February 11 — Psalm 22:22-28
Genesis 40:1-41:16; Matthew 14:1-14

He does not deal with us according to our sins, nor repay us according to our iniquities. Psalm 103:10

To gain remission of our sin, 317r
no work of ours avails;
God's favor we may strive to win,
but all our labor fails;
we're midst our fairest actions lost,
and none 'fore him of aught can boast.
We live alone through mercy.

God saved us and called us with a holy calling, not according to our works but according to his own purpose and grace. This grace was given to us in Christ Jesus before the ages began. 2 Timothy 1:9

Therefore my hope is in his grace, 317r
and not in my own merit;
on him my confidence I place,
instructed by his Spirit;
his precious word has promised me
he will my joy and comfort be;
thereon is my reliance.

Loving Savior, we confess that we can do nothing to earn forgiveness, and we are grateful that you pardon our sins in mercy and grace in accordance with your great love. Thank you, Jesus. Amen.

Tuesday, February 12 — Psalm 22:29-31
Genesis 41:17-57; Matthew 14:15-24

After the suffering of his soul, he will see the light [of life] and be satisfied. Isaiah 53:11 (NIV)

Hail, O once despised Jesus! 330
Hail, O Galilean King!
You have suffered to release us,
hope, salvation, joy to bring.
Hail, O agonizing Savior,
bearer of our sin and shame;
by your merits we find favor;
life is given through your name.

God raised Christ from the dead and seated him at his right hand in the heavenly places, far above all rule and authority and power and dominion, and above every name that is named, not only in this age but also in the age to come. Ephesians 1:20,21

Paschal Lamb, by God appointed, 330
all our sins on you were laid;
by almighty love anointed,
you have full atonement made.
All your people are forgiven
through the virtue of your blood;
opened is the gate of heaven;
we are reconciled to God.

Suffering servant Christ, by your sacrifice we are saved from death and redeemed to serve you. Help us to proclaim your kingship and your kingdom to the world. Amen.

Wednesday, February 13 — Psalm 23
Genesis 42; Matthew 14:25-15:9

You have turned my mourning into dancing; you have taken off my sackcloth and clothed me with joy. Psalm 30:11

Faith in the conscience works for peace, 700
and bids the mourner's weeping cease,
by faith the children's place we claim,
and give all honor to one name.

Bartimaeus regained his sight and followed Jesus on the way. Mark 10:52

Good news! Our Christ has come! 630*
He heals the sad of heart.
He sets the pris'ners free
and helps the blind to see.
God's Spirit works through all who love,
through all who touch the lives of these.

We profess our faith in the one who came to heal the sick, give sight to the blind, and set the captives free. O Christ, help us to reach out in love to the sick and wounded in our midst. Amen.

Thursday, February 14 — Psalm 24
Genesis 43; Matthew 15:10-20

O Lord, our Sovereign, how majestic is your name in all the earth! Psalm 8:1

O Majestic Being, 554
may our souls and bodies,
at all times be at your service!
Like the holy angels
who bow down before you,
may we ceaselessly adore you,
and through grace,
Jesus' grace,
in our whole demeanor,
offer praise and honor.

To the King of kings and Lord of lords, who alone is immortal and who lives in unapproachable light, whom no one has seen or can see. To him be honor and might forever. Amen. 1 Timothy 6:15,16 (NIV)

Immortal, invisible, God only wise, 457
in light inaccessible hid from our eyes,
most blessed, most glorious, O Ancient of Days,
almighty, victorious, your great name we praise.

Sovereign Lord, we love and adore you, we bow down before you, we sing your praises. We worship you as the immortal, invisible God of all creation who crowned humankind with glory and honor; may we be found worthy. Amen.

Friday, February 15 — Psalm 25:1-7
Genesis 44; Matthew 15:21-28

Let no one lose heart. 1 Samuel 17:32 (NIV)

O for a faith that will not shrink, 409r
though pressed by every foe,
that will not tremble on the brink
of any earthly woe.

Set all your hope on the grace that Jesus Christ will bring you when he is revealed. 1 Peter 1:13

Lo! The hosts of evil round us 751*
scorn the Christ, assail his ways!
From the fears that long have bound us,
free our hearts to faith and praise.
Grant us wisdom, grant us courage
for the living of these days,
for the living of these days.

God of grace, in faith we come to you, drawn by your Holy Spirit. Help us to face the challenges of these days with courage and boldness through Jesus Christ our Lord. Amen.

* Used by permission of Elinor Fosdick Downs

Saturday, February 16 — Psalm 25:8-22
Genesis 45; Matthew 15:29-16:4

Do not go after other gods to serve and worship them, and do not provoke me to anger with the work of your hands. Jeremiah 25:6

Forth in your name, O Lord, I go 638
my daily labor to pursue —
you only, Lord, resolved to know
in all I think or speak or do.

Adulterers! Do you not know that friendship with the world is enmity with God? Therefore whoever wishes to be a friend of the world becomes an enemy of God. James 4:4

Christ for the world we sing! 640
The world to Christ we bring
with one accord
with us the work to share,
with us reproach to dare,
with us the cross to bear
for Christ our Lord.

Jesus, you said you did not come into the world to condemn it, but to save it. Therefore, bless us as we bring the saving gospel of Christ to the world, that all might be transformed by your love. Amen.

Second Sunday in Lent

Watchword for the Week — For God so loved the world that he gave his only Son, so that everyone who believes in him may not perish but may have eternal life. John 3:16

Sunday, February 17 — Genesis 12:1-4a; Psalm 121
Romans 4:1-5,13-17; John 3:1-17

Do cool waters from distant sources ever cease to flow? Yet my people have forgotten me. Jeremiah 18:14,15 (NIV)

God of our weary years, God of our silent tears, 707
thou who hast brought us thus far on the way,
thou who hast by thy might led us into the light,
keep us forever in the path, we pray.
Lest our feet stray from the places,
our God, where we met thee,
lest our hearts,
drunk with the wine of the world, we forget thee,
shadowed beneath thy hand,
may we forever stand,
true to our God, true to our native land.

What if some were unfaithful? Will their faithlessness nullify the faithfulness of God? By no means! Romans 3:3,4

How firm a foundation, you saints of the Lord 709
is laid for your faith in his excellent word!
What more can he say than to you he has said,
to you who for refuge to Jesus have fled?

God of truth, forgive our lapses in faith when we stumble and swerve from the path of righteousness. May the truth of your word prevail in our lives and draw us back to you. In Jesus' name. Amen.

Monday, February 18 — Psalm 26
Genesis 46:1-27; Matthew 16:5-20

He will cover you with his pinions, and under his wings you will find refuge. Psalm 91:4

All praise to you, my God, this night 569
for all the blessings of the light.
Keep me, O keep me, King of kings,
beneath the shelter of your wings.

Jesus said to the leader of the synagogue, "Do not fear, only believe." Mark 5:36

Lord, give us such a faith as this, 409r
and then, whate'er may come,
we'll taste e'en here the hallowed bliss
of an eternal home.

Most high God, we dwell in your shadow, secure in your faithfulness. In response to Jesus' words, we pray that our faith might outgrow our unbelief, for in him all things are possible. Amen.

Tuesday, February 19 — Psalm 27:1-6
Genesis 46:28-47:31; Matthew 16:21-28

The light of the moon will be like the light of the sun, and the light of the sun will be sevenfold on the day when the Lord binds up the injuries of his people, and heals the wounds. Isaiah 30:26

O Master, from the mountain side 581
make haste to heal these hearts of pain;
among these restless throngs abide;
O tread the city's streets again.

This slight momentary affliction is preparing us for an eternal weight of glory beyond all measure. 2 Corinthians 4:17

Save us in our soul's distress; 352
be our help to cheer and bless,
while we grow in holiness:
hear us, holy Jesus.

Healer of souls, we confess our wayward and disobedient acts that sever our hearts from you. Bind up our wounds, heal our souls, and let the heart scars remind us of your unconditional love shown in Christ Jesus. Amen.

Wednesday, February 20 — Psalm 27:7-14
Genesis 48; Matthew 17:1-13

My hand laid the foundation of the earth, and my right hand spread out the heavens; when I summon them, they stand at attention. Isaiah 48:13

All your works with joy surround you, 544
earth and heav'n reflect your rays,
stars and angels sing around you,
center of unbroken praise;
field and forest, vale and mountain,
flow'ry meadow, flashing sea,
chanting bird and flowing fountain,
praising you eternally!

In the beginning was the Word, and the Word was with God, and the Word was God. All things came into being through him, and without him not one thing came into being. John 1:1,3

Crown him the Lord of years, 405
the risen Lord sublime,
Creator of the rolling spheres,
the Master of all time.
All hail, Redeemer, hail!
For you have died for me;
your praise and glory shall not fail
throughout eternity.

Eternal Word, we take your creation for granted and fail to worship you in awe as you deserve. Yet amazingly, as Creator of the universe you stooped to become flesh and thereby redeem us from our sin. Thank you, Jesus. Amen.

Thursday, February 21 — Psalm 28
Genesis 49; Matthew 17:14-27

Sing to the Lord, bless his name; tell of his salvation from day to day. Psalm 96:2

Sing hallelujah, praise the Lord! 543
Sing with a cheerful voice;
exalt our God with one accord,
and in his name rejoice.
Ne'er cease to sing, O ransomed host,
praise Father, Son, and Holy Ghost,
until in realms of endless light
your praises shall unite.

With gratitude in your hearts sing psalms, hymns, and spiritual songs to God. Colossians 3:16

Sing alleluia, Christ does live, 364
and peace on earth restore;
come, ransomed souls, and glory give,
sing, worship, and adore:
to him our heartfelt thanks we pay
in deep humility.
It's God alone whose saving way
has set believers free.

Great Jehovah, your name itself is holy; with trembling hearts and voices we bless your name and sing of your glory! Please accept our songs, hymns, and music as a fragrant offering lifted heavenward to you. Amen.

Friday, February 22 — Psalm 29
Genesis 50; Matthew 18:1-14

Let the words of my mouth and the meditation of my heart be acceptable to you, O Lord, my rock and my redeemer. Psalm 19:14

Upon your precepts and your ways 510
my heart will meditate with awe;
your word shall be my chief delight,
and I will not forget your law.

Jesus said, "So I tell you, whatever you ask for in prayer, believe that you have received it, and it will be yours." Mark 11:24

We come to you, our Father, 433
with thoughts of thanks and praise,
for your abundant mercy,
and all your love and grace;
we praise you for your goodness
and for your loving care,
for daily show'rs of blessing,
for answers to our prayers.

Rock and Redeemer, you have saved us by your blood, what more could we ask? Yet you also promised an abundant life with Christ, far exceeding anything we could ask for in prayer. In his name we give thanks. Amen.

Saturday, February 23 — Psalm 30:1-5
Exodus 1:1-2:10; Matthew 18:15-35

O Lord, do your eyes not look for truth? Jeremiah 5:3

You are the truth; your word alone 661
true wisdom can impart;
you only can inform the mind
and purify the heart.

Do not judge by appearances, but judge with right judgment. John 7:24

O, send your Spirit, Lord, 502
now unto me,
that he may touch my eyes
and make me see.
Show me the truth concealed
within your Word,
and in your book revealed
I see my Lord.

Righteous Judge, we confess that our eyes are dimmed by sin, and we cannot see the truth. We pray that your Spirit would convict us, open the eyes of our hearts, and show us the truth and the word, Jesus Christ. Amen.

Third Sunday in Lent

Watchword for the Week — O come, let us worship and bow down, let us kneel before the Lord, our Maker! Psalm 95:6

Sunday, February 24 — Exodus 17:1-7; Psalm 95
Romans 5:1-11; John 4:5-42

Be glad and rejoice in the Lord your God. Joel 2:23

Church, rejoice! 631
Raise your voice,
sing Jehovah's worthy praise;
extol his name forever;
laud him, our God and Savior;
proclaim to ev'ry nation
the tidings of salvation;
bear the witness
to his greatness;
spread the story
of his glory
to the earth's remotest bounds.

Rejoice in the Lord! Let your gentleness be known to everyone. The Lord is near. Philippians 4:4,5

Rejoice, the Lord is King! 372
Your Lord and King adore.
Rejoice, give thanks and sing
and triumph evermore.
Lift up your heart, lift up your voice,
rejoice, again I say, rejoice!

God of peace, help us to express our inner joy through an outward life of gentleness and love. May the world understand our lack of anxiety and worry as evidence of confidence in Christ Jesus to provide all we need. Amen.

Monday, February 25 — Psalm 30:6-12
Exodus 2:11-3:22; Matthew 19:1-12

You are the Lord, you alone; you have made heaven, the heaven of heavens, with all their host, the earth and all that is on it, the seas and all that is in them. To all of them you give life. Nehemiah 9:6

He built the earth, he spread the sky, 171r
and fixed the starry lights on high;
wonders of grace to God belong,
repeat his mercies in your song.

Worship him who made heaven and earth, the sea and the springs of water. Revelation 14:7

Enter his courts with joy; 164r
with fear address the Lord;
he formed us with his hand,
and quickened by his word.
With wide command he spreads his sway,
o'er every sea and every land.

Immortal and eternal God, we confess that our worship falls short of honoring your grandeur. Please accept what we offer, in fear and trembling, as a reflection of our love for you. We bless your holy name. Amen.

Tuesday, February 26 — Psalm 31:1-5
Exodus 4:1-5:9; Matthew 19:13-22

The Lord said to me, "You are my servant, Israel, in whom I will be glorified." Isaiah 49:3

O come, O come, Immanuel, 274
and ransom captive Israel,
that mourns in lowly exile here
until the Son of God appear.
Rejoice! Rejoice! Immanuel
shall come to you, O Israel.

Has God rejected his people? By no means! Romans 11:1

O seed of Israel's chosen race, 403
now ransomed from the fall,
hail him who saves you by his grace,
and crown him Lord of all!
Hail him who saves you by his grace,
and crown him Lord of all!

God of Israel, you preserved a remnant of a disobedient people in order to save the world through Christ. We confess our own disobedience and pray to be counted among the remnant that faithfully serves our Lord. In Jesus' name. Amen.

Wednesday, February 27 — Psalm 31:6-9
Exodus 5:10-6:12; Matthew 19:23-30

Many are saying to me, "There is no help for you in God." But you, O Lord, are a shield around me, my glory, and the one who lifts up my head. Psalm 3:2,3

I have no help but yours, nor do I need 421
another arm but yours to lean upon;
it is enough, O Lord, enough indeed;
my strength is in your might, your might alone.

Paul said, "To this day I have had help from God, and so I stand here, testifying to both small and great." Acts 26:22

A faith that shines more bright and clear, 409r
when tempests rage without,
that when in danger knows no fear,
in darkness feels no doubt.

Our Shield and Defender, we earnestly desire to trust you in all things. But we confess that our faith is sometimes weak and we seek help elsewhere. May your Holy Spirit draw us powerfully back into your sustaining arms. Amen.

Thursday, February 28 — Psalm 31:10-20
Exodus 6:13-7:24; Matthew 20:1-16

Happy are those who keep his decrees, who seek him with their whole heart. Psalm 119:2

Lord, we your presence seek; 584
we ask this blessing true:
give us a pure and lowly heart,
a temple fit for you.

I beg you to lead a life worthy of the calling to which you have been called, with all humility and gentleness, with patience. Ephesians 4:1,2

Join we all with one accord; 525
praise we all our common Lord;
for we all have heard his voice,
all have made his will our choice.
Join we with the saints of old,
no more strangers in the fold,
one the Shepherd who us sought,
one the flock his blood has bought.

Gracious Lord, we confess that we are not worthy of your blessings, yet we are blessed when our hearts truly seek you. We pray for the power of your Holy Spirit to live as Jesus lived; humble and gentle, patient and loving. Amen.

Friday, February 29 — Psalm 31:21-24
Exodus 8; Matthew 20:17-28

He was oppressed, and he was afflicted, yet he did not open his mouth; like a lamb that is led to the slaughter. Isaiah 53:7

Jesus! Heav'nly hosts adore you, 330
seated at your Father's side.
Crucified this world once saw you;
now in glory you abide.
There for sinners you are pleading,
and our place you now prepare,
ever for us interceding,
till in glory we appear.

Christ himself bore our sins in his body on the cross, so that, free from sins, we might live for righteousness; by his wounds you have been healed. 1 Peter 2:24

What wondrous love is this, O my soul, O my soul! 328
What wondrous love is this, O my soul!
What wondrous love is this
 that caused the Lord of bliss
to bear the dreadful curse for my soul, for my soul,
to bear the dreadful curse for my soul?

Lamb of God, you took away the sins of the world by your sacrifice on the cross. What wondrous love, what good news! You went to the cross silently; may we come to the cross singing your praises in thanksgiving! Amen.

March 1, 1457:
Beginning of the Unity of the Brethren in Bohemia

Saturday, March 1 — Psalm 32
Exodus 9; Matthew 20:29-21:11

With weeping they shall come, and with consolations I will lead them back, for I have become a father to Israel. Jeremiah 31:9

God calling yet! I cannot stay; 310r
my heart I yield without delay;
vain world, farewell, from you I part
the voice of God has reached my heart.

In the days of his flesh, Jesus offered up prayers and supplications, with loud cries and tears, to the one who was able to save him from death, and he was heard because of his reverent submission to God. Hebrews 5:7

Perfect submission, all is at rest, 714
I in my Savior am happy and blessed,
watching and waiting, looking above,
filled with his goodness, lost in his love.

Suffering Lord, during your earthly life you have experienced anguish and shame for the sake of humankind. With strong cries and supplication you implored the name of your heavenly father in the garden of Gethsemane. Endow us with your love that we may be steadfast in our faith. Amen.

Fourth Sunday in Lent

Watchword for the Week — Surely goodness and mercy shall follow me all the days of my life, and I shall dwell in the house of the Lord my whole life long. Psalm 23:6

Sunday, March 2 — 1 Samuel 16:1-13; Psalm 23
Ephesians 5:8-14; John 9:1-41

Even heaven and the highest heaven cannot contain you, much less this house that I have built! 1 Kings 8:27

He rules the world with truth and grace, 294
and makes the nations prove
the glories of his righteousness
and wonders of his love,
and wonders of his love,
and wonders, wonders of his love.

Although you have not seen him, you love him; and even though you do not see him now, you believe in him and rejoice with an indescribable and glorious joy. 1 Peter 1:8

When the Lord appears, 594
this my spirit cheers;
when, his love to me revealing
he, the Sun of grace, with healing
in his beams appears,
this my spirit cheers.

Transcendent God, you are above all that we can aspire or imagine being. The heavens cannot contain you. You are not confined to a specific geographical area, but rather you are our dwelling place in all generations. Grant us strength to follow our heart's desire, which is to do your will. Amen.

Monday, March 3 — Psalm 33:1-5
Exodus 10; Matthew 21:12-22

God looks to the ends of the earth, and sees everything under the heavens. Job 28:24

This is my Father's world, 456
and to my list'ning ears
all nature sings and round me rings
the music of the spheres.
This is my Father's world;
I rest me in the thought
of rocks and trees, of skies and seas —
his hand the wonders wrought.

It is not the will of your Father in heaven that one of these little ones should be lost. Matthew 18:14

When through the deep waters I call you to go, 535r
the rivers of woe shall not you overflow;
for I will be with you your troubles to bless,
and sanctify to you your deepest distress.

Loving God, when all seems impossible and without any solution, we are once again reminded that you are the creator of the universe and in you the entire world is contained. Help, O Lord, that we can be assured of your grace and mercy. Amen.

Tuesday, March 4 — Psalm 33:6-11
Exodus 11:1-12:20; Matthew 21:23-32

Do not fear or be dismayed! Joshua 8:1

When we seek relief 799
from a long-felt grief,
when temptations come alluring,
make us patient and enduring;
show us that bright shore
where we weep no more.

Who will harm you if you are eager to do what is good? But even if you do suffer for doing what is right, you are blessed. 1 Peter 3:13,14

In the hour of trial, 419r
Jesus, plead for me;
lest by base denial
I depart from thee;
When you see me waver,
with a look recall,
nor for fear or favor
suffer me to fall.

Merciful God, we try to do your will, which is to love kindness and mercy, and to walk humbly before you. We have come to realize that it is not possible by might nor power but by your Holy Spirit. Help us not to lose heart but to be encouraged by your words that constantly sustain us by knowing that you are still in control. Amen.

Wednesday, March 5 — Psalm 33:12-22
Exodus 12:21-51; Matthew 21:33-46

From the least to the greatest of them, everyone is greedy for unjust gain; and from prophet to priest, everyone deals falsely. They have treated the wound of my people carelessly, saying, "Peace, peace," when there is no peace. Jeremiah 6:13,14

In haunts of wretchedness and need, 581
on shadowed thresholds dark with fears,
from paths where hide the lures of greed
we catch the vision of your tears.

Love is not rude. It does not insist on its own way. 1 Corinthians 13:5

O cross that lifts up my head, 360r
I dare not ask to fly from you;
I lay in dust life's glory dead,
and from the ground there blossoms red
life that shall endless be.

Loving God, in spite of the many ways we are treated by the arrogance and selfish pride of others, we have come to realize that you are always present to offer a helping hand when the entire world appears to be falling on us. Remind us of your mercy and unending love. Amen.

Thursday, March 6 — Psalm 34:1-7
Exodus 13:1-14:18; Matthew 22:1-14

Rise up, O God, plead your cause. Psalm 74:22

O use me, Lord, use even me 394r
just as you will, and when, and where,
until your blessed face I see,
your rest, your joy, your glory share.

Now have come the salvation and the power and the kingdom of our God and the authority of his Messiah. Revelation 12:10

The springs of salvation from Christ, 616
the Rock, bursting
and flowing throughout all the world's wilderness
bring life and salvation to those who are thirsting
to drink from this spring of salvation by grace;
as streams through the desert refresh the ground
and make land once barren with green abound,
the pow'r of his Spirit, our cold hearts o'erflowing,
renews us for service with lives bright and glowing.

Christ the mediator, there is none other like you to plead our case before your heavenly Father. Have compassion on us and forgive our iniquities and sins. Thank you, Lord, for the hope of a new beginning. In your name we pray. Amen.

Friday, March 7 — Psalm 34:8-18
Exodus 14:19-15:21; Matthew 22:15-22

The Lord gave, and the Lord has taken away. Blessed be the name of the Lord. Job 1:21

I fear no foe with you at hand to bless, 807
though ills have weight, and tears their bitterness.
Where is death's sting? Where, grave, your victory?
I triumph still, if you abide with me.

As Jesus approached the gate of the town, a man who had died was being carried out. He was his mother's only son, and she was a widow...When the Lord saw her, he had compassion for her and said to her, "Do not weep." Then he came forward and touched the bier, and the bearers stood still. And he said, "Young man, I say to you, rise!" Luke 7:12-14

Our hope and expectation, p56
O Jesus, now appear!
Arise, the sun so longed for,
o'er this benighted sphere!
With hearts and hands uplifted,
we look, O Lord, to you
for all the earth's redemption,
creation made anew.

All powerful God, there is nothing beyond your understanding or that you cannot do. With a word spoken by your mouth or by a touch of your hands you can restore the sick to health and the dead to life. Make us sensitive to that miraculous touch so we can be healed both spiritually and physically. Through Christ's name we pray. Amen.

Saturday, March 8 — Psalm 34:19-22
Exodus 15:22-16:36; Matthew 22:23-40

O Lord of hosts, you are God, you alone, of all the kingdoms of the earth; you have made heaven and earth. Isaiah 37:16

Praise, my soul, the King of heaven, 529
to his feet your tribute bring.
Ransomed, healed, restored, forgiven,
evermore his praises sing.
Alleluia! Alleluia!
Praise the everlasting King!

From him and through him and to him are all things. To him be the glory forever. Romans 11:36

To God be the glory — great things he has done! 550
So loved he the world that he gave us his Son,
who yielded his life an atonement for sin,
and opened the life-gate that all may go in.

Creator God, you are absolute in nature. You evolved around everything and your whole creation is contained within you. Where there was darkness you established light and where there was desert you established life. How awesome is your transcending love; it surpasses all human understanding. To you almighty God be the glory. Amen.

Fifth Sunday in Lent

Watchword for the Week — I wait for the Lord, my soul waits, and in his word I hope. Psalm 130:5

Sunday, March 9 — Ezekiel 37:1-14; Psalm 130
Romans 8:6-11; John 11:1-45

O Lord, in the morning you hear my voice; in the morning I plead my case to you, and watch. Psalm 5:3

Glorious Lord, yourself impart! 558
Light of light, from God proceeding,
open now our ears and heart,
help us by your Spirit's pleading;
hear the cry that we are raising;
hear, and bless our prayers and praising.

Do not worry about anything, but in everything by prayer and supplication with thanksgiving let your requests be made known to God. Philippians 4:6

Rejoice, then, you sad hearted, 60r
who sit in deepest gloom,
who mourn o'er joys departed,
and tremble at your doom;
he who alone can cheer you
is standing at the door;
he brings his pity near you
and bids you weep no more.

Jesus Christ, our mediator between human being and God, we put our lives in your hands so you can plead our case before the Almighty God. Help us to be constant in our faith in you as the one who is there to support and sustain us. With prayer and supplication we make our concerns known to you. Amen.

Monday, March 10 — Psalm 35:1-10
Exodus 17:1-18:6; Matthew 22:41-23:12

Those who bring thanksgiving as their sacrifice honor me; to those who go the right way I will show the salvation of God. Psalm 50:23

The wise may bring their learning, 658
the rich may bring their wealth,
and some may bring their greatness,
and some their strength and health:
we too would bring our treasures
to offer to the King,
we have no wealth or learning —
what shall we children bring?

Thanks be to God for his indescribable gift! 2 Corinthians 9:15

Rejoice, O pilgrim throng! 786
Rejoice, give thanks and sing:
your festal banner wave on high,
the cross of Christ your king.
Rejoice, rejoice, rejoice, give thanks and sing!

Merciful God, with praise and thanksgiving we lift up your name which is above all names in heaven and on earth. May we be nurtured by your Holy Spirit in knowing that you honor those who are willing to walk in righteousness and in the way of peace. Grant us courage, wisdom, and strength to be steadfast in our relationship with you. Through Christ our Lord. Amen.

Tuesday, March 11 — Psalm 35:11-18
Exodus 18:7-19:9; Matthew 23:13-22

See, I have tested you in the furnace of adversity. Isaiah 48:10

When through fiery trials your pathway shall lie, 709
my grace, all sufficient, shall be your supply.
The flame shall not hurt you; I only design
your dross to consume and your gold to refine.

One man was there who had been ill for thirty-eight years... Jesus said to him, "Stand up, take your mat and walk." John 5:5,8

Trusting only in thy merit, 772
would I seek thy face;
heal my wounded, broken spirit,
save me by thy grace.
Savior, Savior, hear my humble cry;
while on others thou art calling;
do not pass me by.

Healer of both mind and body, we give you thanks for your willingness to give us a second chance by restoring us physically and spiritually. There is nothing we do that you are not willing to forgive. How great you are, healer of the universe. Through Christ, who is our sustainer, redeemer, and comforter. Amen.

Wednesday, March 12 — Psalm 35:19-28
Exodus 19:10-20:21; Matthew 23:23-32

I know that the Lord maintains the cause of the needy, and executes justice for the poor. Psalm 140:12

Where cross the crowded ways of life, 581
where sound the cries of race and clan,
above the noise of selfish strife
we hear your voice, O Son of Man.

Has not God chosen the poor in the world to be rich in faith and to be heirs of the kingdom that he has promised to those who love him? James 2:5

See, from his head, his hands, his feet 350
sorrow and love flow mingled down;
did e'er such love and sorrow meet,
or thorns compose so rich a crown?

Loving God, you have chosen everyone who is willing to love justice and kindness, and to walk in uprightness before you to become heirs of your kingdom. Help us to be steadfast and immovable in serving you. Through Christ, in whom we have redemption and forgiveness for our sins. Amen.

Thursday, March 13 — Psalm 36
Exodus 20:22-21:27; Matthew 23:33-39

Yet, O Lord, you are our Father; we are the clay, and you are our potter; we are all the work of your hand. Isaiah 64:8

"Go forth in all the earth," — 633
your word to us is given:
"Proclaim salvation's worth
to people under heaven."
This holy task, O Lord,
your church must quite fulfill;
to us your grace afford,
and mold us to your will.

For we are what he has made us, created in Christ Jesus for good works, which God prepared beforehand to be our way of life. Ephesians 2:10

To serve the present age, 645
my calling to fulfill,
O may it all my pow'rs engage
to do my master's will.

Creator God, you have formed us from dust and have elaborated a handy work that is beyond all human understanding. We are mindful of who we are and from whence we came. Enable us to reflect your image which is the fruits of the spirit. Thank you, Lord, for making us who we are. Through Christ our Lord and Savior. Amen.

Friday, March 14 — Psalm 37:1-6
Exodus 21:28-22:24; Matthew 24:1-25

He who keeps Israel will neither slumber nor sleep. Psalm 121:4

Keep me through your pow'r 608
so minded each hour
that I naught beside
may know but you only, the Lord crucified.

Our Lord Jesus Christ will strengthen you to the end, so that you may be blameless on the day of our Lord Jesus Christ. 1 Corinthians 1:7,8

Open now the crystal fountain 790
where the healing waters flow;
let the fire and cloudy pillar
lead me all my journeys through.
Strong deliv'rer, strong deliv'rer,
ever be my strength and shield;
ever be my strength and shield.

All powerful God, we are aware that you are our dwelling place in all generations. We know that you are there to guide and sustain us. When we fall, you are there to extend your hand and lift us up. When we fail to walk circumspectly before you, you are willing to forgive us and cleanse us from our iniquities and sins. Thank you for protecting us. In Jesus' name we pray. Amen.

Saturday, March 15 — Psalm 37:7-15
Exodus 22:25-23:26; Matthew 24:26-35

Thus says the Lord, "I will rejoice in doing good to them." Jeremiah 32:41

God is my strong salvation, 769
no enemy I fear;
he hears my supplication,
dispelling all my care;
if he, my head and master,
defend me from above,
what pain or what disaster
can part me from his love?

Jesus said, "The Son of Man is to be betrayed into human hands, and they will kill him, and three days after being killed, he will rise again." Mark 9:31

He that drinks shall live forever; 106r
tis a soul renewing flood.
God is faithful; God will never
break his covenant in blood,
signed when our Redeemer died,
sealed when he was glorified.

Gracious God, we are challenged daily by the need to love and trust others in our homes and in the world at large. Help us to learn from Jesus our Lord. Though he was betrayed he was able to pray for the forgiveness of his betrayers and abusers. Amen.

Palm Sunday

Watchword for the Week — And being found in human form, Jesus humbled himself and became obedient to the point of death — even death on a cross. Philippians 2:7,8

Sunday, March 16 — Isaiah 50:4-9a; Psalm 31:9-16
Philippians 2:5-11; Matthew 21:1-11

And when you turn to the right or when you turn to the left, your ears shall hear a word behind you, saying, "This is the way; walk in it." Isaiah 30:21

O let me hear you speaking 603
in accents clear and still,
above the storms of passion,
the murmurs of self-will.
O speak to reassure me,
to hasten or control;
and speak to make me listen,
O guardian of my soul.

See, we are going up to Jerusalem, and the Son of Man will be handed over. Mark 10:33

Go to dark Gethsemane, 349
all who feel the tempter's pow'r;
your Redeemer's conflict see,
watch with him one bitter hour.
Turn not from his griefs away;
learn of Jesus Christ to pray.

Sacrificial Lamb, we are grateful for your willingness to give your life for the sake of all who are willing to surrender their life to you. It is with your love and example shown that we can now reconcile to you, O God almighty, as the guardian of our soul. Amen.

Monday, March 17 — Psalm 37:16-22
Exodus 23:27-25:9; Matthew 24:36-44

God blessed them, and said to them, "Be fruitful and multiply, and fill the earth and subdue it." Genesis 1:28

We thank you, our Creator, 453
for all things bright and good,
the seed-time and the harvest,
our life, our health, our food;
accept the gifts we offer
for all your love imparts,
and what you most would treasure —
our humble, thankful hearts.

All belong to you, and you belong to Christ, and Christ belongs to God. 1 Corinthians 3:22,23

Take my life, O Lord, renew, 610
consecrate my heart to you.
Take myself, and I will be
yours for all eternity,
yours for all eternity.

Dear Lord, help us this day to realize that you want us to be good stewards of all your wonderful gifts. From creation you gave us your command to be faithful and multiply and care for your world. Give us the grace and strength to be truthful to your will. In Jesus' name we pray. Amen.

Tuesday, March 18 — Psalm 37:23-26
Exodus 25:10-40; Matthew 24:45-51

May those who love your salvation say continually, "Great is the Lord!" Psalm 40:16

Now thank we all our God 533
with heart and hands and voices,
who wondrous things has done,
in whom his world rejoices;
who, from our mother's arms,
has blessed us on our way
with countless gifts of love,
and still is ours today.

Jesus said, "You heard me say to you, 'I am going away, and I am coming to you.' If you loved me, you would rejoice that I am going to the Father, because the Father is greater than I." John 14:28

Our hope and expectation, 256
O Jesus, now appear;
arise, O Sun so longed for
o'er this benighted sphere.
With hearts and hands uplifted,
we look, O Lord, to you
for all the earth's redemption,
creation made anew.

Eternal Savior, as you prepared to leave your disciples to return to your Father, there was a sense of helplessness and fear. However, your reassurance that it was necessary for you to go and prepare a place so there can be a reunion and celebration when you return for your followers provides new hope and expectation. Thank you for your unending love. Amen.

Wednesday, March 19 — Psalm 37:27-33
Exodus 26; Matthew 25:1-13

"Do not be afraid, O little Israel, for I myself will help you," declares the Lord, your Redeemer, the Holy One of Israel. Isaiah 41:14 (NIV)

If you but trust in God to guide you 712
and place your confidence in him,
you'll find him always there beside you
to give you hope and strength within;
for those who trust God's changeless love
build on the rock that will not move.

The Lord Jesus on the night when he was betrayed took a loaf of bread, and when he had given thanks, he broke it and said, "This is my body that is for you. Do this in remembrance of me." In the same way he took the cup also, after supper, saying, "This cup is the new covenant in my blood. Do this, as often as you drink it, in remembrance of me." 1 Corinthians 11:23-25

Thy body broken for my sake, 422
my bread from heav'n shall be;
thy testamental cup I take,
and thus remember thee.

Heavenly Father, these days we live in constant fear of the way things are in our world. There is uncertainty and a complete disregard for the life of humankind. Nevertheless, we are assured by your word that you are always with us to help, protect, and strengthen us. Thank you for your unending mercies. Through Christ our Lord. Amen.

Maundy Thursday

Watchword for the Day — He has gained renown by his wonderful deeds; the Lord is gracious and merciful. Psalm 111:4

Thursday, March 20 — Psalm 37:34-40
Exodus 27:1-28:14; Matthew 25:14-30

Turn now, every one of you, from your evil way and wicked doings. Jeremiah 25:5

Early let us seek your favor; 731
early let us do your will;
blessed Lord and only Savior,
with your love our spirits fill.
Blessed Jesus, blessed Jesus,
you have loved us, love us still.
Blessed Jesus, blessed Jesus,
you have loved us, love us still.

The cock crowed for the second time. Then Peter remembered that Jesus had said to him, "Before the cock crows twice, you will deny me three times." And he broke down and wept. Mark 14:72

How shall I meet my Savior? 269
How shall I truly welcome thee?
What manner of behavior
is by thy love required of me?
I wait for thy salvation;
grant me, O Lord, thy spirit's light;
and may my preparation
be well accepted in thy sight.

Merciful God, we confess that we have not always been the person you expect us to be in Jesus Christ. We have not loved you the way we should. As matter of fact, we have denied you in thoughts, words, and deeds. Help us to amend what we are, and direct us in the way you want us to go. To the glory of your holy name. Amen.

Good Friday

Watchword for the Day — For God so loved the world that he gave his only Son, so that everyone who believes in him may not perish but may have eternal life. John 3:16

Friday, March 21 — Psalm 38:1-8
Exodus 28:15-43; Matthew 25:31-46

Is my hand shortened, that it cannot redeem? Isaiah 50:2

Naught in this world affords true rest 768
but Christ's atoning blood.
This purifies the guilty breast,
and reconciles to God.
Hence flows unending love to him
who came lost sinners to redeem,
and Christ our Savior now appears
daily to us more dear.

Then Jesus gave a loud cry and breathed his last. And the curtain of the temple was torn in two, from top to bottom. Now when the centurion, who stood facing him, saw that in this way he breathed his last, he said, "Truly this man was God's Son!" Mark 15:37-39

Faith finds in Christ our ev'ry need 700
to save or strengthen us indeed;
we now receive the grace sent down,
which makes us share his cross and crown.

Almighty and ever-living God, with your compassionate love you gave your son as the Savior of the world to redeem sinful people from their unrighteousness. You have inspired non-believers with your word. The centurion was able to say, "Truly this man was God's Son!" Give grace to all who proclaim the gospel and comfort the bereaved. Through Christ our Savior. Amen.

Great Sabbath

Saturday, March 22 — Psalm 38:9-16
Exodus 29:1-30; Matthew 26:1-13

He will bless those who fear the Lord, both small and great. Psalm 115:13

All people that on earth do dwell, 539
sing to the Lord with cheerful voice;
serve him with joy, his praises tell,
come now before him and rejoice.

Jesus said, "Let her alone; why do you trouble her? She has performed a good service for me... She has done what she could; she has anointed my body beforehand for its burial. Mark 14:6,8

Hail to the Lord's anointed! 263
Great David's greater Son!
Hail, in the time appointed,
his reign on earth begun!
He comes to break oppression,
to set the captive free,
to take away transgression,
and rule in equity.

Almighty God, in Jesus Christ you have called us to be your disciples; however, we do not want to obey you as our commander. We talk when we shouldn't and keep silent when we should stand up for what is right and pleasing in your sight. Help us to be of sound mind so that in humility we can respond to your calling. Have mercy on us humbly; through Jesus our anointed King. Amen.

Easter Sunday

Watchword for the Week — So if you have been raised with Christ, seek the things that are above, where Christ is, seated at the right hand of God. Colossians 3:1

Sunday, March 23 — Acts 10:34-43; Psalm 118:1-2,14-24
Colossians 3:1-4; John 20:1-18

From the rising of the sun to its setting my name is great among the nations, says the Lord. Malachi 1:11

Lord of all being, throned afar, 464
your glory flames from sun and star;
center and soul of ev'ry sphere,
yet to each loving heart how near!

Now after he rose early on the first day of the week, he appeared first to Mary Magdalene... She went out and told those who had been with him, while they were mourning and weeping. Mark 16:9,10

Christians, dismiss your fear; 356
let hope and joy succeed;
the joyful news with gladness hear:
"The Lord is ris'n indeed!"
The promise is fulfilled
in Christ our only Head;
now justice, mercy, reconciled,
he lives who once was dead.

Risen Lord and Savior, the grave could not hold you because you died without sin. Now seated at the right hand of our Father on high, we know that our faith and trust in you will make us also transcend the power of death. In your name we pray. Amen.

Easter Monday

Monday, March 24 — Psalm 38:17-22
Exodus 29:31-30:16; Matthew 26:14-30

I will instruct you and teach you the way you should go. Psalm 32:8

I need thee ev'ry hour; 740
teach me thy will,
and thy rich promises
in me fulfill.
I need thee, O I need thee,
ev'ry hour I need thee!
O bless me now, my Savior —
I come to thee!

Paul wrote: God, who had set me apart before I was born and called me through his grace, was pleased to reveal his Son to me, so that I might proclaim him among the Gentiles. Galatians 1:15,16

Jesus calls us; o'er the tumult 600
of our life's wild, restless sea,
day by day his voice is sounding,
saying, "Christian, follow me."

Almighty and merciful God, often you have called us and we have not responded to your voice. We have strayed away from you through ignorance or self pride by following the devices of our own heart. We have offended you, O Lord, by our low standard way of living. Have mercy upon us and grant us the strength to walk in holiness and righteousness before your glory. Through Christ our Lord. Amen.

Tuesday, March 25 — Psalm 39:1-6
Exodus 30:17-31:11; Matthew 26:31-35

O Lord, may they who love you be like the sun when it rises in its strength. Judges 5:31 (NIV)

Fair is the sunshine, 470
fair is the moonlight,
bright the sparkling stars on high;
Jesus shines brighter,
Jesus shines purer
than all the angels in the sky.

Jesus said, "Those who love me will keep my word, and my Father will love them, and we will come to them and make our home with them." John 14:23

Thou, Lord, wilt not forsake me, 795
though I am oft to blame;
as thy reward, O take me
anew, just as I am;
grant me henceforth, dear Savior,
through all my pilgrim years
to look to thee and never
give way to anxious fears.

God of love and mercy, we thank you for the assurance of your presence in our lives. When we walk, help us to walk in the footsteps of Jesus our Lord. Help us to shine with a genuine love that can only be earned from you. Amen.

Wednesday, March 26 — Psalm 39:7-13
Exodus 31:12-32:29; Matthew 26:36-46

Noah was a righteous man, blameless in his generation; Noah walked with God. Genesis 6:9

Apostles, prophets, martyrs, p107
and all the sacred throng
who wear the spotless raiment,
who raise the ceaseless song;
for those passed on before us,
our Savior, we adore,
and walking in their footsteps,
would serve you more and more.

God did not spare the ancient world when he brought the flood on its ungodly people, but protected Noah, a preacher of righteousness, and seven others. 2 Peter 2:5 (NIV)

Church unite 631
for the right;
let your foes behold your stand;
rebuke them for their error;
in spite with hope and fervor;
declare the Savior's merit
and how the Holy Spirit
by his power,
ev'ry hour,
will direct us
and protect us
in a world of sin and strife.

Creator and Sustainer of the universe, you made all things in your wisdom. O God, you indicated to all of us that you are the "I Am, who Am." You have always protected your people. You saved steadfast Noah and his family from the flood. Give us courage and strength to be always willing and ready to walk uprightly before you. Through Christ, in whom we have redemption and forgiveness for our sins. Amen.

Thursday, March 27 — Psalm 40:1-8
Exodus 32:30-33:23; Matthew 26:47-58

Why do you contend against him, saying, 'He will answer none of my words'? For God speaks in one way, and in two, though people do not perceive it. Job 33:13,14

My mind enlighten with your light, 379r
that I may understand aright
the glorious gospel mystery,
which shows the way to heaven and thee.

Let anyone with ears to hear listen! Mark 4:23

God calling yet! Shall I not hear? 310r
Earth's pleasures shall I still hold dear?
Shall life's swift passing years all fly,
and still my soul in slumbers lie?

Holy Father, the noise around us tends to drown out the voice of the Holy Spirit you've sent to guide and comfort us. Make us sensitive to your calling, as we take moments from the hustles and tussles of life to listen to you. Beloved Friend, create in us a clean heart and renew a right spirit within us. Amen.

Friday, March 28 — Psalm 40:9-17
Exodus 34; Matthew 26:59-75

Yours, O Lord, are the greatness, the power, the glory, the victory, and the majesty; for all that is in the heavens and on the earth is yours. 1 Chronicles 29:11

Savior, now with contrite hearts 741
we approach your throne of love,
asking pardon for our sins,
peace and comfort from above.
You once suffered on the cross
to atone for sinner's guilt;
may we never, Lord, forget
that for us your blood was spilled.

Whoever speaks must do so as one speaking the very words of God; whoever serves must do so with the strength that God supplies, so that God may be glorified in all things through Jesus Christ. To him belong the glory and the power forever and ever. 1 Peter 4:11

Hear our prayer, O Lord, 825
hear our prayer, O Lord,
incline your ear to us,
and grant us your peace. Amen.

Lord, open our hearts and minds to accept you as the omnipotent, omnipresent, and omniscient God of the universe. Therefore, let your peace dwell in us so that we may speak and live your words. Through Jesus Christ our Lord. Amen.

Saturday, March 29 — Psalm 41
Exodus 35; Matthew 27:1-10

Satisfy us in the morning with your steadfast love, so that we may rejoice and be glad all our days. Psalm 90:14

Worship, honor, glory, blessing, 454
Lord, we offer as our gift;
young and old, your praise expressing,
our glad songs to you we lift.
All the saints in heav'n adore you;
we would join their glad acclaim;
as your angels serve before you,
so on earth we praise your name.

Let us hold fast to the confession of our hope without wavering. Hebrews 10:23

My soul, then, with assurance 177r
hope still, be not dismayed;
he will from each encumbrance
again lift up your head;
beyond your wish extended
his goodness will appear,
when he has fully ended
what caused your needless fear.

Foundation of our faith, we thank you for not only being the author of the human race but also for allowing us free will to follow your instructions and teachings. Encourage us, O God, when we get discouraged and strengthen us when we become weak so we may stand firm on solid ground that is the foundation of our faith. Through Jesus Christ our sustainer and redeemer. Amen.

Second Sunday of Easter

Watchword for the Week — Blessed be the God and Father of our Lord Jesus Christ! By his great mercy he has given us a new birth into a living hope through the resurrection of Jesus Christ from the dead. 1 Peter 1:3

Sunday, March 30 — Acts 2:14a,22-32; Psalm 16
1 Peter 1:3-9; John 20:19-31

For a brief moment I abandoned you, but with great compassion I will gather you. Isaiah 54:7

Jesus, call thou me 285
from the world to thee;
speed me ever, stay me never;
Jesus, call thou me.

The gifts and the calling of God are irrevocable. Romans 11:29

Make my calling and election, 808
Jesus, ev'ry day more sure;
keep me under your direction,
till I, through almighty pow'r,
unto endless glory raised
in your mansions shall be placed.
When in you I end my race,
weeping shall forever cease.

Lord, open our hearts and minds so that we may be attentive to the voice of your calling. Do not leave us desolate or as orphans but help us be the gift of your irrevocable love. Help us to open up our hearts to one another so that you may be glorified. To God be the glory. Amen.

Monday, March 31 — Psalm 42
Exodus 36; Matthew 27:11-31

He will bring me out into the light; I will see his righteousness. Micah 7:9 (NIV)

Lead on, O King eternal; 753
we follow, not with fears,
for gladness breaks like morning
where'er your face appears:
your cross is lifted o'er us;
we journey in its light;
the crown awaits the conquest;
lead on, O God of might!

Once you were darkness, but now in the Lord you are light. Live as children of light. Ephesians 5:8

Light of the world, p68
we worship you;
our gifts to you we bring;
accept our sinful hearts, O Lord,
while praise to you we sing.

Omnipotent God, creator of the universe, we give you thanks and praise for having brought us out of darkness into light. This light has shone to all and lives in each believer. May we be nurtured by your Holy Spirit as we live for you by showing mercy and loving kindness to others. Help us to be just so that there can be peace and so that your manifestation to the human race will not be in vain. Most loving God, in your name we pray. Amen.

Tuesday, April 1 — Psalm 43
Exodus 37; Matthew 27:32-44

If my father and mother forsake me, the Lord will take me up. Psalm 27:10

Sing, pray, and keep his ways unswerving, 712
offer your service faithfully,
and trust his word; though undeserving,
you'll find his promise true to be.
God never will forsake in need
the soul that trusts in him indeed.

The Lord will rescue me from every evil attack and will bring me safely to his heavenly kingdom. To him be glory for ever and ever. 2 Timothy 4:18 (NIV)

Tenderly he shields and spares us, 529
well our feeble frame he knows,
in his hands he gently bears us,
rescues us from all our foes.
Alleluia! Alleluia!
Widely as his mercy flows.

Dear Lord, be with us today at home, school, and work. Rescue us from the pressures, worries, and stress of the day and give us clear minds to know and do your will. Amen.

Wednesday, April 2 — Psalm 44:1-8
Exodus 38; Matthew 27:45-56

Give us life, and we will call on your name. Psalm 80:18

Had I the grace to seek his face 596
in any trying hour!
Help from none will he withhold
who implores his power.

Christ says, "If in my name you ask me for anything, I will do it." John 14:14

Ask and it shall be given unto you, 605
seek and you shall find,
knock and the door shall be opened unto you —
Allelu, alleluia!

O Lord, forgive us for not believing when you say to just ask in your name. This very day we ask you to renew our spirits and fill us with energy to help all those in need. Thank you Lord! Amen.

Thursday, April 3 — Psalm 44:9-16
Exodus 39:1-31; Matthew 27:57-66

Once more I will astound these people with wonder upon wonder; the wisdom of the wise will perish. Isaiah 29:14 (NIV)

All glory to our Lord and God 485
for love so deep, so high, so broad —
the Trinity, whom we adore
forever and forevermore.

Many who heard him were astounded. They said, "Where did this man get all this? What is this wisdom that has been given to him? What deeds of power are being done by his hands!" Mark 6:2

But warm, sweet, tender, even yet, 196r
a present help is he;
and faith has still its Olivet,
and love its Galilee.

Lord Jesus, we are amazed at the wonders you performed and amazed still at the skills you give to physicians to heal. Lord grant each of us kind hands to do your will in this world. Amen.

Friday, April 4 — Psalm 44:17-26
Exodus 39:32-40:23; Matthew 28:1-20

The Lord is at my right hand, I shall not be moved. Psalm 16:8

I fully am persuaded 769
and joyfully declare
I'm never left unaided,
my Father hears my prayer;
his comforts never fail me,
he stands at my right hand;
when tempests fierce assail me,
they're calm at his command.

We make it our aim to please him. 2 Corinthians 5:9

Faithful soul, behold your King 275*
and Lord comes to meet you.
He will comfort and help you
as before the prophets had told you.
Please the Lord in ev'rything you do,
and his peace most sincerely pursue.

Holy Spirit, come upon our congregations and be with us. Help us in our struggles that we might always be faithful to our calling and please you in all that we do in your name. Amen.

Saturday, April 5 — Psalm 45:1-9
Exodus 40:24-Leviticus 1:17; Mark 1:1-8

The Lord said, "I will never again curse the ground because of humankind, for the inclination of the human heart is evil from youth. Genesis 8:21

We plow the fields, and scatter 453
the good seed on the land,
but it is fed and watered
by God's almighty hand;
he sends the snow in winter,
the warmth to swell the grain,
the breezes and the sunshine
and soft refreshing rain.
All good gifts around us
are sent from heav'n above;
then thank the Lord,
O thank the Lord for all his love.

We urge you not to receive God's grace in vain. 2 Corinthians 6:1 (NIV)

Witness here to all around you 515
of your Savior's dying love;
tell them how he sought and found you,
gave you grace from heav'n above.

Lord, we are grateful for all you have given us — the good earth where we can plant our seeds, the spring rains, and the warming sun. May we use all your gifts wisely as we witness for you. Amen.

Third Sunday of Easter

Watchword for the Week — You have been born anew, not of perishable but of imperishable seed, through the living and enduring word of God. 1 Peter 1:23

Sunday, April 6 — Acts 2:14a,36-41; Psalm 116:1-4,12-19
1 Peter 1:17-23; Luke 24:13-35

Ah, Lord, great and awesome God, keeping covenant and steadfast love with those who love you and keep your commandments, we have sinned and done wrong. Daniel 9:4,5

Hear then, dear Lord Jesus, 746
hear our earnest prayer,
grant your loving mercy,
keep us in your care.
All that is displeasing
unto you, forgive;
more to your name's glory
may we henceforth live.

Forgive us our debts, as we also have forgiven our debtors. Matthew 6:12

Pardon, Lord, and are there those 779
who my debtors are, or foes?
I, who by forgiveness live,
here their trespasses forgive.

Dear heavenly Father, forgive us in all our wrong doings. Give us courage to forgive others and not hold grudges. Cleanse our hearts that we may begin a new week with a clean slate. Amen.

Monday, April 7 — Psalm 45:10-17
Leviticus 2,3; Mark 1:9-20

Noah found favor in the sight of the Lord. Genesis 6:8

The Lord bless and keep you in his favor 446
as his chosen, cherished heir;
the Lord make his face shine on you ever
and enfold you in his care.
The Lord lift his countenance upon you,
may where-e'er you go his Spirit lead you,
and his peace on you bestow;
Amen, Amen, be it so.

By faith Noah, being warned by God about things not yet seen, in reverence prepared an ark for the salvation of his household. Hebrews 11:7 (NASB)

Gracious Father, bless this congregation 444
as the purchase of your Son;
for his sake behold us with compassion,
and us all your children own;
Jesus, grant to us your peace and favor;
Holy Spirit, dwell with us forever,
and to us Christ's love explain;
hear us, Lord our God! Amen.

Dear Lord, may we be like Noah — strong in faith and ready to do your will. May we find favor in your sight as we labor in your kingdom. Amen.

Tuesday, April 8 — Psalm 46
Leviticus 4; Mark 1:21-34

But as for me, I will look to the Lord, I will wait for the God of my salvation; my God will hear me. Micah 7:7

Had I the grace to seek his face 596
in any trying hour!
Help from none will he withhold
who implores his power.

As servants of God we have commended ourselves in every way: through great endurance, in afflictions, hardships, calamities. 2 Corinthians 6:4

God of church and God of hist'ry, 637*
pour your blessings on our deeds.
Grant endurance for our ventures,
give us strength to serve and lead.
Alleluia! Our Creator,
Christ and Spirit — this our creed.

We thank you this day, O Lord, for all those who accepted your promise of salvation, heard your call, and risked all to follow in your footsteps. Be with all those this day who are enduring hardship, affliction, and calamity. Strengthen them with your spirit. Amen.

Wednesday, April 9 — Psalm 47
Leviticus 5:1-6:13; Mark 1:35-45

For as the earth brings forth its shoots, and as a garden causes what is sown in it to spring up, so the Lord God will cause righteousness and praise to spring up before all the nations. Isaiah 61:11

We'll crowd your gates with thankful songs, 455
high as the heav'n our voices raise;
and earth, with her ten thousand tongues,
shall fill your courts with sounding praise.

He who supplies seed to the sower and bread for food will supply and multiply your seed for sowing and increase the harvest of your righteousness. 2 Corinthians 9:10

He only is the Maker of all things near and far; 453
he paints the wayside flower,
he lights the evening star;
the winds and waves obey him,
by him the birds are fed;
much more to us, his children,
he gives our daily bread.

Great Sower of seeds, we thank you for springtime and the opportunity it brings to renew our souls, plant seeds of faith, and trust in your name. Lord, bless our work and grant us a bountiful harvest. Amen.

Thursday, April 10 — Psalm 48
Leviticus 6:14-7:21; Mark 2:1-12

The decrees of the Lord are sure, making wise the simple. Psalm 19:7

The church from her dear master 237r
received the gift divine,
and still that light she lifteth
o'er all the earth to shine.
It is the golden casket
where gems of truth are stored;
it is the heaven-drawn picture
of Christ, the living word.

For since, in the wisdom of God, the world did not know God through wisdom, God decided, through the foolishness of our proclamation, to save those who believe. 1 Corinthians 1:21

I am trusting you to guide me; 542r
you alone shall lead,
every day and hour supplying
all my need.

Ageless God, we thank you for your wisdom. We thank you for the senior members of our congregations who have shared their wisdom with us over many years. Bless them for their continual faithful service. May your spirit be with them and lift them up. Amen.

Friday, April 11 — Psalm 49:1-12
Leviticus 7:22-8:17; Mark 2:13-28

O save your people, and bless your heritage; be their shepherd, and carry them forever. Psalm 28:9

Come, faithful Shepherd, bind me 795
with cords of love to thee,
and evermore remind me
that thou hast died for me;
O may the Holy Spirit
set this before my eyes,
that I thy death and merit
above all else may prize.

Jesus saw a great crowd; and he had compassion for them, because they were like sheep without a shepherd; and he began to teach them many things. Mark 6:34

Praise to the Savior for his deep compassion, 383
graciously caring for his chosen people;
young men and women, aging folk and children,
praise to the Savior!

Faithful and compassionate Shepherd, be with us. We need you to take us by your strong hands and lead us through each hour. Bring us safely to our rest at the end of the day. Amen.

Saturday, April 12 — Psalm 49:13-20
Leviticus 8:18-9:11; Mark 3:1-12

It is vain for you to rise up early, to retire late, to eat the bread of painful labors; for He gives to His beloved even in his sleep. Psalm 127:2 (NASB)

Day by day, at home, away, 723
Jesus is my staff and stay.
When I hunger, Jesus feeds me,
into pleasant pastures leads me;
when I thirst, he bids me go
where the quiet waters flow.

Jesus said to the disciples, "When I sent you out without a purse, bag, or sandals, did you lack anything?" They said, "No, not a thing." Luke 22:35

Show'rs of blessings, show'rs of blessing 636
from the Lord proceed,
strength supplying, strength supplying
in the time of need;
for no servant of our King
ever lacked for anything.
He will never, he will never
break the bruised reed.

Dear Jesus, we thank you for supplying all our needs each day. Forgive us when we want more than we really need. Move our hearts to share our abundance with those less fortunate. Amen.

Fourth Sunday of Easter

Watchword for the Week — Jesus says, "I am the gate. Whoever enters by me will be saved, and will come in and go out and find pasture." John 10:9

Sunday, April 13 — Acts 2:42-47; Psalm 23
1 Peter 2:19-25; John 10:1-10

Must I not take care to say what the Lord puts into my mouth? Numbers 23:12

Lord speak to me that I may speak 646
in living echoes of your tone.
As you have sought, so let me seek
your erring children lost and lone.

Jesus said, "I say to you that listen: Love your enemies, do good to those who hate you." Luke 6:27

Love is a gift, a present sweet, 536*
love unfailing and complete.
Bonded in love, we are to stand,
guided by the great command.
Love one another, bear no ill,
share of the bounty, do God's will.
Let us by action love profess,
with our deeds as evidence.

Lord, open our mouths that we may sing praises to you. Open our hearts and loosen our tongues that we may tell others of your wonderful love for us. Amen.

Monday, April 14 — Psalm 50:1-6
Leviticus 9:12-10:20; Mark 3:13-19

May the Lord give you increase, both you and your children. Psalm 115:14

Bless, O Lord, we pray, your congregation; 445
bless each home and family;
bless the youth, the rising generation;
blessed may your dear children be;
bless your servants, grant them help and favor;
you to glorify be their endeavor.
Lord, on you we humbly call;
let your blessing rest on all.

Jesus said, "Let the little children come to me; do not stop them; for it is to such as these that the kingdom of God belongs." And he took them up in his arms, laid his hands on them, and blessed them. Mark 10:14,16

Gracious Savior, gentle Shepherd, 660
children all are dear to you;
may your loving arms enfold them
in your care their whole life through;
fondly tend and safely keep them
in your mercy strong and true.

Father of all, we thank you this day for our children. May we be mindful of your example to care for our children at home, at school, and in our congregations. May we be faithful in our promise to love and nurture our children. Amen.

Tuesday, April 15 — Psalm 50:7-15
Leviticus 11:1-28; Mark 3:20-34

Shower, O heavens, from above, and let the skies rain down righteousness; let the earth open, that salvation may spring up, and let it cause righteousness to sprout up also; I the Lord have created it. Isaiah 45:8

He shall come down like showers 263
upon the fruitful earth,
and love, joy, hope, like flowers,
spring in his path to birth;
before him on the mountains
shall Peace, the herald, go;
and righteousness, in fountains,
from hill to valley flow.

Pursue righteousness, faith, love, and peace, along with those who call on the Lord from a pure heart. 2 Timothy 2:22

Lord, we your presence seek; 584
we ask this blessing true:
give us a pure and lowly heart,
a temple fit for you.

As the showers of springtime rain down upon the earth, O Lord, may your love rain down upon us, bringing salvation and renewed faith to our family and congregation. Let it pour, Lord! Amen.

Wednesday, April 16 — Psalm 50:16-23
Leviticus 11:29-13:8; Mark 4:1-20

The Lord is my light and my salvation; whom shall I fear? Psalm 27:1

Christians, dismiss your fear; 356
let hope and joy succeed;
the joyful news with gladness hear:
"The Lord is ris'n indeed!"
The promise is fulfilled
in Christ our only Head;
now justice, mercy, reconciled,
he lives who once was dead.

You were bought with a price; do not become slaves of human masters. 1 Corinthians 7:23

They live to him who bought them 516
with his blood,
baptized them with his Spirit, pure and good;
and in true faith and everburning love,
their hearts and hopes ascend to seek above
th'eternal good.

Light of the world, shine down on us this day and open our eyes to the needs of those around us. Grant us the desire to work for you bringing your hope to those around us. Amen.

Thursday, April 17 — Psalm 51:1-6
Leviticus 13:9-46; Mark 4:21-29

The Lord said to Abram, "I will bless you and you will be a blessing." Genesis 12:2 (NIV)

"I'll bless you, and you shall be set for a blessing!" 616
Thus said God, the Lord, to his servant of old;
O may we, in grace and in number increasing,
through work show our faith and in service be bold;
upon your truth founded, we shall not move,
let us ever follow, and fearless prove;
so shall we in doctrine, in word and behavior,
to ev'ryone witness that Christ is our Savior.

Do not repay evil for evil or abuse for abuse; but, on the contrary, repay with a blessing. It is for this that you were called — that you might inherit a blessing. 1 Peter 3:9

We now forgive each other's faults 785*
as we our own confess,
that we may love each other well
in Christian gentleness.

Giver of blessings, you have given us so much. May we be worthy of your gifts by showing understanding, forgiveness, and love to all with whom we come in contact today. Amen.

Friday, April 18 — Psalm 51:7-12
Leviticus 13:47-14:18; Mark 4:30-41

My soul clings to you; your right hand upholds me. Psalm 63:8

All praise to you my God this night 569
for all the blessings of the light.
Keep me, O keep me, King of kings,
beneath the shelter of your wings.

Moved with pity, Jesus stretched out his hand and touched the leper, and said to him, "I do choose. Be made clean!" Mark 1:41

That we may care, as you have cared 475br
for sick and lame, for deaf and blind,
and freely share, as you have shared,
in all the sorrows of mankind.

Great Healer, be with those among us this day who are awaiting test results, suffering from painful ailments, and are terminally ill. Comfort them in their hour of need. Our lives are in your loving hands. Amen.

Saturday, April 19 — Psalm 51:13-19
Leviticus 14:19-57; Mark 5:1-20

So teach us to count our days that we may gain a wise heart. Psalm 90:12

All our days, O Jesus, 770
hallow unto you;
may our lives be given
in your service true;
let us all experience,
to the end of days;
your abiding presence
and your loving grace.

Christ died for all, so that those who live might live no longer for themselves, but for him who died and was raised for them. 2 Corinthians 5:15

Sing alleluia, Christ does live, 364
and peace on earth restore;
come ransomed souls, and glory give,
sing, worship and adore:
to him our heartfelt thanks we pay
in deep humility.
It's God alone whose saving way
has set believers free.

Dear Lord, we thank you for the beauty of this day. May we use our time wisely today, sharing your love with others and giving glory and honor to you. Amen.

Fifth Sunday of Easter

Watchword for the Week — Jesus says, "I am the way, and the truth, and the life. No one comes to the Father except through me." John 14:6

Sunday, April 20 — Acts 7:55-60; Psalm 31:1-5,15-16
1 Peter 2:2-10; John 14:1-14

O Lord, how manifold are your works! In wisdom you have made them all; the earth is full of your creatures. Psalm 104:24

Each little flow'r that opens, 467
each little bird that sings —
God made their glowing colors,
God made their tiny wings.
All things bright and beautiful,
all creatures great and small,
all things wise and wonderful —
the Lord God made them all.

You are worthy, our Lord and God, to receive glory and honor and power, for you created all things. Revelation 4:11

Holy, holy, holy Lord God Almighty! 381
All thy works shall praise thy name
in earth and sky and sea.
Holy, holy, holy, merciful and mighty!
God in three persons, blessed Trinity!

Great Creator, we come to you with heavy hearts. You created a beautiful earth for us and we have really made a mess of it. Forgive us, Lord. Prod us to smarten up, wake up, and clean up. Amen.

Monday, April 21 — Psalm 52
Leviticus 15:1-24; Mark 5:21-43

The earth, O Lord, is full of your steadfast love; teach me your statutes. Psalm 119:64

Lead us to Christ, the living way, 157br
nor let us from his pastures stray;
lead us to holiness, the road
that we must take to dwell with God.

Christ says, "The Advocate, the Holy Spirit, whom the Father will send in my name, will teach you everything, and remind you of all that I have said to you." John 14:26

Teach us to know the Father, Son, 226r
and you, of both, to be but one;
that through the ages all along,
your praise may be our endless song.

Holy Spirit, come and be with us and lift us up. Open our minds to receive the message of God's love. Guide us and set us free to do your will. Amen.

Tuesday, April 22 — Psalm 53
Leviticus 15:25-16:25; Mark 6:1-6

Maintain justice, and do what is right, for soon my salvation will come, and my deliverance be revealed. Isaiah 56:1

For the herald's voice is crying 264
in the desert far and near,
calling us to true repentance,
since the Kingdom now is here.
O, that warning cry obey!
Now prepare for God a way!
Let the valleys rise to meet him,
and the hills bow down to greet him!

See, now is the acceptable time; see, now is the day of salvation! 2 Corinthians 6:2

Create in me a clean heart, O God, p79
and renew a right Spirit within me.
Cast me not away from your presence,
and take not your Holy Spirit from me.
Restore unto me the joy of salvation;
anoint me with your Spirit free.
Create in me a clean heart, O God,
and renew a right spirit within me.

Dear heavenly Father, we repent our sinful ways and are ready to receive salvation. Create a clean heart within us and fill us with your Spirit. Amen.

Wednesday, April 23 — Psalm 54
Leviticus 16:26-18:5; Mark 6:7-13

They have turned their backs to me, and not their faces. But in the time of their trouble they say, "Come and save us!" Jeremiah 2:27

Let every thought, and work, and word 342r
to you be ever given;
then life shall be your service, Lord,
and death the gate of heaven.

We will devote ourselves to prayer and to serving the word. Acts 6:4

Called by Christ, redeemed, accepted, 624*
we are blessed with work to do.
By the Spirit we're empowered:
"Tell the good news, life renew."
Our lives now reveal Christ's presence;
we will show God's love and grace.
Faith in action, ever, always,
while on earth we run our race.

Savior, we are sorry we turned our backs on you. Forgive us and save us from ourselves. Send Your Holy Spirit to encourage us to do your will. Amen.

Thursday, April 24 — Psalm 55:1-8
Leviticus 18:6-19:11; Mark 6:14-29

Who are they that fear the Lord? He will teach them the way that they should choose. Psalm 25:12

Lord Jesus, think on me, 764
nor let me go astray;
through darkness and perplexity
point out your chosen way.

Jesus said, "Follow me and I will make you fish for people." Mark 1:17

Let the people praise you, Lord; 384br
be by all that live adored;
let the nations shout and sing
glory to their Savior King;
at your feet their tribute pay,
and your holy will obey.

Holy Jesus, we know there will be many risks and surprises when we follow you. Fill us with your Spirit that we may accept the challenge to become fishers of those wishing to follow you. Amen.

Friday, April 25 — Psalm 55:9-15
Leviticus 19:12-20:8; Mark 6:30-44

Relieve the troubles of my heart, and bring me out of my distress. Psalm 25:17

Rejoice, then, ye sad hearted, 60r
who sit in deepest gloom,
who mourn o'er joys departed,
and tremble at your doom;
he who alone can cheer you
is standing at the door;
he brings his pity near you
and bids you weep no more.

Christ says, "In this world you will have trouble. But take heart! I have overcome the world." John 16:33 (NIV)

How good the name of Jesus sounds 487
to all believing ears!
It soothes our sorrows, heals our wounds,
and drives away our fears.
It makes the wounded spirit whole,
and calms the troubled mind;
his manna for each hungry soul,
the lost and weary find.

Precious Savior, how happy we are to know you will relieve us of our troubles. Give us the faith to leave our burdens and troubles with you. Calm our troubled hearts and be with us through the challenges of this day. Amen.

Saturday, April 26 — Psalm 55:16-19
Leviticus 20:9-21:12; Mark 6:45-56

The Lord our God may not leave us or abandon us. 1 Kings 8:57

Whate'er my God ordains is right; 549r
he never will deceive me;
he leads me by the proper path;
I know he will not leave me,
and take content
what he has sent,
his hand can turn my griefs away,
and patiently I wait his day.

The two disciples urged Jesus strongly, saying, "Stay with us, because it is almost evening and the day is now nearly over." So he went in to stay with them. Luke 24:29

When two friends on Easter day 112br
to Emmaus bent their way,
on that paschal eventide
Christ was walking at their side.
Then their hearts within them glowed
when himself to them he showed,
in the scriptures, as a king
glorified by suffering.

Holy Spirit, be with us this day. Do not leave us. Be with us as we witness to others. May the lonely feel your Spirit surrounding them and may those who are anxious feel your comfort. Amen.

Sixth Sunday of Easter

Watchword for the Week — Make a joyful noise to God, all the earth; sing the glory of his name; give to him glorious praise. Psalm 66:1,2

Sunday, April 27 — Acts 17:22-31; Psalm 66:8-20
1 Peter 3:13-22; John 14:15-21

For the Lord is good; his steadfast love endures forever, and his faithfulness to all generations. Psalm 100:5

Because the Lord our God is good, 539
his mercy is forever sure.
His truth at all times firmly stood,
and shall from age to age endure.

From his fullness we have all received, grace upon grace. John 1:16

My lips shall be employed to bless 370ow
the Lord who is my righteousness;
my pleasure, only to pursue
his steps and his blest will to do.

Amazing God, today we sing with joy and praise your name for all the goodness you have bestowed upon our congregations. May we always be faithful in our service to you. Amen.

Monday, April 28 — Psalm 55:20-23
Leviticus 21:13-22:16; Mark 7:1-8

**David said to the Lord, "I have sinned greatly in what I have done. But now, O Lord, I pray you, take away the guilt of your servant."
2 Samuel 24:10**

My faith looks trustingly 705
to Christ of Calvary,
my Savior true!
Lord, hear me while I pray,
take all my guilt away,
strengthen in ev'ry way
my love for you!

**Jesus said, "Those who are well have no need of a physician, but those who are sick; I have come to call not the righteous but sinners."
Mark 2:17**

Christ bids each afflicted soul 416
"Come that I may soothe your grief.
No one who is strong and whole
needs a doctor for relief;
therefore have no fear, draw nigh,
that your want I may supply."

Great Physician, like David, we ask that you forgive us our sins and remove all our guilt. Heal us and make us whole again so that we can do your will today. Amen.

Tuesday, April 29 — Psalm 56:1-8
Leviticus 22:17-23:22; Mark 7:9-23

My tears have been my food day and night, while people say to me continually, "Where is your God?" Psalm 42:3

He built the earth, he spread the sky, 26br
and fixed the starry lights on high:
wonders of grace to God belong,
repeat his mercies in your song.

At three o'clock Jesus cried out with a loud voice, "My God, my God, why have you forsaken me?" Mark 15:34

Christ, who on the cross forsaken, 699*
like a lamb to slaughter led,
suffered under Pontius Pilate,
he descended to the dead.
We believe in Jesus risen,
heaven's king to rule and reign,
to the Father's side ascended
till as judge he comes again.

Eternal God, how often we have wandered away and lost sight of you. But you are always here waiting for us to come back to you. We long to worship you Lord. Thank you for not forsaking us. Amen.

Wednesday, April 30 — Psalm 56:9-13
Leviticus 23:23-24:9; Mark 7:24-37

Our soul waits for the Lord; he is our help and shield. Psalm 33:20

O God, our help in ages past, 461
our hope for years to come,
remain our guard while life shall last,
and our eternal home.

If we hope for what we do not see, we wait for it with patience. Romans 8:25

Rely on God, your Savior, 177r
so shall you safe go on;
build on his grace and favor,
so shall your work be done.
You can make no advances
by self-consuming care;
but he his help dispenses,
when called upon by prayer.

Everlasting God, springtime reminds us of your great love for us. From plain brown bulbs spring unique and beautiful flowers. Give us hope that we too will become unique and beautiful in your sight, ready to witness for you. Amen.

Ascension Day
National Day of Prayer

Watchword for the Day — Christ says, "I, when I am lifted up from the earth, will draw all people to myself." John 12:32

Thursday, May 1 — Psalm 57:1-6
Leviticus 24:10-25:17; Mark 8:1-13

Ascension of the Lord — Acts 1:1-11; Psalm 47
Ephesians 1:15-23; Luke 24:44-53

Turn my eyes from looking at vanities. Psalm 119:37

Each little flow'r that opens, 467
each little bird that sings —
God made their glowing colors,
God made their tiny wings.
All things bright and beautiful,
all creatures great and small,
all things wise and wonderful —
the Lord God made them all.

The Lord Jesus, after he had spoken to the disciples, was taken up into heaven and sat down at the right hand of God. And they went out and proclaimed the good news everywhere. Mark 16:19,20

The word of God, which ne'er shall cease, 509
proclaims free pardon, grace, and peace,
salvation shows in Christ alone,
the perfect will of God makes known.

Lord Jesus, may we see the real world about us rather than our human perception. May we react, as did the disciples, to the fact that the you have ascended by sharing the gospel everywhere. Amen.

Friday, May 2 — Psalm 57:7-11
Leviticus 25:18-55; Mark 8:14-21

Full of honor and majesty is his work, and his righteousness endures forever. Psalm 111:3

But now the bonds of death are burst, 374
the ransom has been paid;
and you are on your Father's throne
in majesty arrayed.
All praise to you, ascended Lord,
all glory ever be
to Father, Son, and Spirit now,
and through eternity.

Without any doubt, the mystery of our religion is great: He was revealed in flesh, vindicated in spirit, seen by angels, proclaimed among Gentiles, believed in throughout the world, taken up in glory. 1 Timothy 3:16

Great things he has taught us, 550
great things he has done,
and great our rejoicing through Jesus the Son:
but purer, and higher, and greater will be
our wonder, our transport when Jesus we see.

Lord, the mystery of God's plan helps us to seek to understand more of God's works all about us. Growing in understanding God's ways, we are overwhelmed by his greatness in all things. Continue to stretch our faith. Amen.

Saturday, May 3 — Psalm 58
Leviticus 26:1-35; Mark 8:22-38

Our God turned the curse into a blessing. Nehemiah 13:2

Those who are by Christ directed, 717
trusting the Good Shepherd's care,
from all harm will be protected,
and no danger need to fear.

In Christ God was reconciling the world to himself, not counting their trespasses against them, and entrusting the message of reconciliation to us. 2 Corinthians 5:19

Maker of all things, Lord our God, p73
now veiled in feeble flesh and blood,
to reconcile and set us free
from endless woe and misery.

We thank you, Lord Jesus, for helping us see into God's heart. We have learned your testing is to make us stronger. God's love sent you to us as a suffering servant so reconciliation for us is to share love with others. Amen.

Ascension Sunday
Seventh Sunday of Easter

Watchword for the Week — Cast all your anxiety on him, because he cares for you. 1 Peter 5:7

Sunday, May 4 — Acts 1:6-14; Psalm 68:1-10,32-35
1 Peter 4:12-14,5:6-11; John 17:1-11

He shall be the one of peace. Micah 5:5

Drop thy still dews of quietness, 739
till all our strivings cease.
Take from our souls the strain and stress;
and let our ordered lives confess
the beauty of thy peace.

Christ says: Peace I leave with you; my peace I give to you. I do not give to you as the world gives. Do not let your hearts be troubled, and do not let them be afraid. John 14:27

Grant we beseech thee, merciful Lord, *
grant to thy faithful people pardon and peace.
Sweet peace, sweet peace.

Mighty God, we live in a violent world that has had peace for only a few years in a century. Make peace-making our calling. Let us not forget that though Jesus lived peace, he was put to death in violence. Amen.

* Taken from the Bluefields Nicaragua Archives, by J. H. Tenney. Used by permission.

Monday, May 5 — Psalm 59:1-9
Leviticus 26:36-27:15; Mark 9:1-10

Hear, you peoples, all of you; listen, O earth, and all that is in it; and let the Lord God be a witness against you. Micah 1:2

The law and prophets there have place, 327
two chosen witnesses of grace;
the Father's voice from out the cloud
proclaims his only Son aloud.

In the past God spoke to our forefathers through the prophets at many times and in various ways, but in these last days he has spoken to us by his Son. Hebrews 1:1,2 (NIV)

We walk by faith and not by sight; 713
no gracious words we hear
from Christ, who spoke as none e'er spoke;
but we believe him near.

We are grateful, Lord Jesus, for your words that are recorded in scripture, and for the teaching done through your acts. Continue to witness to us in our hearts. Amen.

Tuesday, May 6 — Psalm 59:10-17
Leviticus 27:16-Numbers 1:16; Mark 9:11-29

Only fear the Lord, and serve him faithfully with all your heart; for consider what great things he has done for you. 1 Samuel 12:24

To God be the glory — 550
great things he has done!
So loved he the world that he gave us his Son,
who yielded his life an atonement for sin,
and opened the life gate that all may go in.
Praise the Lord, praise the Lord,
let the earth hear his voice!
Praise the Lord, praise the Lord,
let the people rejoice!
O come to the Father through Jesus the Son,
And give him the glory —
great things he has done!

The church throughout Judea, Galilee, and Samaria had peace and was built up. Living in the fear of the Lord and in the comfort of the Holy Spirit, it increased in numbers. Acts 9:31

Come as a messenger of peace, 432
filled with the Spirit, fired with love;
live to behold our large increase,
and die to meet us all above.

Dear God, we are convinced of your love for us by the miracles you performed in the past and the miracles we experience daily. These cause us to praise you every day. Amen.

Wednesday, May 7 — Psalm 60
Numbers 1:17-54; Mark 9:30-37

There is no Holy One like the Lord, no one besides you. 1 Samuel 2:2

Holy, holy, holy! 381
Though the darkness hide thee,
though the eye made blind by sin
thy glory may not see,
only thou art holy; there is none beside thee,
perfect in pow'r, in love, and purity.

As he who called you is holy, be holy yourselves in all your conduct. 1 Peter 1:15

Come then, come, O flock of Jesus, 673
covenant with him anew;
unto him, who conquered for us,
pledge we love and service true;
and should our love's union holy
firmly linked no more remain,
wait ye at his footstool lowly,
till he draw it close again.

Lord Jesus, we cannot be holy like you, because only you are unique. But we can turn our lives over to you, so you can help us love others. In your precious name we pray. Amen.

Thursday, May 8 — Psalm 61
Numbers 2; Mark 9:38-50

Praise the Lord! I will give thanks to the Lord with my whole heart, in the company of the upright, in the congregation. Psalm 111:1

Gracious Father, bless this congregation 444
as the purchase of your Son;
for his sake behold us with compassion,
and us all your children own;
Jesus, grant to us your peace and favor;
Holy Spirit, dwell with us forever,
and to us Christ's love explain;
hear us, Lord our God! Amen.

Let no evil talk come out of your mouths, but only what is useful for building up, as there is need, so that your words may give grace to those who hear. Ephesians 4:29

O teach me, Lord, that I may teach 646
the precious truths which you impart.
And wing my words that they may reach
the hidden depths of many a heart.

Our talk, dear God, is formed among the faithful, but we need to share these kind words we learn, to teach those who seek to know you personally. In your name. Amen.

Friday, May 9 — Psalm 62
Numbers 3:1-32; Mark 10:1-12

Consider my affliction and my trouble, and forgive all my sins. Psalm 25:18

Hear then, dear Lord Jesus, 746
hear our earnest prayer,
grant your loving mercy,
keep us in your care.
All that is displeasing
unto you, forgive;
more to your name's glory
may we henceforth live.

The saying is sure and worthy of full acceptance, that Christ Jesus came into the world to save sinners. 1 Timothy 1:15

To avert from us God's wrath, 416
Jesus suffered in our stead;
by an ignominious death
he a full atonement made;
and by his most precious blood
brought us, sinners, nigh to God.

When we are discouraged with our ineffective lives, dear Lord, we are grateful that you came into this world to save sinners like us. We are cleansed daily and abundantly. Thank you! Amen.

Saturday, May 10 — Psalm 63
Numbers 3:33-4:14; Mark 10:13-31

Those who know your name put their trust in you, for you, O Lord, have not forsaken those who seek you. Psalm 9:10

Jesus' name, Jesus' name, 324
source of life and happiness!
In this name true consolation
mourning sinners may possess;
here is found complete salvation.
Blessed Jesus, we your name will praise
all our days, all our days.

Peter said, "Repent, and be baptized every one of you in the name of Jesus Christ so that your sins may be forgiven; and you will receive the gift of the Holy Spirit." Acts 2:38

They live to him who bought them 516
with his blood,
baptized them with his Spirit, pure and good;
and in true faith and everburning love,
their hearts and hopes ascend to seek above
th'eternal good.

Dear Lord, as on the miracle of Pentecost, the Holy Spirit powerfully began a new phase of God's plan, you can still call us to new life. Give us the gifts we need. Amen.

Day of Pentecost

Watchword for the Week — Now there are varieties of gifts, but the same Spirit; and there are varieties of services, but the same Lord. 1 Corinthians 12:4,5

Sunday, May 11 — Acts 2:1-21; Psalm 104:24-34,35b
1 Corinthians 12:3b-13; John 20:19-23

The righteousness of the righteous shall not save them when they transgress; and as for the wickedness of the wicked, it shall not make them stumble when they turn from their wickedness. Ezekiel 33:12

O Spirit, our Lord God, 376
in this appointed hour,
as on the day of Pentecost,
descend with all your pow'r.

As Jesus was walking along, he saw Levi, son of Alphaeus, sitting at the tax booth, and he said to him, "Follow me." And he got up and followed him. Mark 2:14

Jesus, still lead on 799
till our rest be won;
and although the way be cheerless,
we will follow calm and fearless;
guide us by your hand
to the promised land.

Lord, you have always dealt with humanity as we struggled without your power. You called leaders to plant seeds, to move mountains, and dream dreams. We still need your spirit and power. Amen.

Monday, May 12 — Psalm 64
Numbers 4:15-49; Mark 10:32-45

You drink wine by the bowlful and use the finest lotions, but you do not grieve over the ruin of Joseph. Amos 6:6 (NIV)

They walked with God in peace and love 396
but failed with one another;
while sternly for the faith they strove,
they fell out with each other.
But he in whom they put their trust,
who knew their frames, that they were dust,
with pity healed their weakness.

Do not be mismatched with unbelievers. For what partnership is there between righteousness and lawlessness? Or what fellowship is there between light and darkness? 2 Corinthians 6:14

Then forth they went, with tongues of flame 396
in one blessed theme delighting;
the love of Jesus, and his name,
God's children all uniting.
That love our theme and watchword still;
the law of love may we fulfill —
give love as love we're given.

God, when the people in Herrnhut realized they could not fellowship with one another, you brought them together by the brotherly agreement which gave new hope. Heal our churches today. Amen.

Tuesday, May 13 — Psalm 65:1-8
Numbers 5; Mark 10:46-52

Put my tears in your bottle. Are they not in your record? Psalm 56:8

Faith in the conscience works for peace, 700
and bids the mourner's weeping cease,
by faith the children's place we claim,
and give all honor to one name.

God will wipe every tear from their eyes. Revelation 21:4

May we faithful, may we faithful 636
in our service be,
truly careful, truly careful
in our ministry;
keep us to your church fast bound,
in the faith preserve us sound,
often weeping, often weeping
grateful tears of joy.

Create in us a new heart, O Lord, and as you dry our tears, open our eyes to the possibilities that you have for our churches today. We pray in Jesus' name. Amen.

Wednesday, May 14 — Psalm 65:9-13
Numbers 6; Mark 11:1-11

I will remember my covenant with you in the days of your youth, and I will establish with you an everlasting covenant. Ezekiel 16:60

We covenant with hand and heart p183
to follow Christ our Lord;
with world, and sin, and self to part,
and to obey his word;
to love each other heartily,
in truth and with sincerity,
and under cross, reproach, and shame,
to glorify his name.

My sheep hear my voice. I know them, and they follow me. I give them eternal life, and they will never perish. No one will snatch them out of my hand. John 10:27,28

Jesus makes my heart rejoice, 662
I'm his sheep and know his voice;
he's a Shepherd, kind and gracious,
and his pastures are delicious;
constant love to me he shows,
yea, my very name he knows.

The close relationship you have with us, O Lord, is based on your gift and our response. As we follow your will, your pastoral grace saves us from disaster. Speak your word, we are listening. Amen.

Thursday, May 15 — Psalm 66:1-7
Numbers 7:1-35; Mark 11:12-26

They rejoice before you as with joy at the harvest. Isaiah 9:3

All your works with joy surround you, 544
earth and heav'n reflect your rays,
stars and angels sing around you,
center of unbroken praise;
field and forest, vale and mountain,
flow'ry meadow, flashing sea,
chanting bird and flowing fountain,
praising you eternally!

The crowds with one accord listened eagerly to what was said by Philip... So there was great joy in that city. Acts 8:6,8

God gave us faithful ones to lead 519
and help us in our time of need;
but, Lord, all pow'r is yours alone,
and you the work must carry on.

Lord, out of Philip's lips you brought joy to believers — but those with hate-filled hearts brought martyrdom to Philip. We are thankful you changed Saul into Paul. Such faithfulness moves hearts by your spirit. Amen.

Friday, May 16 — Psalm 66:8-15
Numbers 7:36-71; Mark 11:27-12:12

My people have committed two evils: they have forsaken me, the fountain of living water, and dug out cisterns for themselves, cracked cisterns that can hold no water. Jeremiah 2:13

I heard the voice of Jesus say, 606
"Behold, I freely give
the living water; thirsty one,
stoop down and drink and live."
I came to Jesus, and I drank
of that life-giving stream;
my thirst was quenched, my soul revived,
and now I live in him.

You cannot serve God and wealth. Matthew 6:24

Take my life, O Lord, renew, 647
consecrate my heart to you;
take my moments and my days;
let me sing your ceaseless praise.

Lord Jesus, we are grateful you always give us choices. But with the choices, you give us grace and faithful friends to help us choose the higher way. Give us long-term wisdom. Amen.

Saturday, May 17 — Psalm 66:16-20
Numbers 7:72-8:4; Mark 12:13-17

Daniel was taken up out of the den, and no kind of harm was found on him, because he had trusted in his God. Daniel 6:23

Standing by a purpose true, heeding God's command, *
Honor them, the faithful few!
All hail to Daniel's Band!
Dare to be a Daniel, dare to stand alone!
Dare to have a purpose firm!
Dare to make it known!

Do not fear what you are about to suffer. Be faithful until death, and I will give you the crown of life. Revelation 2:10

No condemnation now I dread, 773
for Christ, and all in him, is mine!
Alive in him, my living Head,
and clothed in righteousness divine,
bold I approach the eternal throne
and claim the crown, through Christ, my own.

Thankfully, Lord Jesus, we view the martyrs of the past. We wonder what we would do if we were faced with such a choice. Keep us faithful, make us strong, should such a calling come to us. Amen.

* by Philip P. Bliss. Used by permission.

Trinity Sunday

Watchword for the Week — O Lord, our Sovereign, how majestic is your name in all the earth! Psalm 8:9

Sunday, May 18 — Genesis 1:1-2:4a; Psalm 8
2 Corinthians 13:11-13; Matthew 28:16-20

Remember the wonderful works he has done, his miracles, and the judgments he uttered. Psalm 105:5

Holy, holy, holy Lord God Almighty! 381
All thy works shall praise thy name
in earth and sky and sea.
Holy, holy, holy, merciful and mighty!
God in three persons, blessed Trinity!

He has done everything well; he even makes the deaf to hear and the mute to speak. Mark 7:37

Thou, O Christ, art all I want; 724
more than all in thee I find;
raise the fallen, cheer the faint,
heal the sick and lead the blind.
Just and holy is thy name,
I am all unrighteousness,
false and full of sin I am,
thou are full of truth and grace.

Lord Jesus, we come to you in the name of the Father and in the Spirit to celebrate the power of your creation, your redemption, and your renewal of us all. How great you are! Amen.

Monday, May 19 — Psalm 67
Numbers 8:5-9:14; Mark 12:18-34

Do not devise evil in your hearts against one another. Zechariah 7:10

We've a song to be sung to the nations, 621
that shall lift their hearts to the Lord,
a song that shall conquer evil
and shatter the spear and sword.

Rid yourselves, therefore, of all malice, and all guile, insincerity, envy, and all slander. 1 Peter 2:1

Mine is the sin, but yours the righteousness; 421
mine is the guilt, but yours the cleansing blood;
here is my robe, my refuge, and my peace,
your blood, your righteousness, O Lord, my God.

In your creation of humanity, Lord Jesus, you gave us freedom to choose between good and evil, truth and falsehood, love and hate. We thank you for being with us in all our decisions. Amen.

Tuesday, May 20 — Psalm 68:1-6
Numbers 9:15-10:36; Mark 12:35-44

You intended to harm me, but God intended it for good. Genesis 50:20 (NIV)

Manifest in making whole 313
palsied limbs and fainting soul;
manifest in valiant fight,
quelling all the devil's might;
manifest in gracious will,
ever bringing good from ill;
anthems be to you addressed,
God in flesh made manifest.

God opposes the proud, but gives grace to the humble. 1 Peter 5:5

Restrain me lest I harbor pride, 733
lest I in my own strength confide;
though I am weak, show me anew
I have my pow'r, my strength from you.

The deeds of Joseph's brothers intended harm, O God, and we have done harmful acts, and spoken harmful words. Give grace, as you did to Joseph, to turn those sins into blessings for all. Amen.

Wednesday, May 21 — Psalm 68:7-18
Numbers 11; Mark 13:1-13

The Lord our God be with us, as he was with our ancestors. 1 Kings 8:57

God with us, God with us, 324
God made known in human frame;
in his name rejoice with gladness,
since to save the lost he came;
none need sink in hopeless sadness,
for Immanuel is now with us,
God with us, God with us.

Paul said, "We bring you the good news that what God promised to our ancestors, he has fulfilled for us, their children, by raising Jesus." Acts 13:32,33

We know that Christ is raised and dies no more. 366
Embraced by death he broke its fearful hold;
and our despair he turned to blazing joy.
Alleluia!

We are blessed by these words, Lord, because we can trace your promises to our ancestors, fulfilled through the early church, and to us today. What a blessing! Amen.

Thursday, May 22 — Psalm 68:19-27
Numbers 12:1-13:16; Mark 13:14-27

It is better to take refuge in the Lord than to put confidence in mortals. Psalm 118:8

If you but suffer God to guide you, 544r
and hope in Him through all your ways,
he'll give you strength, what e'er betide you,
and bear you through the evil days;
who trusts in God's unchanging love
builds on the rock that nought can move.

For God all things are possible. Mark 10:27

The peace of Christ makes fresh my heart, 701
a fountain ever springing!
All things are mine since I am his!
How can I keep from singing?

As you led your disciples in singing, Lord Jesus, your daily leading builds our confidence so that we cannot keep from singing. Thank you for the path you give us every day. Amen.

Friday, May 23 — Psalm 68:28-35
Numbers 13:17-33; Mark 13:28-37

Who observes my ordinances, and follows my statutes; he shall not die for his father's iniquity. Ezekiel 18:17

Breathe on me, breath of God, 494
fill me with life anew,
that I may love the things you love
and do what you would do.
Breathe on me, breath of God,
so shall I never die,
but live with you the perfect life
of your eternity.

You also must consider yourselves dead to sin and alive to God in Christ Jesus. Romans 6:11

Holy Spirit, ever dwelling 495
in the holiest realms of light;
Holy Spirit, ever brooding
o'er a world of gloom and night;
Holy Spirit, ever raising
those of earth to thrones on high;
living, life-imparting Spirit,
you we praise and magnify.

"There is a balm in Gilead to make the wounded whole, there is a balm in Gilead to heal the sin-sick soul.*" Thank you for making us alive. In the name of Jesus. Amen.

* Moravian Book of Worship, 500.

Saturday, May 24 — Psalm 69:1-12
Numbers 14; Mark 14:1-11

If you are returning to the Lord with all your heart, then put away the foreign gods. 1 Samuel 7:3

Prayer is the contrite sinner's voice 749
returning from his ways,
while angels in their songs rejoice,
and cry, "Behold he prays!"

We know that no idol in the world really exists, and that there is no God but one. 1 Corinthians 8:4

Before the Lord's eternal throne, 455
you nations, bow with sacred joy;
know that the Lord is God alone;
he can create, and he destroy.

Lord Jesus, many of us grew up with our parents' faith, but when we left home we realized it was not ours, and we groped about. But when we returned to you we rejoiced with the angels! Amen.

Second Sunday after Pentecost

Watchword for the Week — For the Lord has comforted his people, and will have compassion on his suffering ones. Isaiah 49:13

Sunday, May 25 — Isaiah 49:8-16a; Psalm 131
1 Corinthians 4:1-5; Matthew 6:24-34

I am surely going to teach the nations, this time I am going to teach them my power and my might, and they shall know that my name is the Lord. Jeremiah 16:21

O blessed Lord, teach me your law, 510
your righteous judgments I declare;
your testimonies make me glad,
for they are wealth beyond compare.

It has now been revealed to his holy apostles and prophets by the Spirit: that is, the Gentiles have become fellow heirs, members of the same body, and sharers in the promise in Christ Jesus through the gospel. Ephesians 3:5,6

The Lord bless and keep you in his favor 446
as his chosen, cherished heir;
the Lord make his face shine on you ever
and enfold you in his care.
The Lord lift his countenance upon you,
may where-e're you go his Spirit lead you,
and his peace on you bestow;
Amen, Amen, be it so.

The spirit of the law has been given to your beloved people, Lord Jesus, and we are heirs of all the promises. Your peace is bestowed on us daily and abundantly. What a privilege! Amen.

Monday, May 26 — Psalm 69:13-21
Numbers 15:1-31; Mark 14:12-31

Remember your creator in the days of your youth, before the days of trouble come, and the years draw near when you will say, "I have no pleasure in them." Ecclesiastes 12:1

Now in the days of youth, 509r
when life flows fresh and free,
you Lord of all our hearts and lives,
we give ourselves to you;
Our fervent gift receive,
and fit us to fulfill,
through all our days, in all our ways,
our heavenly Father's will.

Paul wrote to Timothy: Let no one despise your youth, but set the believers an example in speech and conduct, in love, in faith, in purity. 1 Timothy 4:12

Just as I am, young, strong, and free, 503r
to be the best that I can be
for truth, and righteousness, and you,
Lord of my life, I come.

Lord God, no matter what phase of life we are in, we need your encouragement to do our best. Especially help the youth as they grow, aid the aged as they mature, and bless us all. Amen.

Tuesday, May 27 — Psalm 69:22-29
Numbers 15:32-16:27; Mark 14:32-42

Depart from evil, and do good; seek peace, and pursue it. Psalm 34:14

All our knowledge, sense, and sight 558
lie in deepest darkness shrouded,
till your Spirit breaks our night
with the beams of truth unclouded;
you alone to God can win us;
you must work all good within us.

Rejoice, be made complete, be comforted, be like-minded, live in peace; and the God of love and peace shall be with you.
2 Corinthians 13:11 (NASB)

So to our God we sing praises, 316
who all our spirits upraises,
and we rejoice in the telling
of his dear grace in us dwelling.

Gracious God, your way of life is clear and comforting, but distractions lead us astray. Keep us close to you so we will always have your guidance and grace. Amen.

Wednesday, May 28 — Psalm 69:30-36
Numbers 16:28-17:13; Mark 14:43-52

I will not leave you until I have done what I have promised you. Genesis 28:15

Just as I am; thou wilt receive, 762
wilt welcome, pardon, cleanse, relieve;
because thy promise I believe,
O Lamb of God, I come, I come!

God, who never lies, promised eternal life before the ages began. Titus 1:2

Thy word, O God, declares 568r
no man has seen or heard
the joys our God prepares
for them that love their Lord.
Their eyes shall see your glory,
your face, your throne, your might;
with shouts shall they adore you,
the true, eternal light.

You are a God of promises, Lord Jesus, and we know that you are faithful in all your promises. We follow because we know you have prepared a place for us. Amen.

Thursday, May 29 — Psalm 70
Numbers 18:1-24; Mark 14:53-65

Then God said, "Let there be light;" and there was light. Genesis 1:3

God, whose almighty word 380
chaos and darkness heard,
and took their flight:
hear us, we humbly pray.
And where the gospel day
sheds not its glorious ray,
let there be light!

Christ says, "I am the light of the world. Whoever follows me will never walk in darkness but will have the light of life." John 8:12

I heard the voice of Jesus say, 369r
"I am this dark world's Light;
look unto me, your morn shall rise,
and all your day be bright."
I looked to Jesus, and I found
in him my Star, my Sun;
and in that Light of life I'll walk,
till traveling days are done.

We often stumble with our flashlights of faith, O Lord, when you bring the floodlight of your presence. As we seek to follow in your footsteps, you are the Lamp and the Light of life! In gratitude, we pray. Amen.

Friday, May 30 — Psalm 71:1-8
Numbers 18:25-19:22; Mark 14:66-72

Long ago you laid the foundation of the earth, and the heavens are the work of your hands. Psalm 102:25

The heavens are telling the Lord's endless glory, *
through all the earth his praise is found.
The seas re-echo the marvelous story:
let all repeat that glorious sound!

Hallelujah! Salvation and glory and power to our God. Revelation 19:1

Sing hallelujah, praise the Lord! 543
Sing with a cheerful voice;
exalt our God with one accord,
and in his name rejoice.
Ne'er cease to sing, O ransomed host,
praise Father, Son, and Holy Ghost,
until in realms of endless light
your praises shall unite.

From debating the creation of the earth, O Lord, with the academic theories of evolution, we all are overwhelmed with the unimaginable complexity of our universe. Just to imagine it is awesome! Thank you. Amen.

* Salem Easter Sunrise Ode. Used by permission.

Saturday, May 31 — Psalm 71:9-18
Numbers 20:1-21:9; Mark 15:1-20

O God, from my youth you have taught me, and I still proclaim your wondrous deeds. Psalm 71:17

Church, rejoice! Raise your voice, 631
sing Jehovah's worthy praise;
extol his name forever;
laud him, our God and Savior;
proclaim to ev'ry nation
the tidings of salvation;
bear the witness to his greatness;
spread the story of his glory
to the earth's remotest bounds.

Paul wrote to Timothy: Continue in what you have learned and firmly believed. 2 Timothy 3:14

O give me Samuel's mind! 609
A sweet unmurm'ring faith,
obedient and resigned
to thee in life and death,
that I may read with childlike eyes
truths that are hidden from the wise.

Lord, you called Samuel in the temple to a lifetime of faithfulness. You gave him and a confused Israel wisdom and insight. Give us that faith to appreciate the truths beyond our mind's comprehension. Amen.

Third Sunday after Pentecost

Watchword for the Week — Blessed be the Lord, for he has wondrously shown his steadfast love to me. Psalm 31:21

Sunday, June 1—Deuteronomy 11:18-21,26-28; Psalm 31:1-5,19-24 Romans 1:16-17,3:22b-28,(29-31); Matthew 7:21-29

How awesome is this place! This is none other than the house of God, and this is the gate of heaven. Genesis 28:17

God reveals his presence; 554
let us now adore him
and with awe appear before him.
God is in His temple;
all in us keep silence
and before him bow with reverence.
Him alone God we own;
he's our Lord and Savior.
Praise his name forever.

Christ says, "I am the gate. Whoever enters by me will be saved." John 10:9

You are the way; to you alone 661
from sin and death we flee;
and those who would the Father seek
your followers must be.

God, where we are is your house. Where we are is the gate of heaven. This is the place of worship. This is the place of the Spirit. Father, we've come to worship you. Amen.

Monday, June 2 — Psalm 71:19-24
Numbers 21:10-22:6; Mark 15:21-32

The Lord said to Gideon, "Peace be to you; do not fear, you shall not die." Then Gideon built an altar there to the Lord, and called it, The Lord is peace. Judges 6:23,24

"Fear not, I am with you; O be not dismayed, 709
for I am your God and will still give you aid;
I'll strengthen you, help you and cause you to stand
upheld by my righteous, omnipotent hand."

Strive to be found by him at peace, without spot or blemish. 2 Peter 3:14

Jesus, Prince of peace, be near us; 13r
fix in all our hearts your home;
with your gracious presence cheer us;
let your sacred kingdom come;
raise to heaven our expectation,
give our favored souls to prove
glorious and complete salvation
in the realms of bliss above.

Father, you are a strong and faithful God. Raise the spirits of the downcast and restore those who have fallen away that your Church may continually sing of your saving help; through Jesus Christ our Lord. Amen.

Tuesday, June 3 — Psalm 72:1-11
Numbers 22:7-41; Mark 15:33-47

I shall not be put to shame, having my eyes fixed on all your commandments. Psalms 119:6

O Jesus, I have promised 603
to serve you to the end;
be now and ever near me,
my master and my friend.
I shall not fear the battle
if you are by my side,
nor wander from the pathway
if you will be my guide.

Guard what has been entrusted to you. 1 Timothy 6:20

O Jesus, you have promised 603
to all who follow you
that where you are in glory
your servants shall be too.
And Jesus, I have promised
to serve you to the end;
O give me grace to follow,
my master and my friend.

God, help us to be Christians who remain faithful to the gospel until the end. May we guard what has been entrusted to us and entrust it to others faithfully, not because we are great, but because your great grace has been asked for, trusted in, and received. Amen.

Wednesday, June 4 — Psalm 72:12-20
Numbers 23; Mark 16:1-13

With the Lord on my side I do not fear. What can mortals do to me? Psalm 118:6

Love divine, all loves excelling, 474
joy of heav'n, to earth come down!
Fix in us you humble dwelling,
all your faithful mercies crown.
Jesus, you are all compassion,
pure unbounded love impart!
Visit us with your salvation,
enter ev'ry trembling heart.

There is no fear in love, but perfect love casts out fear. 1 John 4:18

Finish, then, your new creation; 474
pure and spotless let us be;
let us see your great salvation
perfectly restored and free.
Changed from glory into glory,
till in heav'n we take our place,
till we cast our crowns before you,
lost in wonder, love, and praise.

Oh Lord, take any fear from our hearts so we will be able to live real love without fear. Help us to be children of faith with passionate love for you, not giving in to worries, fears, or an uptight and anxious spirit. Amen.

Thursday, June 5 — Psalm 73:1-12
Numbers 24,25; Mark 16:14-Luke 1:4

Wash me thoroughly from my iniquity, and cleanse me from my sin. Psalm 51:2

Just as I am, and waiting not 762
to rid my soul of one dark blot,
to thee, whose blood can cleanse each spot,
O Lamb Of God, I come, I come!

Jesus said, "The tax collector, standing far off, would not even look up to heaven, but was beating his breast and saying, 'God, be merciful to me, a sinner!' I tell you, this man went down to his home justified." Luke 18:13,14

Just as I am; thou wilt receive, 762
wilt welcome, pardon, cleanse, relieve;
because thy promise I believe,
O Lamb Of God, I come, I come!

Father, thank you for making it possible for us to come to you through Jesus. We come as works in progress, not claiming to have already achieved. Receive us, Lord, just as we are, and walk with us on our journey. Amen.

Friday, June 6 — Psalm 73:13-20
Numbers 26:1-24; Luke 1:5-25

Love the Lord, all you his saints. Psalm 31:23

O could we but love that Savior, 589
who loves us so ardently,
as we ought, our souls would ever
full of joy and comfort be;
if we, by his love incited,
could ourselves and all forget,
then, with Jesus Christ united,
we should heav'n anticipate.

If I have prophetic powers and understand all mysteries and all knowledge, and if I have all faith, so as to remove mountains, but do not have love, I am nothing. 1 Corinthians 13:2

When love unfeigned our actions truly show, 415br
the God of peace his blessing will bestow;
O Lord, unite your Church for Jesus' sake,
and bless what in your name we undertake.

Father, all too often we do not love at all; when we do love, we love within certain boundaries. Lord Jesus, forgive our lovelessness, and teach us to love others as you have loved us. Amen.

Saturday, June 7 — Psalm 73:21-28
Numbers 26:25-56; Luke 1:26-38

Those who oppress the poor insult their maker. Proverbs 14:31

O brother man, fold to your heart your brother; 488r
where pity dwells, the peace of God is there;
to worship rightly is to love each other,
each smile a hymn, each kindly deed a prayer.

In humility regard others as better than yourselves. Philippians 2:3

May it to the world appear 487r
that we your disciples are
by our loving mutually,
by our being on in thee.

Father, you are the one who holds our lives in your hands. Give not what we so desire in economics and renown, but give us the things that will make us rich in Christ. In Jesus' name. Amen.

Fourth Sunday after Pentecost

Watchword for the Week — God desires steadfast love and not sacrifice, the knowledge of God rather than burnt offerings. Hosea 6:6

Sunday, June 8 — Hosea 5:15-6:6; Psalm 50:7-15
Romans 4:13-25; Matthew 9:9-13,18-26

Be gracious to me, O Lord, for I am languishing; O Lord, heal me, for my soul is struck with terror. Psalm 6:2,3

Come now, almighty King, 555
help us you name to sing,
help us to praise.
Father all glorious,
ever victorious,
come and reign over us,
Ancient of Days.

God's Spirit helps us in our weakness. Romans 8:26

Come, holy Comforter, 555
your sacred witness bear
in this glad hour.
Your grace to us impart,
now rule in ev'ry heart,
never from us depart,
Spirit of pow'r!

Lord, we praise you for your faithfulness and love toward us. Thank you for being willing to take charge of our problems in every difficult situation. Help us to walk in your truth and to help others to also be victorious. Amen.

Monday, June 9 — Psalm 74:1-9
Numbers 26:57-27:23; Luke 1:39-45

Do not be wise in your own eyes; fear the Lord, and turn away from evil. Proverbs 3:7

Guide me, O my great Redeemer, 790
pilgrim through this barren land.
I am weak, but you are mighty;
hold me with your pow'rful hand.
Bread of heaven, bread of heaven,
feed me now and evermore,
feed me now and evermore.

Where is the one who is wise? Where is the scribe? Where is the debater of this age? Has not God made foolish the wisdom of the world? 1 Corinthians 1:20

When I tread the verge of Jordan, 790
bid my anxious fears subside;
death of death and hell's destruction,
land me safe on Canaan's side.
Songs of praises, songs of praises,
I will sing forevermore;
I will sing forevermore.

Lord, help us to never be content just the way we are. Give us a holy restlessness that motivates us to move on to greater things for you. This we ask through Jesus Christ, who leads us on to greater things. Amen.

Tuesday, June 10 — Psalm 74:10-17
Numbers 28:1-29:6; Luke 1:46-56

When you have eaten and are satisfied, praise the Lord your God. Deuteronomy 8:10 (NIV)

Be present at our table, Lord; 816
be here and everywhere adored;
from your all-bounteous hand our food
may we receive with gratitude.

God created food to be received with thanksgiving. 1 Timothy 4:3

Praise God, who gives our daily bread 816
and has again our table spread.
May he with all his gifts impart
his crowning gift, a thankful heart.

O gracious God, you lavish our lives with goodness. Remind us often of how much you cherish us, of how abundantly you have offered gifts to us, especially during the difficult moments and chapters in our lives. Amen.

Wednesday, June 11 — Psalm 74:18-23
Numbers 29:7-40; Luke 1:57-66

You have given me the shield of your salvation, and your right hand has supported me. Psalm 18:35

My hope is built on nothing less 771
than Jesus' blood and righteousness;
no merit of my own I claim
but wholly lean on Jesus' name.
On Christ the solid rock I stand;
all other ground is sinking sand,
all other ground is sinking sand.

Thanks be to God, who in Christ always leads us in triumphal procession. 2 Corinthians 2:14

When he shall come with trumpet sound, 771
O may I then in him be found
clothed in his righteousness alone,
redeemed to stand before the throne.
On Christ the solid rock I stand;
all other ground is sinking sand,
all other ground is sinking sand.

Father, you are our salvation, our strength, and our shield. Answer us in the day of trouble; send us help from your holy place. Come in the glory of your saving light and shine upon our pathways. Through Jesus Christ our Lord. Amen.

Thursday, June 12 — Psalm 75
Numbers 30:1-31:12; Luke 1:67-80

The Lord will be your everlasting light, and your God will be your glory. Isaiah 60:19

Morning Star, O cheering sight! 281
Ere thou cam'st, how dark earth's night!
Morning Star, O cheering sight!
Ere thou cam'st, how dark earth's night!

Jesus said, "You are the light of the world." Matthew 5:14

Jesus mine, in me shine; 281
in me shine, Jesus mine;
fill my heart with light divine.

Lord Jesus, you once took on the weakness of our human condition to be the light of the world. Help us now as your disciples to be your light for those who do not see, strength for the wavering, and comfort for the troubled heart. Amen.

Friday, June 13 — Psalm 76
Numbers 31:13-47; Luke 2:1-20

The Lord has punished me severely, but he did not give me over to death. Psalm 118:18

Breathe, O breathe your loving Spirit p124
into ev'ry troubled breast,
let us all in you inherit,
let us find the promised rest.
Take away the love of sinning;
Alpha and Omega be;
end of faith, as its beginning,
set our hearts at liberty.

Those who suffer according to God's will should commit themselves to their faithful Creator and continue to do good. 1 Peter 4:19 (NIV)

Savior, now for strength we plead, 417r
in your love together banded,
to advance where you did lead
doing what you have commanded.
Heart and hand we pledge you here;
give us grace to persevere.

Dear Lord, keep watch with those who work, watch, or weep this day. Tend to the sick, give rest to the weary, bless the dying, soothe the suffering, pity the afflicted, and shield the joyous. Help them sense your presence, peace, and power. Amen.

Saturday, June 14 — Psalm 77:1-9
Numbers 31:48-32:27; Luke 2:21-32

Show us your steadfast love, O Lord, and grant us your salvation. Psalm 85:7

Sing to the Lord most high; 164r
let every land adore.
With grateful voice make known
his goodness and his power.
Let cheerful songs declare his ways,
and let his praise inspire your tongues.

You were washed, you were sanctified, you were justified in the name of the Lord Jesus Christ and in the Spirit of our God. 1 Corinthians 6:11

Take time to be holy, 378r
speak oft with your Lord;
abide in him always,
and feed on his word.
Make friends of God's children;
help those who are weak,
forgetting in nothing
his blessing to seek.

Father, we come before you with both boldness and humility. We come with humility because we can make no boast of how well we have done. Yet we also come with boldness, because you are the God of love as well as of holiness. Amen.

Fifth Sunday after Pentecost

Watchword for the Week — The Lord is good; his steadfast love endures forever, and his faithfulness to all generations. Psalm 100:5

Sunday, June 15 — Exodus 19:2-8a; Psalm 100
Romans 5:1-8; Matthew 9:35-10:8,(9-23)

I have spoken to you again and again, yet you have not obeyed me. Jeremiah 35:14 (NIV)

Sing praise to God, who reigns above, p15
the God of all creation,
the God of power, the God of love,
the God of our salvation;
with healing balm my soul he fills,
and ev'ry faithless murmur stills.
To God all praise and glory!

Nathanael said, "Can anything good come out of Nazareth?" Philip said to him, "Come and see." John 1:46

The Lord is never far away, p15
but through all grief distressing,
an ever-present help and stay,
our peace, and joy, and blessing,
as with a mother's tender hand,
he leads his own, his chosen band.
To God all praise and glory!

Faithful, steadfast, and loving God, we are your people, the sheep of your pasture. Deliver us from faithlessness, our resolute God. Impart a willing spirit within us for your kingdom and glory. Amen.

Monday, June 16 — Psalm 77:10-15
Numbers 32:28-33:9; Luke 2:33-40

You are the God of my salvation; for you I wait all day long. Psalm 25:5

Your incarnation, wounds, and death 327r
I will confess while I have breath,
till I shall see you face to face,
arrayed with your righteousness.

This is the boldness we have in him, that if we ask anything according to his will, he hears us. 1 John 5:14

No condemnation now I dread, 773
for Christ, and all in him, is mine!
Alive in him, my living Head,
and clothed in righteousness divine,
bold I approach the eternal throne
and claim the crown, through Christ, my own.

Ever-present Father, we are so grateful for your presence in our lives. Thank you for the power you have bestowed upon us so that we are able to live an abundant life with your help. Help us sense the presence, the peace, and the power only you can give. Amen.

Tuesday, June 17 — Psalm 77:16-20
Numbers 33:10-56; Luke 2:41-52

Do not fear, for I have redeemed you; I have called you by name, you are mine. Isaiah 43:1

I am thine, O Lord — I have heard thy voice, 607
and it told thy love to me;
but I long to rise in the arms of faith
and be closer drawn to thee.

Many tax collectors and sinners came and were sitting with Jesus and his disciples. Matthew 9:10

Consecrate me now to thy service, Lord, 607
by the pow'r of grace divine;
let my soul look up with a steadfast hope
and my will be lost in thine.

God of grace, you loved the world so much that you gave your only Son to be our Savior. Help us to rejoice in our salvation by showing mercy and truth and by walking in the way of righteousness and peace. Amen.

Wednesday, June 18 — Psalm 78:1-8
Numbers 34; Luke 3:1-20

You shall not steal. Exodus 20:15

Take my wealth, all I possess, 647
make me rich in faithfulness.
Take my mind that I may use
ev'ry pow'r as you should choose.

Do not seek your own advantage, but that of the other. 1 Corinthians 10:24

Take my motives and my will, 647
all your purpose to fulfill.
Take my heart — it is your own;
it shall be your royal throne.

Loving God, you made us for yourself that we might worship you, yet we often get lost in our own wishes, wants, and motives. Turn us back to the path that places you first. Amen.

Thursday, June 19 — Psalm 78:9-16
Numbers 35:1-30; Luke 3:21-38

In your hand are power and might, so that no one is able to withstand you. 2 Chronicles 20:6

Let me at thy throne of mercy 772
find a sweet relief;
kneeling there in deep contrition,
help my unbelief.

I believe; help my unbelief! Mark 9:24

Trusting only in thy merit, 772
would I seek thy face;
heal my wounded, broken spirit,
save me by thy grace.

Lord Jesus Christ, Son of the living God, teach us to walk in your way more trustfully, to accept your truth more faithfully, and to share your life more lovingly. Amen.

Friday, June 20 — Psalm 78:17-31
Numbers 35:31-Deuteronomy 1:18; Luke 4:1-13

Comfort, O comfort my people, says your God.
Isaiah 40:1

When peace, like a river, attendeth my way, 754
when sorrows like sea billows roll;
whatever my lot, you have taught me to say,
it is well, it is well with my soul.

Paul wrote: As you share in our sufferings,
so also you share in our consolation.
2 Corinthians 1:7

Though Satan should buffet, 754
though trials should come,
let this blessed assurance control,
that Christ has regarded my helpless estate,
and has shed his own blood for my soul.

Heavenly Father, all around us is the bustle and activity of a world struggling with conflicts of armies, nations, and persons. May we be your voice helping those around us to never lose sight of your sovereignty. Amen.

Saturday, June 21 — Psalm 78:32-39
Deuteronomy 1:19-46; Luke 4:14-21

O Lord God, you have only begun to show your servant your greatness and your might! Deuteronomy 3:24

I am trusting you, Lord Jesus; 542r
never let me fall;
I am trusting you forever
and for all.

All of us, with unveiled faces, seeing the glory of the Lord as though reflected in a mirror, are being transformed into the same image from one degree of glory to another. 2 Corinthians 3:18

May your rich grace impart 705
strength to my fainting heart,
my zeal inspire;
as you have died for me,
my love, adoringly,
pure, warm and changeless be,
a living fire!

O Lord God, not because of us, but because of you and your glory, are we transformed into your image. May we, now and always, look up to you and, in faith, glorify you in all our ways. We praise you in Jesus' name. Amen.

Sixth Sunday after Pentecost

Watchword for the Week — Jesus says, "Those who find their life will lose it, and those who lose their life for my sake will find it." Matthew 10:39

Sunday, June 22 — Jeremiah 20:7-13; Psalm 69:7-10,(11-15),16-18 Romans 6:1b-11; Matthew 10:24-39

Correct me, O Lord, but in just measure; not in your anger, or you will bring me to nothing. Jeremiah 10:24

Be still, my soul: the Lord is on your side. 757
Bear patiently the cross of grief and pain;
leave to your God to order and provide;
in ev'ry change God faithful will remain.
Be still, my soul: your best, your heav'nly friend
through thorny ways leads to a joyful end.

The Lord knows how to rescue the godly from temptation. 2 Peter 2:9 (NASB)

Savior, now for strength we plead, 417r
in your love together banded,
to advance where you do lead
doing what you have commanded.
Heart and hand we pledge you here;
give us grace to persevere.

Father, daily we are weakened by the shortcomings of human nature, intimidated by the influences of society, and pressured to conform. Forgive our self-satisfaction, and inspire us to be conscious of your claim on our lives. Amen.

Monday, June 23 — Psalm 78:40-55
Deuteronomy 2; Luke 4:22-30

Be glad and rejoice forever in what I am creating. Isaiah 65:18

The strife is o'er, the battle done, 361
the victory of life is won;
the song of triumph has begun.
Alleluia! Alleluia! Alleluia!

Jesus came among the disciples and said, "Peace be with you." After he said this, he showed them his hands and his side. Then the disciples rejoiced when they saw the Lord. John 20:19,20

Lord, by your wounds on Calvary 361
from death's dread sting your servants free,
that we may live eternally.
Alleluia! Alleluia! Alleluia!

Sacrificial Lord, our Savior, we are amazed and grateful. You are worthy; we praise and honor you! All our lives adore you. Amen.

Tuesday, June 24 — Psalm 78:56-64
Deuteronomy 3; Luke 4:31-44

The Lord says, "Those who love me, I will deliver." Psalm 91:14

There is a balm in Gilead 500
to make the wounded whole,
there is a balm in Gilead
to heal the sin sick soul.

Jesus said to the healed man, "Get up and go on your way; your faith has made you well." Luke 17:19

Sometimes I feel discouraged, 500
and think my work's in vain,
but then the Holy Spirit revives my soul again.

Patient Father, we confess that we not only sin, but often resist the attempts of others, even you, to help us. Forgive our arrogance, stubbornness, and pride, and enable us to accept with gratitude your saving grace. Amen.

Wednesday, June 25 — Psalm 78:65-72
Deuteronomy 4:1-31; Luke 5:1-11

Surely, God is my helper; the Lord is the upholder of my life. Psalm 54:4

O God, our help in ages past, 461
our hope for years to come,
our shelter from the stormy blast,
and our eternal home!

We know that the one who raised the Lord Jesus will raise us also with Jesus. 2 Corinthians 4:14

My faith looks trustingly 705
to Christ of Calvary,
my Savior true!
Lord, hear me while I pray,
take all my guilt away,
strengthen in ev'ry way
my love for you!

Father Creator, O Lord, our God, we praise you for the wonderful things you have done. Grant us the strength to follow you so we may know the delight of doing your will. In the name of Jesus Christ we pray. Amen.

Thursday, June 26 — Psalm 79:1-8
Deuteronomy 4:32-5:21; Luke 5:12-26

I will rejoice in the Lord; I will exult in the God of my salvation. Habakkuk 3:18

Rejoice, O pilgrim throng! 786
Rejoice, give thanks and sing:
your festal banner wave on high,
the cross of Christ your king.

Paul wrote: I am confident about all of you, that my joy would be the joy of all of you. 2 Corinthians 2:3

Rejoice! Rejoice! 786
Rejoice, give thanks and sing!

Lord, we don't pretend to understand the complexity and precision of your ways. But we put our trust in you and your Son, Jesus Christ, to keep us safe through the hard times to come. Amen.

Friday, June 27 — Psalm 79:9-13
Deuteronomy 5:22-6:25; Luke 5:27-39

The Lord is near to all who call on him, to all who call on him in truth. Psalm 145:18

Jesus, call thou me 285
from the world to thee;
speed me ever, stay me never;
Jesus, call thou me.

Bartimaeus began to shout out and say, "Jesus, Son of David, have mercy on me!" Jesus stood still and said, "Call him here." And they called the blind man, saying to him, "Take heart; get up, he is calling you." Mark 10:47,49

Behold, the Master passes by! 307r
O see you not his pleading eye?
With low, sad voice he calls you,
"Leave this vain world and follow me."

We are grateful to you, O God, for the blessing of your forgiveness. We thank you that in Christ, you set us free from the guilt and blindness of the past, and give us hope for the future. Amen.

Saturday, June 28 — Psalm 80:1-7
Deuteronomy 7; Luke 6:1-11

Sing and rejoice, O daughter Zion! For lo, I will come and dwell in your midst, says the Lord. Zechariah 2:10

Sing hallelujah, praise the Lord! p114
Sing with a cheerful voice;
exalt our God with one accord,
and in his name rejoice.
Ne'er cease to sing, O ransomed host;
praise Father, Son, and Holy Ghost,
until in realms of endless light
your praises shall unite.

John wrote: I heard a loud voice from the throne saying, "See, the home of God is among mortals. He will dwell with them as their God; they will be his peoples, and God himself will be with them." Revelation 21:3

There we to all eternity p114
shall join th'angelic lays
and sing in perfect harmony
to God our Savior's praise;
he has redeemed us by his blood,
and made us kings and priests to God;
for us, for us, the Lamb was slain!
Praise ye the Lord! Amen.

O God, thank you for all the ways the gospel may be proclaimed. Help us to see and make use of the opportunities that come in cultural disguises for welcoming people into the faith. In Jesus' name. Amen.

Seventh Sunday after Pentecost

Watchword for the Week — Happy are the people who know the festal shout, who walk, O Lord, in the light of your countenance. Psalm 89:15

Sunday, June 29 — Jeremiah 28:5-9; Psalm 89:1-4,15-18
Romans 6:12-23; Matthew 10:40-42

You shall know that I am the Lord, when I deal with you for my name's sake, not according to your evil ways, or corrupt deeds. Ezekiel 20:44

Lord, nothing from your arms of love p147
shall your own people sever.
Our helper never will remove;
our God will fail us never.
Your people, Lord, have dwelt secure;
our dwelling place you will endure
forever and forever.

All this is for your benefit, so that the grace that is reaching more and more people may cause thanksgiving to overflow to the glory of God. 2 Corinthians 4:15 (NIV)

Lord, you have been our dwelling place p147
in ev'ry generation.
Your people still have known your grace
and your blessed consolation.
Through ev'ry age you heard our cry,
through ev'ry age we found you nigh,
our strength and our salvation.

Father of peace, we are joyful in your word, your Son, Jesus Christ, who reconciles us to you. Let us hasten forward with the eagerness of new found faith and love. Amen.

Monday, June 30 — Psalm 80:8-11
Deuteronomy 8:1-9:6; Luke 6:12-26

**The Lord opens the eyes of the blind.
Psalm 146:8**

People in darkness are looking for light, 266*
come, come, come Jesus Christ;
people with blindness are longing for sight,
come, Lord Jesus Christ.
These days of adventure when all people wait
are days for the advent of Love.

John's disciples said to him, "Are you the one who is to come, or are we to wait for another?" Jesus answered them, "Go and tell John what you hear and see: the blind receive their sight, the lame walk, the lepers are cleansed, the deaf hear, the dead are raised, and the poor have good news brought to them. Matthew 11:3-5

Good news! Our Christ has come! 630**
He heals the sad of heart.
He sets the pris'ners free
and helps the blind to see.
God's Spirit works through all who love,
through all who touch the lives of these.

Lord of all, we pray now for those in our midst and also for those in other parts of the world, particularly the oppressed, who need miracles of healing and faith in Christ. Amen.

Tuesday, July 1 — Psalm 80:12-19
Deuteronomy 9:7-10:22; Luke 6:27-38

The days are surely coming, says the Lord, when the city shall be rebuilt for the Lord. Jeremiah 31:38

Risen Lord, shall yet the city 697*
be the city of despair?
Come today, our judge, our glory;
be its name, "The Lord is there!"

And I saw the holy city, the new Jerusalem, coming down out of heaven from God, prepared as a bride adorned for her husband. Revelation 21:2

How lovely is that city, 814
the home of God's elect!
How beautiful the country
that eager hearts expect!
O Christ, in mercy bring us
to that eternal shore
where Father, Son, and Spirit
are worshiped evermore.

Compassionate Savior, you who wept over the ancient city of Jerusalem, help us to feel your broken heart for the cities of today. Encourage and empower those within our cities who witness to your love. And fill us all with longing for the coming of your holy city. Amen.

Wednesday, July 2 — Psalm 81:1-5
Deuteronomy 11; Luke 6:39-49

Remember your congregation, which you acquired long ago, which you redeemed to be the tribe of your heritage. Psalm 74:2

Highly favored congregation, 515
loved by Jesus and esteemed,
ne'er forget your destination,
why from this vain world redeemed.

Christ Jesus gave himself a ransom for all. 1 Timothy 2:6

Witness here to all around you 515
of your Savior's dying love;
tell them how he sought and found you,
gave you grace from heav'n above.

Lord Jesus, we pray for our church — your church — ransomed by your shed blood. Give us a fresh understanding of the depth of your love for us. May we share the love you've given with the hurting people we meet this day. Amen.

Thursday, July 3 — Psalm 81:6-10
Deuteronomy 12; Luke 7:1-17

He grants peace within your borders. Psalm 147:14

Where charity and love prevail, 785*
there God is ever found;
brought here together by Christ's love
by love we thus are bound.

Christ is our peace. Ephesians 2:14

Let strife among us be unknown; 785*
let all contentions cease.
Be God's the glory that we seek;
be his our only peace.

Prince of peace, give us your gift of peace this day. Bring healing, we pray, to broken or strained relationships. For your sake and for our own sake, enable us to truly forgive those who have wronged us. And in being set free from past hurts, may we enter fully into your peace. Amen.

Friday, July 4 — Psalm 81:11-16
Deuteronomy 13:1-14:21; Luke 7:18-30

Remember the former things of old; for I am God, and there is no other; I am God, and there is no one like me. Isaiah 46:9

Here I find my greatest treasure; 782
hither by thy help I've come;
and I hope, by thy good pleasure,
safely to arrive at home.
Jesus sought me when a stranger,
wand'ring from the fold of God;
he, to rescue me from danger,
bought me with his precious blood.

Paul wrote: By the grace of God I am what I am. 1 Corinthians 15:10

O, to grace how great a debtor 782
daily I'm constrained to be!
Let that grace, Lord, like a fetter,
bind my wand'ring heart to thee.
Prone to wander, Lord, I feel it,
prone to leave the God I love,
here's my heart, O take and seal it;
seal it for thy courts above.

Beloved Savior, were it not for you, we would be lost. Yet you have sought us out, you have saved us, you are making us new according to your wondrous love. May the love you have shown us bind our hearts to you forever. Amen.

Saturday, July 5 — Psalm 82:1-4
Deuteronomy 14:22-15:18; Luke 7:31-38

O Lord my God, you are very great. You are clothed with honor and majesty, wrapped in light as with a garment. Psalm 104:1,2

The people who in darkness walked 320
have seen a glorious light;
on them broke forth the heav'nly dawn
who dwelt in death and night.

For it is the God who said, "Let light shine out of darkness," who has shone in our hearts to give the light of the knowledge of the glory of God in the face of Jesus Christ. 2 Corinthians 4:6

Morning Star, thy glory bright 281
far excels the sun's clear light.
Morning Star, thy glory bright
far excels the sun's clear light.
Jesus be, constantly,
constantly, Jesus be
more than thousand suns to me.

Light of the world, shine upon our hearts this day. Dispel any darkness within us. Enlighten us with a greater understanding of you, in all your glory and wonder. Amen.

Eighth Sunday after Pentecost

Watchword for the Week — The Lord is gracious and merciful, slow to anger and abounding in steadfast love. Psalm 145:8

Sunday, July 6 — Zechariah 9:9-12; Psalm 145:8-14
Romans 7:15-25a; Matthew 11:16-19,25-30

John Hus Festival† — Isaiah 49:1-7; Psalm 135:1-13
1 Corinthians 1:18-24; Matthew 5:1-12

For God will bring every deed into judgment, including every secret thing, whether good or evil. Ecclesiastes 12:14

Out of the deep I cry to you, 317r
my God with heart's contrition;
bow down your ear in grace to me,
and hear you my petition;
for if in judgment you will try
man's sin and great iniquity,
ah, who can stand before you?

Therefore do not pronounce judgment before the time, before the Lord comes, who will bring to light the things now hidden in darkness and will disclose the purposes of the heart. Then each one will receive commendation from God. 1 Corinthians 4:5

Lord, for thy coming us prepare; p8
may we, to meet thee without fear,
at all times ready be;
in faith and love preserve us sound;
O let us day and night be found
waiting with joy to welcome thee.

Holy God, how often we have missed the mark! How often we have acted wrongly. How often our deeds appeared noble, yet were driven by selfish motives. But now, Lord, we confess our sin, seeking your pardon. By your grace may we enter your presence forgiven, without fear. Amen.

† On July 6, 1415, John Hus was martyred at the Council of Constance.

Monday, July 7 — Psalm 82:5-8
Deuteronomy 15:19-17:7; Luke 7:39-50

What are human beings that you are mindful of them, mortals that you care for them? Psalm 8:4

Frail children of dust, and feeble as frail, 566
in you we do trust, nor find you to fail;
your mercies how tender, how firm to the end,
our maker, defender, redeemer, and friend.

See what love the Father has given us that we should be called children of God; and that is what we are. 1 John 3:1

From him there goes forth virtue, that we may 325r
with confidence to God the Father pray.
And then we shall ourselves to all proclaim
the heirs of God through faith in Jesus' name.

Infinite God, to think that you are mindful of us, that you care for us, that you love us so much as to call us your children — this is a wondrous thing! May you deepen our understanding of your astonishing love for us. Amen.

Tuesday, July 8 — Psalm 83:1-8
Deuteronomy 17:8-18:22; Luke 8:1-15

You shall rejoice in the Lord; in the Holy One of Israel you shall glory. Isaiah 41:16

Stand up, and bless the Lord, 531
you people of his choice!
Stand up and bless the Lord your God,
with heart and soul and voice.

We boast in God through our Lord Jesus Christ, through whom we have now received reconciliation. Romans 5:11

God is our strength and song, 531
and his salvation ours;
then be his love in Christ proclaimed
with all our ransomed pow'rs.

Lord, you are amazing. You are powerful beyond all measure, wise beyond our comprehension, truly and completely good. To think that you care for ones such as us; we are humbled and filled with joy. May we live this day filled with gratitude and praise. Amen.

Wednesday, July 9 — Psalm 83:9-12
Deuteronomy 19:1-20:09; Luke 8:16-25

**Come and see what God has done:
he is awesome in his deeds among mortals.
Psalm 66:5**

Praise the Lord! You heav'ns adore him, 454
praise him, angels in the height;
sun and moon, rejoice before him;
praise him, all you stars and light.
Praise the Lord! For he has spoken;
worlds his mighty voice obeyed;
laws which never shall be broken
for their guidance he has made.

Jesus said to her, "Daughter, your faith has made you well; go in peace, and be healed of your disease." Mark 5:34

Faith is a living power from heav'n 700
that grasps the promise God has giv'n,
a trust that can't be overthrown
fixed heartily on Christ alone.

Awesome God, with you all things are possible. Give us the faith to ask simply and directly from you what we need this day. Through Christ our Lord we pray. Amen.

Thursday, July 10 — Psalm 83:13-18
Deuteronomy 20:10-21:23; Luke 8:26-39

Here is my servant, whom I uphold, my chosen, in whom my soul delights. Isaiah 42:1

We pray you, bless them all, 288r
and prosper their endeavor,
in their important call
to serve you, gracious Savior;
you listen to our prayers,
and surely will uphold
the faithful ministers
of your redeemed fold.

To the Israelites belong the adoption, the glory, the covenants, the giving of the law, the worship, and the promises; to them belong the patriarchs, and from them, according to the flesh, comes the Messiah. Romans 9:4,5

O come, O come, Immanuel, 274
and ransom captive Israel,
that mourns in lowly exile here
until the Son of God appear.
Rejoice! Rejoice! Immanuel
shall come to you, O Israel.

God of Israel, remember your chosen people. Lead them, and all nations, into greater understanding of your divine purpose. Hasten the day when all peoples, together, will unite in worship before you and your Messiah. Amen.

Friday, July 11 — Psalm 84:1-7
Deuteronomy 22; Luke 8:40-56

Plead my cause and redeem me; give me life according to your promise. Psalm 119:154

Holy Spirit, peace divine, 164br
still this restless heart of mine;
speak to calm this tossing sea,
stayed in your tranquility.

You will do well to be attentive to the prophetic message as to a lamp shining in a dark place, until the day dawns and the morning star rises in your hearts. 2 Peter 1:19

Again, as evening's shadow falls, 43r
we gather in these hallowed walls;
and evening hymn and evening prayer
rise mingling on the holy air.

Living God, speak your message to our hearts. May we recognize your voice this day through the pages of scripture, through the words of brothers and sisters, through the still small voice of your Spirit. Speak Lord, we are listening. Amen.

Saturday, July 12 — Psalm 84:8-12
Deuteronomy 23:1-24:13; Luke 9:1-11

Thus shall you say to one another, among yourselves, "What has the Lord answered?" or "What has the Lord spoken?" Jeremiah 23:35

Keep me from saying words 615
that later need recalling;
guard me, lest idle speech
may from my lips be falling;
but when, within my place,
I must and ought to speak,
then to my words give grace,
lest I offend the weak.

Encourage one another and build up each other. 1 Thessalonians 5:11

Let us each for others care, 672
each another's burden bear,
to your church a pattern give,
showing how believers live.

Living Word, give us the wisdom to know when we should speak, and when we should be silent. When we do speak, may our words be used only for good, to build others up in you. Amen.

Ninth Sunday after Pentecost

Watchword for the Week — There is therefore now no condemnation for those who are in Christ Jesus. Romans 8:1

Sunday, July 13 — Isaiah 55:10-13; Psalm 65:(1-8), 9-13
Romans 8:1-11; Matthew 13:1-9,18-23

Do not withhold good from those to whom it is due, when it is in your power to do it. Proverbs 3:27

We lose what on ourselves we spend; 406r
we have as treasure without end
whatever, Lord, to you we lend,
who givest all.

At the present time your plenty will supply what they need, so that in turn their plenty will supply what you need. Then there will be equality. 2 Corinthians 8:14 (NIV)

Lord of hosts, we ask your aid, 392r
keep us ever unafraid;
hold us loyal, hold us true
to the task we have to do;
lead us on to victory;
we shall triumph praising you.

O Lord, our provider, enable us to freely share with others all that we have first received from you. This day, help us to be generous with our time, our attention, our kind words to others, and our offerings to you. Amen.

Monday, July 14 — Psalm 85:1-7
Deuteronomy 24:14-25:19; Luke 9:12-27

All the Israelite men and women whose hearts made them willing to bring anything for the work that the Lord had commanded by Moses to be done, brought it as a freewill offering to the Lord. Exodus 35:29

O Lord of heaven and earth and sea, 406r
to you all praise and glory be!
How shall we show our love to you,
who givest all?

Each of you must give as you have made up your mind, not reluctantly or under compulsion, for God loves a cheerful giver. 2 Corinthians 9:7

And we believe your word, 657
though dim our faith may be.
Whate'er we do for you, O Lord,
we do it gratefully.

God, you have been so generous to us. Forgive us when we are less than generous in response. Forgive us, as well, when we have given much, yet with proud or begrudging hearts. Make us examples of true generosity, for your glory. Amen.

Tuesday, July 15 — Psalm 85:8-12
Deuteronomy 26:1-27:13; Luke 9:28-36

Create in me a clean heart, O God, and put a new and right spirit within me. Psalm 51:10

Create in me a clean heart, O God, p79
and renew a right Spirit within me.
Cast me not away from your presence,
and take not your Holy Spirit from me.
Restore unto me the joy of salvation;
anoint me with your Spirit free.
Create in me a clean heart, O God,
and renew a right Spirit within me.

It is well for the heart to be strengthened by grace. Hebrews 13:9

May your rich grace impart 705
strength to my fainting heart,
my zeal inspire;
as you have died for me,
my love, adoringly,
pure, warm and changeless be,
a living fire!

Merciful God, we give you thanks for your incredible gift of grace. We are clean within, not because of what we have done, but because of what you have done for us. We are deeply grateful. Amen.

Wednesday, July 16 — Psalm 86:1-10
Deuteronomy 27:14-28:24; Luke 9:37-50

Then the nations that are left all around you shall know that I, the Lord, have rebuilt the ruined places, and replanted that which was desolate. Ezekiel 36:36

Praise to the Lord, who will prosper 530
your work and defend you;
surely his goodness and mercy
shall daily attend you.
Ponder anew
what the almighty can do
if with his love he befriend you.

Paul wrote: There is no longer Jew or Greek, there is no longer slave or free, there is no longer male and female; for all of you are one in Christ Jesus. Galatians 3:28

In Christ there is no east or west — 781
he breaks all barriers down:
by Christ redeemed, by Christ possessed,
in Christ we live as one.

Savior of the world, open the eyes of all people that they might see you and know you for who you are. May men and women from all classes, races, and nations unite in loving and worshiping you. Amen.

Thursday, July 17 — Psalm 86:11-17
Deuteronomy 28:25-57; Luke 9:51-62

You have taken up my cause, O Lord, you have redeemed my life. Lamentations 3:58

You have cancelled my transgression, p202
Jesus, by your precious blood;
may I find therein salvation,
happiness, and peace with God;
and since you, for sinners suff'ring
on the cross were made an off'ring,
from all sin deliver me,
that I wholly yours may be.

Our Savior Jesus Christ gave himself for us that he might redeem us from all iniquity. Titus 2:14

O Eternal Word, 473
Jesus Christ, our Lord!
While the hosts heav'n adore you,
we with awe fall down before you,
and with rapture raise
songs of love and praise.

Lord Jesus, there is no one like you. The fact that you would give yourself for us is overwhelming. We cherish this most precious gift and celebrate our relationship with you. May what you have done for us inspire us each day to make our piece of this world the place you want it to be. Amen.

Friday, July 18 — Psalm 87
Deuteronomy 28:58-29:21; Luke 10:1-16

Those who are far off shall come and help to build the temple of the Lord. Zechariah 6:15

Gracious Lord, gracious Lord, 528
blessed is our lot indeed
in your ransomed congregation;
here we on your merits feed,
and the well-springs of salvation,
all the needy to revive and cheer,
stream forth here, stream forth here.

Like living stones, let yourselves be built into a spiritual house, to be a holy priesthood, to offer spiritual sacrifices acceptable to God through Jesus Christ. 1 Peter 2:5

We entreat, we entreat, 528
Lord, lift up your countenance
on your ransomed congregations;
grace to ev'ry soul dispense.
May we in our situations
daily in your great salvation share.
Hear our prayer, hear our prayer.

Living God, we look in the mirror and think we are not enough, we are convinced by our culture that we have to be more: more beautiful, more wealthy, more powerful. Help us to look in the mirror and know we are enough because we are yours. Lord, remind us that because we are yours, we are called to build your kingdom, joyfully serving you all the days of our lives. Amen.

Saturday, July 19 — Psalm 88:1-5
Deuteronomy 29:22-31:8; Luke 10:17-24

Lord, great is your faithfulness. Lamentations 3:23

O God, our faithful God, p124r
your fountain ever flowing,
without whom nothing is,
all perfect gifts bestowing;
a pure and healthy frame
O give him, and within
a conscience free from blame,
a soul unhurt by sin.

Grace to you and peace from him who is and who was and who is to come. Revelation 1:4

Grace and peace from God, our blessed Savior, 444
be with all who love his name;
church of Christ, his service deem a favor,
joyfully his death proclaim,
be prepared for rest or for employment,
from activity derive enjoyment,
serve with zeal and faithfulness,
filled with love his name confess.

Parenting God, we so often overlook your help and guidance. You have been with us throughout all our days. We praise you, O God, and will remember that everything we are and everything we do is a reflection of your grace to us. Amen.

Tenth Sunday after Pentecost

Watchword for the Week — Thus says the Lord, the King of Israel, and his Redeemer, the Lord of hosts: I am the first and I am the last; besides me there is no god. Isaiah 44:6

Sunday, July 20 — Isaiah 44:6-8; Psalm 86:11-17
Romans 8:12-25; Matthew 13:24-30,36-43

The Lord gives the sun for light by day and the fixed order of the moon and the stars for light by night; he stirs up the sea so that its waves roar. Jeremiah 31:35

Praise the Lord! You heav'ns adore him, 454
praise him, angels in the height;
sun and moon, rejoice before him;
praise him, all you stars and light.
Praise the Lord! For he has spoken;
worlds his mighty voice obeyed;
laws which never shall be broken
for their guidance he has made.

So do not be foolish, but understand what the will of the Lord is. Ephesians 5:17

Mighty God, we humbly pray, 586
let your pow'r now lead the way
that in all things we may show
that we in your likeness grow.

We renew our commitment to you, O God, and seek to understand what your will is for us as we serve you. Open our hearts and minds to your Spirit. May we feel you leading us through this day. Amen.

Monday, July 21 — Psalm 88:6-12
Deuteronomy 31:9-32:9; Luke 10:25-42

I have loved you, says the Lord. Malachi 1:2

Great Father of glory, pure Father of light, 457
your angels adore you, all veiling their sight;
all praise we would render, O lead us to see
the light of your splendor, your love's majesty.

Jesus' clothes became dazzling white. Then a cloud overshadowed them, and from the cloud there came a voice, "This is my Son, the Beloved; listen to him!" Mark 9:3,7

O wondrous sight! O vision fair 327
of glory that the church shall share,
which Christ upon the mountain shows,
where brighter than the sun he glows!

Through the ages you have loved us. Thank you, God. You loved us enough to sacrifice your son so that we might live eternally. Thank you, God. You love us today and will love us forever. Thank you, God. You love us so much that you do not leave us alone, but send your spirit to reveal yourself to us. Thank you God. Amen.

Tuesday, July 22 — Psalm 88:13-18
Deuteronomy 32:10-43; Luke 11:1-13

In your great mercies you did not make an end of your people or forsake them. Nehemiah 9:31

To God whose mercy knows no bounds, 541
we gratefully direct our sounds,
O praise him, alleluia!
Within this space and then beyond
his presence stirs us to respond,
Alleluia!

Regard the patience of our Lord as salvation. 2 Peter 3:15

In mercy, Lord, this grace bestow, 643
that in your service we may do
with gladness and a willing mind
whatever is for us assigned.

Gracious God, you bless us more than we know. Your patience with us is unending. We gratefully accept your love and mercy and pray that we might show others a glimpse of your unending love. Amen.

Wednesday, July 23 — Psalm 89:1-8
Deuteronomy 32:44-33:17; Luke 11:14-28

Why is my pain unceasing, my wound incurable, refusing to be healed? Truly, you are to me like a deceitful brook, like waters that fail. Jeremiah 15:18

> Be still my soul: the Lord is on your side. 757
> Bear patiently the cross of grief or pain;
> leave to your God to order and provide;
> in ev'ry change God faithful will remain.
> Be still, my soul: your best, your heav'nly friend
> through thorny ways leads to a joyful end.

And a man lame from birth was being carried in... When he saw Peter and John about to go into the temple, he asked them for alms... but Peter said, "I have no silver or gold, but what I have I give you; in the name of Jesus Christ of Nazareth, stand up and walk." Acts 3:2,3,6

> That we may care as you have cared, 475br
> for sick and lame, for deaf and blind,
> and freely share, as you have shared,
> in all the sorrows of mankind.

Comforting God, help us to release our pain to you. Open our hearts so that we might receive your healing power. Amen.

Thursday, July 24 — Psalm 89:9-18
Deuteronomy 33:18-34:12; Luke 11:29-36

O Lord, you are my refuge, my portion in the land of the living. Psalm 142:5

We hail you as our Savior, Lord, 267
our refuge and our great reward;
without your grace we waste away
like flow'rs that wither and decay.

Blessed be the God and Father of our Lord Jesus Christ! By his great mercy he has given us a new birth into a living hope through the resurrection of Jesus Christ from the dead. 1 Peter 1:3

Great things he has taught us, 550
great things he has done,
and great our rejoicing through Jesus the Son:
but purer, and higher, and greater will be
our wonder, our transport when Jesus we see.

Lord God, with you in our lives we have everything we need. With you in our lives we can let go of anger, pain, suffering, loss, and greed. With you in our lives we become new people. With you we are fully satisfied. Amen.

Friday, July 25 — Psalm 89:19-29
Joshua 1,2; Luke 11:37-54

He who scattered Israel will gather them and will watch over his flock like a shepherd. Jeremiah 31:10 (NIV)

Tender Shepherd, never leave them, 660
never let them go astray;
by your warning love directed,
may they walk the narrow way!
Thus direct them, thus defend them,
lest they fall an easy prey.

Christ says, "I am the good shepherd. I know my own and my own know me." John 10:14

O Christ, the church's Head and Lord, p200
you as a Shepherd lead us,
your flock, and richly with your word
and sacrament still feed us.
What shall we say? Lost in amaze,
our hearts bow down before you;
for none sufficiently can praise,
love, honor, or adore you.

Shepherding God, our desire is to know you better. We are humbled by your ability to care for us so lovingly. We praise your name. We receive your grace and mercy and we walk with you anew this day. Amen.

Saturday, July 26 — Psalm 89:30-37
Joshua 3,4; Luke 12:1-12

My house shall be called a house of prayer for all peoples. Isaiah 56:7

To your temple, Lord, I come, 553
for it is my worship home.
This earth has no better place,
here I see my Savior's face.

Jesus entered the temple and began to drive out those who were selling and those who were buying in the temple, and he overturned the tables of the money changers and the seats of those who sold doves. Mark 11:15

Within the Father's house 318
the Son has found his home,
and to his temple suddenly
the Lord of life has come.

Lord God, we are so blessed to be able to come to you in prayer. We humbly acknowledge that we are in need of your presence in our lives. Drive out all those things in us that keep us from truly being with you. Help us to see ourselves as your people. Help others to see you in us as we live our lives. Amen.

Eleventh Sunday after Pentecost

Watchword for the Week — God, turn to me and be gracious to me, as is your custom toward those who love your name. Psalm 119:132

Sunday, July 27 — 1 Kings 3:5-12; Psalm 119:129-136
Romans 8:26-39; Matthew 13:31-33,44-52

O land, land, land, hear the word of the Lord! Jeremiah 22:29

O word of God incarnate, 505
O wisdom from on high,
O truth unchanged, unchanging,
O light of our dark sky:
we praise you for the radiance
that from the scripture's page,
a lantern to our footsteps,
shines on from age to age.

Those are the ones on whom seed was sown on the good soil; and they hear the word and accept it, and bear fruit. Mark 4:20 (NASB)

When seed falls on good soil, 501
it's born through quiet toil;
where soil receives, the earth conceives
the blade, the stem, the fruit, the leaves.
Good soil, O mother earth,
the womb, where seeds take birth.

Nurturing God, plant the seeds of your scripture in our hearts and minds so that we might grow in your wisdom. May all that we do and all that we say be a response to your word. May we bear fruit that honors you. In Jesus' name. Amen.

Monday, July 28 — Psalm 89:38-45
Joshua 5,6; Luke 12:13-21

In God's hand is the life of every living thing. Job 12:10

For the beauty of the earth, 538
for the glory of the skies,
for the love which from our birth
over and around us lies,
Lord of all, to you we raise
this our hymn of grateful praise.

Do you not know that you are not your own? 1 Corinthians 6:19

Take my life, O Lord, renew, 610
consecrate my heart to you.
Take my self, and I will be
yours for all eternity,
yours for all eternity.

God, we are alive because of you. We celebrate with all creation your glory and awesome nature. As we serve you, Lord, we remember the blessing you give us each day and we marvel at your greatness. May we honor you with our lives. Amen.

Tuesday, July 29 — Psalm 89:46-52
Joshua 7; Luke 12:22-34

Wait for the Lord; be strong, and let your heart take courage; wait for the Lord! Psalm 27:14

Who trusts in God, a strong abode 427r
in heaven and earth possesses;
who looks in love to Christ above,
no fear his heart oppresses.
In you alone, dear Lord, we own
sweet hope and consolation,
our shield from foes, our balm for woes,
our great and sure salvation.

The disciples woke Jesus up and said to him, "Teacher, do you not care that we are perishing?" He woke up and rebuked the wind, and said to the sea, "Peace! Be still!" Then the wind ceased. Mark 4:38,39

Be still my soul: your God will undertake 757
to guide the future, as in ages past.
Your hope, your confidence let nothing shake;
all now mysterious shall be bright at last.
Be still, my soul: the waves and winds still know
the Christ who ruled them while he dwelt below.

We hear the words of scripture calling us to be still. We want to simply wait for the Lord, but our fast paced lives break in and ask us to do something, anything. Help us, O Lord, to put aside everything and look to you. Peace! Be still! Wait for the Lord. Amen.

Wednesday, July 30 — Psalm 90
Joshua 8:1-29; Luke 12:35-48

I lie down and sleep; I wake again, for the Lord sustains me. Psalm 3:5

Lord, may I be at rest in you 569
and sweetly sleep the whole night through.
Refresh my strength, for your own sake,
so I may serve you when I wake.

Christ says, "My Father, who has given my sheep to me, is greater than all; no one can snatch them out of my Father's hand." John 10:29 (NIV)

'Tis the most blessed and needful part 768
to have in Christ a share,
and to commit our way and heart
unto his faithful care;
this done, our steps are safe and sure,
our hearts' desires are rendered pure,
and naught can pluck us from his hand,
which leads us to the end.

We belong to you Lord God. We trust your love and look to you to sustain us as we move through our earthly lives. For if we live, it is for you that we live, and if we die, it is for you that we die. So whether we live or we die we remain in your care. Amen.

Thursday, July 31 — Psalm 91:1-8
Joshua 8:30-9:27; Luke 12:49-59

The spirit of the Lord shall rest on him, the spirit of wisdom and understanding, the spirit of counsel and might, the spirit of knowledge and the fear of the Lord. Isaiah 11:2

Of the Father's love begotten 483
ere the worlds began to be,
he is Alpha and Omega –
he the source, the ending he
of the things that are, that have been,
and that future years shall see
evermore and evermore.

John the Baptizer said, "He whom God has sent speaks the words of God, for God gives the Spirit without measure." John 3:34

Holy Spirit! All divine, 231r
dwell within this heart of mine;
cast down every idol throne,
reign supreme, and reign alone.

Spirit God, you give us everything we need: food, shelter, your word, family, talents, gifts, wisdom, understanding — the list goes on and on. Thank you for blessing us with your Spirit. May we be open to receiving this gift and may we use it to promote your holy name in our world. Amen.

Friday, August 1 — Psalm 91:9-16
Joshua 10:1-28; Luke 13:1-17

I will call to mind the deeds of the Lord; I will meditate on all your work, and muse on your mighty deeds. Psalm 77:11,12

Life-giving Creator of both great and small; 457
of all life the maker, the true life of all;
we blossom, then wither like leaves on the tree,
but you live forever who was and will be.

Jesus said to the man who had been healed, "Go home to your friends, and tell them how much the Lord has done for you, and what mercy he has shown you." Mark 5:19

Unresting, unhasting, and silent as light, 457
nor wanting, nor wasting, you rule day and night;
your justice like mountains high soaring above
your clouds which are fountains
of goodness and love.

Jesus our brother, though you have done so much for us we are hesitant to share, even with our friends, what your love means in our lives. Give us grace to speak the words of your mercy and courage to do the acts of your justice. In your name we pray. Amen.

Saturday, August 2 — Psalm 92:1-8
Joshua 10:29-11:23; Luke 13:18-30

They read from the Book of the Law of God, making it clear and giving the meaning so that the people could understand what was being read. Nehemiah 8:8 (NIV)

O teach us all your perfect will 734
to understand and to fulfill;
when human insight fails, give light;
this will direct our steps aright.

Do the work of an evangelist; carry out your ministry fully. 2 Timothy 4:5

Proclaim to ev'ry people, tongue, and nation 618
that God, in whom they live and move, is love;
tell how he stooped to save his lost creation,
and died on earth that we might live in love.
Publish glad tidings, tidings of peace,
tidings of Jesus, redemption, and release.

Holy One, you have made each of us with our own ability to read your word and apply it as you give direction. You refresh our understanding and renew our faith through daily, disciplined prayer and study. Use us today to refresh and renew those we live with and those we meet. Amen.

Twelfth Sunday after Pentecost

Watchword for the Week — The Lord is good to all, and his compassion is over all that he has made. Psalm 145:9

Sunday, August 3 — Isaiah 55:1-5; Psalm 145:8-9,14-21
Romans 9:1-5; Matthew 14:13-21

Lord, you are righteous, but this day we are covered with shame. Daniel 9:7 (NIV)

O sacred head, now wounded, 345
with grief and shame weighed down,
now scornfully surrounded
with thorns your only crown.
O sacred head, what glory
and blessing you have known!
Yet, though despised and gory,
I claim you as my own.

Christ prays, "I am not asking you to take them out of the world, but I ask you to protect them from the evil one." John 17:15

Holy Spirit, truth divine, p223a
shine upon these eyes of mine;
send your radiance from above,
let me know my Savior's love.

Creating God, sometimes our shame-based theology keeps us from seeing your image in ourselves and in others. As we worship you today, help us embrace your forgiveness and help us lift up our sisters and brothers who also need to recognize they are worthy of your love. Amen.

Monday, August 4 — Psalm 92:9-15
Joshua 12:1-13:7; Luke 13:31-14:6

Serve the Lord with all your heart; and do not turn aside after useless things that cannot save, for they are useless. 1 Samuel 12:20,21

To serve the present age, 645
my calling to fulfill,
O may it all my pow'rs engage
to do my Master's will.

Do not love the world or the things in the world. The love of the Father is not in those who love the world. 1 John 2:15

The peace of Christ makes fresh my heart, 701
a fountain ever springing!
All things are mine since I am his!
How can I keep from singing?
No storm can shake my inmost calm,
while to that Rock I'm clinging.
Since love is Lord of heaven and earth,
how can I keep from singing?

We burden ourselves, God, not just with things but with the wanting of more things. Guide our decision so that our tithing, giving, purchasing, investing, family life, speaking for those who have no voice, caring for the earth, and sharing our hope in you may bring you delight and bring justice to this, your world. Thank you for such opportunities to express our faith. Amen.

Tuesday, August 5 — Psalm 93
Joshua 13:8-14:5; Luke 14:7-24

Spare your people, O Lord, and do not make your heritage a mockery. Joel 2:17

They walked with God in peace and love 396
but failed with one another;
while sternly for the faith they strove,
they fell out with each other.
But he in whom they put their trust,
who knew their frames, that they were dust,
with pity healed their weakness.

The Lord has helped his servant Israel, in remembrance of his mercy. Luke 1:54

As we are taught of Jesus 434*
we celebrate the faith
built up by those before us
and passed through us today.
Thus our lives are established
in time and history.
We know who we are called to be:
the church, empowered in ministry
to serve all people lovingly. Alleluia!

Gracious God, sometimes we get stuck in the past and cannot bring the energy of your living word to bear on the needs of the world today. Forgive us and help us celebrate our heritage by challenging future generations with our own faithful efforts to live out your good news. We remember your mercy by being merciful. Amen.

Wednesday, August 6 — Psalm 94:1-11
Joshua 14:6-15:19; Luke 14:25-35

Surely it was for my welfare that I had great bitterness; but you have held back my life from the pit of destruction, for you have cast all my sins behind your back. Isaiah 38:17

Christ came from heaven's throne 482
salvation to bestow,
but people scorned and none
the longed-for Christ would know.
But O my friend,
my friend indeed,
who at my need
his life did spend.

Paul wrote: For just as the sufferings of Christ are abundant for us, so also our consolation is abundant through Christ. 2 Corinthians 1:5

For the joy you came to give 336*
you meekly went to die,
teaching us to bear our cross
to know your kind of joy.
Give us faith to follow you
through cross to faith's reward,
loving as you showed us how,
our humble Servant Lord.

Lord Jesus, sometimes life is just so hard we become heavy with despair and bitterness. You know first-hand about suffering and in you we are able to find consolation, uncover hope, and discover abundant compassion. Speak through us that others may find in you what they need to live. Amen.

Thursday, August 7 — Psalm 94:12-23
Joshua 15:20-63; Luke 15:1-10

Six days you shall labor and do all your work. But the seventh day is a Sabbath to the Lord your God; you shall not do any work. Exodus 20:9,10

This day is holy to the Lord; 821
this day the Lord has made;
we will rejoice with one accord
and in his name be glad.
Come, let us worship and bow down,
with thanks appear before his throne;
he to our songs of praise and prayer
will lend a gracious ear.

Jesus said, "The Sabbath was made for humankind, and not humankind for the Sabbath." Mark 2:27

O Majestic Being, 554
may our souls and bodies
at all times be at your service!
Like the holy angels
who bow down before you,
may we ceaselessly adore you,
and through grace, Jesus' grace,
in our whole demeanor,
offer praise and honor.

Lord of the Sabbath, it is the middle of the week and some of us are busy, bored, or bound up with things that appear to be more important than they are. Our focus has become distorted. You translate our prayers and worship into the rest and renewal we need. So, Lord, let our daily living reflect the healthy balance of our faith. Amen.

Friday, August 8 — Psalm 95
Joshua 16,17; Luke 15:11-32

I will leave in the midst of you a people humble and lowly. They shall seek refuge in the name of the Lord. Zephaniah 3:12

God with us, God with us, 324
God made known in human frame;
in his name rejoice with gladness,
since to save the lost he came;
none need sink in hopeless sadness,
for Immanuel is now with us,
God with us, God with us.

Be all the more eager to confirm your call and election, for if you do this, you will never stumble. 2 Peter 1:10

Christ for the world we sing! 640
The world to Christ we bring
with loving zeal;
the poor and them that mourn,
the faint and overborne,
sin-sick and sorrow worn,
whom Christ does heal.

Immanuel, God with us, guide us into ministries of compassion, keeping us from the fear of stumbling, making mistakes, and taking gospel directed risks. Place your claim on us and help us trust you. Keep us respectful of the world's needs but unafraid and eager to minister in your name. Amen.

Saturday, August 9 — Psalm 96:1-9
Joshua 18:1-19:9; Luke 16:1-15

The Lord will vindicate his people, and have compassion on his servants. Psalm 135:14

Christ shall the banquet spread 399r
with his own royal hand
and raise that faithful servant's head
amid the angelic band.

His master said, "Well done, good and trustworthy slave; you have been trustworthy in a few things, I will put you in charge of many things." Matthew 25:21

O happy servant he 399r
in such a posture found!
He shall his Lord with rapture see
and be with honor crowned.

Lord, we want to be good and trustworthy members of your family. When we bring our personal struggles to you in prayer, you bless us. When we share your good news, you bless us. When we stand on the side of justice, you bless us. Bless others through us today. Amen.

Thirteenth Sunday after Pentecost

Watchword for the Week — Jesus spoke to the disciples and said, "Take heart, it is I; do not be afraid." Matthew 14:27

Sunday, August 10 — 1 Kings 19:9-18; Psalm 85:8-13
Romans 10:5-15; Matthew 14:22-33

Even when you turn gray I will carry you. I have made, and I will bear; I will carry and will save. Isaiah 46:4

Though naught of your great power 434r
may move my soul,
with you through night and darkness
I reach the goal.
Take, then my hand, O Father,
and lead you me
until my journey endeth
eternally.

I am the Alpha and the Omega, the beginning and the end. To the thirsty I will give water as a gift from the spring of the water of life. Revelation 21:6

Trusting his mild staff always, 662
I go in and out in peace;
he will feed me with the treasure
of his grace in richest measure;
When athirst to him I cry,
living water he'll supply.

It is Sunday, Lord. We are children, teenagers, adults, elderly, and we all praise you. No matter how old we are, keep us outraged at the oppression and abuse your people of all ages suffer and help us to share the water of life we have found in you. Amen.

Monday, August 11 — Psalm 96:10-13
Joshua 19:10-39; Luke 16:16-31

O my God, I cry by day, but you do not answer; and by night, but find no rest. Psalm 22:2

Much forgiven, may I learn 779
love for hatred to return;
then my heart assured shall be
you, my God, have pardoned me.

Jesus said, "And will not God grant justice to his chosen ones who cry to him day and night? Will he delay long in helping them? I tell you, he will quickly grant justice to them." Luke 18:7,8

Pray justice may come rolling down 696*
as in a mighty stream,
with righteousness in field and town
to cleanse us and redeem.
For God is longing to restore
an earth where conflicts cease,
a world that was created for
a harmony of peace.

Help us, Lord, to look beyond both the comfort we have and the comfort we desire. Give us courage to confront the systems in our society that enslave and demean our sisters and brothers and give us hearts of compassion rooted in your gospel of justice, mercy, and peace. Amen.

Tuesday, August 12 — Psalm 97:1-6
Joshua 19:40-21:8; Luke 17:1-10

Be merciful to me, O God, be merciful to me, for in you my soul takes refuge. Psalm 57:1

Most holy Lord and God, p6
holy, almighty God,
Holy and most merciful Savior,
our Eternal God!
Grant that we may never
lose the comforts from your death.
Have mercy, O Lord.

God is love, and those who abide in love abide in God, and God abides in them. 1 John 4:16

May the mind of Christ my Savior 585
live in me from day to day,
by his love and pow'r controlling
all I do and say.

Creating One, your expressions of love in creation delight and stretch us. Redeeming One, your example of putting love into action startles and humbles us. Sustaining One, your presence in our attempts at sharing love and mercy encourages and empowers us. Show us how to serve the neighbors we have from you. Amen.

Wednesday, August 13 — Psalm 97:7-12
Joshua 21:9-45; Luke 17:11-19

August Thirteenth Festival† — Joshua 24:16-24; Psalm 133
1 John 4:1-13; John 17:1-2,6-19

O grant us help against the foe, for human help is worthless. Psalm 60:11

Lead us, Jesus, gently day by day. 418*
Lead us, Jesus, show us each the way
to walk your diff'rent walk,
from fears and hungers freed,
O, lead us, Jesus, lead us.

When Jesus was at the table with the disciples, he took bread, blessed and broke it, and gave it to them. Then their eyes were opened, and they recognized him. Luke 24:30,31

Feed us, Jesus, we in hunger stand. 418*
Feed us, Jesus, from your timeless hand:
the broken bread of life,
the love that we all need,
O, feed us, Jesus, feed us.

Jesus, even as we pray this prayer there are so many people who are hungry, homeless, discouraged, in pain, losing loved ones, facing addictions, struggling with finances, or unhappy in their faith community. You stand in the middle of today and offer yourself, bread and cup, mercy and grace. Help us stand with you to feed and love unconditionally these who are precious to you. Amen.

† At the conclusion of a Holy Communion service in the church at Berthelsdorf, Germany, on August 13, 1727, the residents of Herrnhut were united into the Renewed Brethren's Church through the Spirit of God.

Thursday, August 14 — Psalm 98
Joshua 22; Luke 17:20-25

Give generously to your needy brother and do so without a grudging heart. Deuteronomy 15:10 (NIV)

Follow with reverent steps the great example 488r
of him whose holy work was doing good;
so shall the wide earth seem our Father's temple,
each loving life a psalm of gratitude.

The measure you give will be the measure you get. Mark 4:24

For he whom Jesus loved has truly spoken: 488r
the holier worship which he deigns to bless
restores the lost, and binds the spirit broken,
and feeds the widow and the fatherless.

We are confronted, Lord of the cross, with the measure of yourself you have given for us. Inspire our sense of generosity that we may share the energy, intelligence, imagination, and love we have from you. Make us cheerful givers not from our abundance but from the needs of others. Amen.

Friday, August 15 — Psalm 99
Joshua 23:1-24:13; Luke 17:26-37

God, I think of you on my bed, and meditate on you in the watches of the night. Psalm 63:6

O Christ, by whom we come to God, 749
the life, the truth, the way!
The path of prayer you also trod;
Lord, teach us how to pray.

Pray in the Spirit at all times in every prayer and supplication. To that end keep alert and always persevere in supplication for all the saints. Ephesians 6:18

Lord, teach us how to pray aright, 750
with rev'rence and with fear;
though dust and ashes in your sight,
we may, we must draw near.

Holy Spirit, we love to pray when we are filled with an awareness of your presence, sometimes excited and joyful, sometimes silent and hopeful. During those other times when we are barely able to believe, thank you for hearing the unspoken prayers of our hearts and minds. Breathe on us, breath of God. Amen.

Saturday, August 16 — Psalm 100
Joshua 24:14-Judges 1:16; Luke 18:1-17

God says, "My purpose shall stand, and I will fulfill my intention." Isaiah 46:10

Cast your burden on the Lord; 538r
only lead upon his word;
you shall soon have cause to bless
his eternal faithfulness.

It is impossible for God to lie. Hebrews 6:18 (NIV)

Peace and goodwill are now to man 174r
most gloriously displayed,
and life eternal we obtain
from God in Christ our head.

Jesus, trustworthy Savior, our lives are rooted in the truth of your love. Many in the world today are the victims of lies, lies that result in economic enslavement, lies that bind us up in conspicuous consumption, or advertising lies that sow the seeds of insecurity. Make us bold in sharing the hope and courage of your good news. Help us tell the truth. Amen.

Fourteenth Sunday after Pentecost

Watchword for the Week — Let the peoples praise you, O God; let all the peoples praise you. Psalm 67:5

Sunday, August 17 — Isaiah 56:1,6-8; Psalm 67
Romans 11:1-2a,29-32; Matthew 15:(10-20),21-28

He put a new song in my mouth, a song of praise to our God. Psalm 40:3

We have received Christ Jesus, 434*
the Lord who sets us free
as sisters and as brothers
in one community,
a people deeply rooted
in Jesus' love and life.
We know who we are called to be:
Christ's body given melody
to sing God's praise resoundingly. Alleluia!

If anyone is in Christ, there is a new creation: everything old has passed away; see, everything has become new! 2 Corinthians 5:17

A new creation comes to life and grows 366
as Christ's new body takes on flesh and blood.
The universe restored and whole will sing:
Alleluia!

You have placed a new song in our hearts, dear and awesome Savior. Speak through the alleluias we sing and shout. Speak as well through those we ponder and whisper. On this day of worship, may those who hear your song of love let go of what is holding them back and embrace the newness of life we have in you. Amen.

Monday, August 18 — Psalm 101
Judges 1:17-2:23; Luke 18:18-30

**You have made the Lord your refuge.
Psalm 91:9**

O God, our help in ages past, 461
our hope for years to come,
remain our guard while life shall last,
and our eternal home.

**God, who has promised is faithful.
Hebrews 10:23**

Praise him for his grace and favor 529
to his people in distress.
Praise him, still the same forever,
slow to chide, and swift to bless.
Alleluia! Alleluia!
Glorious his faithfulness!

God of us all, our refuge, our rock, the center of our faith, you empower us to love mercy, do justice, and walk humbly with you. Keep us relying on you for clear direction. Great is your faithfulness, Lord. We would be faithful to you. And all God's people said a quiet "Amen."

Tuesday, August 19 — Psalm 102:1-11
Judges 3; Luke 18:31-43

Nations shall come to your light, and kings to the brightness of your dawn. Isaiah 60:3

Thy glad beams, thou Morning Star, 281
cheer the nations near and far.
Thy glad beams, thou Morning Star,
cheer the nations near and far.
Thee we own, Lord alone,
Lord alone, thee we own,
our dear Savior, God's dear Son.

Our Savior Christ Jesus abolished death and brought life and immortality to light through the gospel. 2 Timothy 1:10

Hymns of praise then let us sing, alleluia! 358
Unto Christ our heavenly King, alleluia!
Who endured the cross and grave, alleluia!
Sinners to redeem and save. Alleluia!

In a time when nation struggles against nation, religion against religion, and race against race, help us focus our lives and our ministries on your gospel, Lord. Through your love, give us words of peace and the courage to speak them. Give us hearts willing to be broken for those you love for you love us all. In the name of Jesus. Amen.

Wednesday, August 20 — Psalm 102:12-22
Judges 4; Luke 19:1-10

Restore us, O Lord God of hosts; let your face shine, that we may be saved. Psalm 80:19

Praise to the Lord, who will prosper 530
your work and defend you;
surely his goodness and mercy
shall daily attend you.
Ponder anew
what the almighty can do
if with his love he befriend you.

Jesus took with him Peter and James and John, and led them up a high mountain apart, by themselves. And he was transfigured before them... then Peter said to Jesus, "Rabbi, it is good for us to be here." Mark 9:2,5

How good, Lord, to be here! 326
Your glory fills the night;
your face and garments, like the sun,
shine with unborrowed light.

When we are feeling inspired and safe in the sanctuaries of our own making, remind us of the needs of your people. In the beautiful darkness of night and in the stunning light of day, shine through us, for you, Lord Jesus, are the light of the world. Shine, Jesus, through us. Amen.

Thursday, August 21† — Psalm 102:23-28
Judges 5; Luke 19:11-27

I will forgive their iniquity, and remember their sin no more. Jeremiah 31:34

Lord, have mercy, Lord, have mercy 636
on each land and place
where your servants, where your servants
preach the word of grace;
life and pow'r on them bestow,
them with needful strength endow,
that with boldness, that with boldness
they may you confess.

God desires everyone to be saved and to come to the knowledge of the truth. 1 Timothy 2:4

You're our strength and motivation, 622*
Christ, you send us out to serve.
We hold back, but your salvation
gives us energy and nerve.
You still find us with your Spirit;
lift us up on eagle's wings.
Give your call, we gladly hear it;
in your work our spirit sings.

Child of Joseph and Mary, who will go? Who will speak your words of grace? Who will care for the wounded? Who will stand with those who despair? Who will share their own pain to encourage others? Who will speak the truth? We will go, Lord, as you lead us. Amen.

† On this day in 1732, the first missionaries departed from Herrnhut bound for St. Thomas.

Friday, August 22 — Psalm 103:1-5
Judges 6; Luke 19:28-44

Daniel went home to his upstairs room where the windows opened toward Jerusalem. Three times a day he got down on his knees and prayed, giving thanks to his God. Daniel 6:10 (NIV)

O Christ, by whom we come to God, 749
the life, the truth, the way!
The path of prayer you also trod;
Lord, teach us how to pray.

Rejoice in hope, be patient in suffering, persevere in prayer. Romans 12:12

Rejoice, rejoice, God's will stands firm 260*
throughout all time and space.
It is a quiet, steady force
pervading every place.
It snaps the brittleness of hate,
unties the bonds of greed.
It holds out love abundant
which never fails our needs.

Holy One, you give us hope and we live as Easter people. Holy One, you understand our suffering and we care for those in pain of many kinds. Holy One, you hear our prayer, and we listen to one another. You work in mysterious ways your wonders to accomplish. And all God's people said, "Amen!"

Saturday, August 23 — Psalm 103:6-18
Judges 7; Luke 19:45-20:8

What more was there to do for my vineyard that I have not done in it? When I expected it to yield grapes, why did it yield wild grapes? Isaiah 5:4

God is working his purpose out, 194br
as year succeeds to year,
God is working his purpose out,
and the time is drawing near;
nearer and nearer draws the time,
the time that shall surely be,
when the earth shall be filled with the glory
of God,
as the waters cover the sea.

Our people must learn to devote themselves to doing what is good, in order that they may provide for daily necessities and not live unproductive lives. Titus 3:14 (NIV)

Praise aloud the God who calls us 637*
through the life and death of Christ.
Ministries we offer gladly
as we journey towards the light.
Alleluia! Bless your people;
by your Spirit give them sight.

God of purpose and power, you call us to lives of devotion, doing what is good not just for ourselves but for the earth and all who live on it. We live out our faith in the small details of each day. May others see, through them, the larger picture of your justice and grace. In the name of Jesus. Amen.

Fifteenth Sunday after Pentecost

Watchword for the Week — Do not be conformed to this world, but be transformed by the renewing of your minds, so that you may discern what is the will of God — what is good and acceptable and perfect. Romans 12:2

Sunday, August 24 — Isaiah 51:1-6; Psalm 138
Romans 12:1-8; Matthew 16:13-20

Elijah said, "How long will you go limping with two different opinions? If the Lord is God, follow him; but if Baal, then follow him." 1 Kings 18:21

Name him, Christians, name him — 480
strong your love as death —
but with awe and wonder,
and with life-filled breath;
he is God the Savior,
he is Christ the Lord,
ever to be worshiped,
evermore adored.

The Son of God, Jesus Christ, was not "Yes and No;" but in him it is always "Yes." 2 Corinthians 1:19

O bless his holy name, 452
and joyful thanks proclaim
through all the earth;
be grateful and receive
God's blessing; and believe;
his love does not deceive.
Now share your mirth!

Lord of the church, you are the affirmation on which our faith is built. Keep us strong, open, and welcoming of all people, unafraid to resonate with your good news. Help us bring your affirmation through our genuine concern for others. Amen.

Monday, August 25 — Psalm 103:19-22
Judges 8; Luke 20:9-19

At the command of the Lord they would camp, and at the command of the Lord they would set out. Numbers 9:23

Who puts his trust in God most just 537r
has built his house securely;
he who relies on Jesus Christ,
heaven shall be his most surely.

Jesus said to them, "Cast the net to the right side of the boat, and you will find some." So they cast it, and now they were not able to haul it in because there were so many fish. John 21:6

Open then our hearts and senses 684*
to your Spirit's varied ways.
Overcome our self defenses
so we hear the prayer and praise
which the folk of countless cultures
in new worlds and rhythms raise.

Jesus the Christ, you are the truth. You stretch us to reach out, beyond our own understanding, into the rich depths of your love where we find abundant good news to share. When we get stuck on one side of the boat, challenge us to turn around and get to work where the needs and resources are. Thank you, Lord. Amen.

* Ted Wilde (1984). Used by permission.

Tuesday, August 26 — Psalm 104:1-9
Judges 9:1-33; Luke 20:20-26

Great is our Lord, and abundant in power; his understanding is beyond measure. Psalm 147:5

Immortal, invisible, God only wise, 457
in light inaccessible hid from our eyes,
most blessed, most glorious, O Ancient of Days,
almighty, victorious, your great name we praise.

God's foolishness is wiser than human wisdom, and God's weakness is stronger than human strength. 1 Corinthians 1:25

Great Father of glory, pure Father of light, 457
your angels adore you, all veiling their sight;
all praise we would render, O lead us to see
the light of your splendor, your love's majesty.

God of wisdom and understanding, many of us are gearing up for school — wondering, anticipating, and curious. Thank you for the gift of learning as we develop our intelligence and compassion. Thank you for those who are foolish enough to teach, strong enough to ask questions, humble enough to learn, angry enough to want to bring change, focused enough to care effectively, and wise enough to pray. Amen.

Wednesday, August 27 — Psalm 104:10-18
Judges 9:34-10:18; Luke 20:27-40

See, you shall call nations that you do not know, and nations that do not know you shall run to you, because of the Lord your God. Isaiah 55:5

God's word alive and active 503*
is offered free to all,
in every tribe and nation
so all will hear God's call
to feed the hungry children,
give drink to those who thirst,
and serve the human fam'ly
by putting God's will first.

Jesus said, "The kingdom of God is as if someone would scatter seed on the ground, and would sleep and rise night and day, and the seed would sprout and grow, he does not know how." Mark 4:26,27

All the world is God's own field, 450
fruit unto his praise to yield,
wheat and weeds together sown,
unto joy or sorrow grown;
first the blade, and then the ear,
then the full corn shall appear;
Lord of harvest, grant that we
wholesome grain and pure may be.

Holy One, may your kingdom come, your will be done, on earth as it is in heaven. Move through us as we feed your hungry children, give drink to those who thirst and serve the human family by putting your will first. Thank you that you are able to grow love in and through us. Amen.

Thursday, August 28 — Psalm 104:19-23
Judges 11:1-27; Luke 20:41-21:4

Sow with a view to righteousness, reap in accordance with kindness. Hosea 10:12 (NASB)

Joyful, joyful, we adore you, 544
God of glory, Lord of love;
hearts unfold like flow'rs before you,
op'ning to the sun above.
Melt the clouds of sin and sadness;
drive the dark of doubt away;
giver of immortal gladness,
fill us with the light of day!

Take no part in the unfruitful works of darkness, but instead expose them. Ephesians 5:11

"When through fiery trials your pathway shall lie, 709
my grace, all sufficient, shall be your supply.
The flame shall not hurt you; I only design
your dross to consume and your gold to refine."

Jesus of Nazareth, you once stood with strong conviction and exposed the corruption of the money-lenders at the temple. Forgive us when we are afraid to challenge familiar, oppressive systems in government, society, and the church. Keep your righteousness before us and be our guide. Amen.

Friday, August 29 — Psalm 104:24-30
Judges 11:28-12:15; Luke 21:5-28

The Lord said to Jonah, "You had compassion on the plant for which you did not work, which came up overnight and perished overnight. And should I not have compassion on Nineveh, that great city?" Jonah 4:10,11 (NASB)

He came down to earth from heaven 292
who is God and Lord of all,
and his shelter was a stable,
and his cradle was a stall;
with the poor and meek and lowly
lived on earth our Savior Holy.

God has imprisoned all in disobedience so that he may be merciful to all. Romans 11:32

Praise to the Lord, who o'er all things 530
wondrously reigning,
shelt'ring you under his wings,
O, so gently sustaining.
Have you not seen
all you have needed has been
met by his gracious ordaining.

Beautiful Savior, you overwhelm us with your unending compassion. Today, as once in that great city Ninevah, there are people chained up in self-doubt, ignorance, poverty, pollution, addiction, and abuse — how your heart must break. Work your chain-breaking compassion through us. Lord, have mercy. Amen.

Saturday, August 30 — Psalm 104:31-35
Judges 13; Luke 21:29-38

If you obey the Lord your God: Blessed shall you be in the city, and blessed shall you be in the field. Deuteronomy 28:2,3

"I'll bless you, and you shall be set for a blessing!" 616
Thus said God, the Lord, to his servant of old;
O may we, in grace and in number increasing,
through work show our faith and
in service be bold;
upon your truth founded, we shall not move,
let us ever follow, and fearless prove;
so shall we in doctrine, in word and behavior,
to ev'ryone witness that Christ is our Savior.

With many such parables Jesus spoke the word to them, as they were able to hear it. Mark 4:33

God's word alive and active, 503*
declared the whole world round,
in tongues of many peoples
and signed without a sound.
This word of hope and freedom
speaks deeply to the soul
of those who long for oneness
and yearn to be made whole.

Like the disciples, Lord, sometimes we hear but don't understand. You continue to challenge us through your parables and example, for your word is alive and active, able to overcome oppression and injustice. As we hear your word, so may we obey you and be a blessing to others in the city and in the field, at school and in the mall, at work and at play, in church and in our families. Amen.

Sixteenth Sunday after Pentecost

Watchword for the Week — Jesus says, "If any want to become my followers, let them deny themselves and take up their cross and follow me." Matthew 16:24

Sunday, August 31 — Jeremiah 15:15-21; Psalm 26:1-8
Romans 12:9-21; Matthew 16:21-28

You must therefore be careful to do as the Lord your God has commanded you; you shall not turn to the right or to the left. Deuteronomy 5:32

May we in service to our God 696*
act out the living word,
and walk the road the saints have trod
till all have seen and heard.
As stewards of the earth may we
give thanks in one accord
to God who calls us all to be
disciples of the Lord.

"The most important one," said Jesus, "is this: 'Hear, O Israel, the Lord our God, the Lord is one. Love the Lord your God with all your heart and with all your soul and with all your mind and with all your strength.' The second is this: 'Love your neighbor as yourself.' There is no commandment greater than these." Mark 12:29-31 (NIV)

Mortals join the mighty chorus, 544
which the morning stars began;
God's own love is reigning o'er us,
joining people hand in hand.
Ever singing, march we onward,
victors in the midst of strife;
joyful music leads us sunward
in the triumph song of life.

Thank you, God for the balance we experience when we love you first and share that love with our neighbor. Bless those today who live your commandments. Amen.

Monday, September 1 — Psalm 105:1-7
Judges 14,15; Luke 22:1-13

Moses implored the Lord his God, and said, "O Lord, turn from your fierce wrath; change your mind and do not bring disaster on your people." Exodus 32:11,12

O God of unrelenting grace, 738*
whose judgment yet we daily face,
forgive us now, good Lord.
You are so distant and so near;
for you we long, yet you we fear,
O known, and yet beyond record.

Paul wrote: I urge that supplications, prayers, intercessions, and thanksgivings be made for everyone. 1 Timothy 2:1

Now we bring ourselves to you; 741
cleanse us, Lord, we humbly pray;
undeserving though we be,
draw us closer ev'ry day.
Lord, our refuge, hope, and strength!
Keep, O keep us safe from harm,
shield us through our earthly life
by your everlasting arm.

O God of the listening heart, hear our prayers this day. Place in our hearts those for whom we would pray. Use us to answer the prayers of others. Bless this day in our prayer to you. Amen.

Tuesday, September 2 — Psalm 105:8-15
Judges 16,17; Luke 22:14-23

My eyes are awake before each watch of the night that I may meditate on your promise. Psalm 119:148

O, send your Spirit, Lord, 502
now unto me,
that he may touch my eyes
and make me see.
Show me the truth concealed
within your Word,
and in your book revealed
I see my Lord.

Jesus said, "If you continue in my word, you are truly my disciples." John 8:31

On him we'll venture all we have, 479
our lives, our all, to him we owe.
None else is able us to save,
naught but the Savior will we know;
this we subscribe with heart and hand,
resolved through grace thereby to stand.

Hope of the world, protect us from distractions. Give us eyes to see you in the events of daily life. Convict our spirits to embody you in all we do. Amen.

Wednesday, September 3 — Psalm 105:16-22
Judges 18; Luke 22:24-38

Trust in the Lord forever, for in the Lord God you have an everlasting rock. Isaiah 26:4

It is enough: earth's struggles soon shall cease 710
and Jesus calls us to heaven's perfect peace.

All things can be done for the one who believes. Mark 9:23

Help then, O Lord, our unbelief; 713
and may our faith abound
to call on you when you are near
and seek where you are found.

Ever-present Lord, this day is a gift to us. Looking forward or looking back you have been with us. Through your steadfast love, strengthen our faith in you that we might live boldly. Amen.

Thursday, September 4 — Psalm 105:23-36
Judges 19; Luke 22:39-51

Why have you despised the word of the Lord, to do what is evil in his sight? 2 Samuel 12:9

O Master, let me walk with you 735
in lowly paths of service true;
tell me your secret; help me bear
the strain of toil, the fret of care.

Whoever says, "I abide in Jesus Christ," ought to walk just as he walked. 1 John 2:6

The cov'nant is made 608
with you as my Head.
Lord, grant my request,
to love and to serve you
till with you I rest.

God of mercy, we are imperfect beings called to do your will. As individuals, as families, as communities, as nations — the world, guide our feet that we might walk in your way. Amen.

Friday, September 5 — Psalm 105:37-45
Judges 20:1-31; Luke 22:52-62

The hand of our God was upon us, and he delivered us. Ezra 8:31

For God, in grace and tenderness, 519
regarded us in our distress;
yea, to our aid himself he came;
let all adore God's holy name.

The Lord stood by me and gave me strength, so that through me the message might be fully proclaimed. 2 Timothy 4:17

Be with me, Lord, where'er I go; 733
teach me what you would have me do;
suggest whate'er I think or say;
direct me in the narrow way.

Divine Truth, encourage our hearts with your words of hope and healing. Are there those around us whose hearts are burdened? Open our mouths to speak your words of comfort. Amen.

Saturday, September 6 — Psalm 106:1-5
Judges 20:32-21:25; Luke 22:63-71

Rend your hearts and not your clothing. Return to the Lord, your God. Joel 2:13

Spirit of God, who dwells within my heart, 490
wean it from sin, through all its pulses move.
Stoop to my weakness, mighty as you are,
and make me love you as I ought to love.

A poor widow came and put into the treasury two small copper coins. Then Jesus called his disciples and said to them, "Truly I tell you, this poor widow has put in more than all those who are contributing to the treasury. For all of them have contributed out of their abundance; but she out of her poverty has put in everything she had, all she had to live on." Mark 12:42-44

We give you but your own 657
in any gifts we bring;
all that we have is yours alone,
a trust from you, our King.

Precious Savior, you came to us so that we might have a place in God's heart. Today we come to you with God in our hearts. Let our joy in you be so obvious to the world that others might see you in us. Amen.

Seventeenth Sunday after Pentecost

Watchword for the Week — Give me understanding, O God, that I may keep your law and observe it with my whole heart. Psalm 119:34

Sunday, September 7 — Ezekiel 33:7-11; Psalm 119:33-40
Romans 13:8-14; Matthew 18:15-20

Thus says the Lord, "Seek me and live." Amos 5:4

God, whose giving knows no ending, 652*
from your rich and endless store;
nature's wonder, Jesus' wisdom,
costly cross, grave's shattered door,
gifted by you, we turn to you,
off'ring up ourselves in praise;
thankful song shall rise forever,
gracious donor of our days.

They brought to him all who were sick or possessed with demons. And the whole city was gathered around the door. And he cured many who were sick with various diseases. Mark 1:32-34

Life and health are in the name 699br
of Jesus Christ our Lord:
Father, forth from you he came
to be the healing word.
Now our hearts rejoice to know,
marking his life as man with men,
nought there is weal of woe
that lies beyond his ken.

All-wise God, you lay your hand upon us; the sick, the weak, the proud, the sinful, and empower us to do what we can not do on our own. We glorify your name, for even in our brokenness we are made whole in you. Amen.

Monday, September 8 — Psalm 106:6-12
Ruth 1; Luke 23:1-12

Woe to the shepherds who only take care of themselves! Should not shepherds take care of the flock? Ezekiel 34:2 (NIV)

Called by Christ, redeemed, accepted, 624*
we are blessed with work to do.
By the Spirit we're empowered:
"Tell the good news, life renew."
Our lives now reveal Christ's presence;
we will show God's love and grace.
Faith in action, ever, always;
while on earth we run our race.

I exhort the elders among you to tend the flock of God that is in your charge, exercising the oversight, not under compulsion but willingly, as God would have you do it — not for sordid gain but eagerly. 1 Peter 5:1,2

Sing, pray, and keep his ways unswerving, 712
offer your service faithfully,
and trust his word; though undeserving,
you'll find his promise true to be.
God never will forsake in need
the soul that trusts in him indeed.

Good Shepherd, you watch over us faithfully. You call us to tend your flock. Who will you place in our care today? Fill us with the desire to be shepherds in your name. Amen.

Tuesday, September 9 — Psalm 106:13-23
Ruth 2,3; Luke 23:13-31

The Lord will reply to his people, "I am sending you grain, new wine and oil, enough to satisfy you fully." Joel 2:19 (NIV)

Breathe on me, breath of God, 494
fill me with life anew,
that I may love the things you love
and do what you would do.

Cast all your anxiety on him, because he cares for you. 1 Peter 5:7

Come now, O Lord, and as in days of old 742
to us your Spirit gracefully unfold;
pour forth your love and all-abounding grace
till we in spirit see you face to face.

Almighty God, there is nothing greater than you. All our concerns are within your power to resolve. You are the light and the joy of our lives. At any given moment your smile is upon us. We thank you Lord. Amen.

Wednesday, September 10 — Psalm 106:24-31
Ruth 4; Luke 23:32-43

The Lord will judge the ends of the earth; he will give strength to his king. 1 Samuel 2:10

A charge to keep I have, 645
a God to glorify,
a never-dying soul to save
and fit it for the sky.

All of us must appear before the judgment seat of Christ, so that each may receive recompense for what has been done in the body, whether good or evil. 2 Corinthians 5:10

Arm me with jealous care, 645
as in your sight to live;
and O your servant, Lord, prepare
the strict account to give.

Lord Jesus, we give ourselves to you. We confess you as Lord and Savior. We strive to live life for you; yet, at times, we make poor choices. We confess to you, not wallowing in the burden of our sin but basking in your life-giving forgiveness. Today we begin anew. Amen.

Thursday, September 11 — Psalm 106:32-39
1 Samuel 1:1-2:11; Luke 23:44-56

They have made themselves gods of gold. Please forgive their sin. Exodus 32:31,32 (NIV)

Lord, forgive me, day by day, 779
debts I cannot hope to pay,
duties I have left undone,
evils I have failed to shun.

Gods made with hands are not gods. Acts 19:26

Lifegiving Creator of both great and small; 457
of all life the maker, the true life of all;
we blossom, then wither like leaves on the tree,
but you live forever who was and will be.

Loving Creator, there is much in life that desires our loyalty. We are tempted by things that could become gods for us. But you see the good in us. You whisper to the spirit in us that praises your name. If we do not hear your whisper, Lord, please shout! For you are our one true God. Amen.

Friday, September 12 — Psalm 106:40-48
1 Samuel 2:12-36; Luke 24:1-12

Have mercy on me, O God, according to your steadfast love; according to your abundant mercy blot out my transgressions. Psalm 51:1

Spirit of God, who dwells within my heart, 490
wean it from sin, through all its pulses move.
Stoop to my weakness, mighty as you are,
and make me love you as I ought to love.

The Son of Man has authority on earth to forgive sins. Mark 2:10

Christ is our Master, Lord, and God, 479
the fullness of the Three in One.
His life, death, righteousness, and blood
our faith's foundation are alone;
his Godhead and his death shall be
our theme to all eternity.

Holy Redeemer, your capacity to forgive is greater than our capacity to sin. Never let us take this gift for granted. Amen.

Saturday, September 13 — Psalm 107:1-9
1 Samuel 3,4; Luke 24:13-27

The word of the Lord is upright, and all his work is done in faithfulness. Psalm 33:4

For the beauty of the earth, 538
for the glory of the skies,
for the love which from our birth
over and around us lies,
Lord of all, to you we raise
this our hymn of grateful praise.

Christ says, "Anyone who hears my word and believes him who sent me has eternal life." John 5:24

My life flows on in endless song, 701
above earth's lamentation,
I hear the real, though far off hymn
that hails a new creation.
No storm can shake my inmost calm,
while to that Rock I'm clinging.
Since love is Lord of heaven and earth,
how can I keep from singing?

Lord of all, we pray in private but you hear us as a chorus. Our life of faith is preparation for the eternal song of praise we will sing in your kingdom. Sing hallelujah, praise the Lord! Amen.

Eighteenth Sunday after Pentecost

Watchword for the Week — Bless the Lord, O my soul, and do not forget all his benefits. Psalm 103:2

Sunday, September 14 — Genesis 50:15-21; Psalm 103:(1-7),8-13 Romans 14:1-12; Matthew 18:21-35

Not one of all the good promises that the Lord had made to the house of Israel had failed; all came to pass. Joshua 21:45

My soul, then, with assurance 177r
hope still, be not dismayed;
he will from each encumbrance
again lift up your head;
beyond your wish extended
his goodness will appear,
when he has fully ended
what caused your needless fear.

Paul wrote: You are children of the promise, like Isaac. Galatians 4:28

Come then, come, O flock of Jesus, 673
covenant with him anew;
unto him, who conquered for us,
pledge we love and service true;
and should our love's union holy
firmly linked no more remain,
wait ye at his footstool lowly,
till he draw it close again.

Divine promise keeper of all that we rely on in this life, your son is the one promise that remains true. May your church be a faithful messenger of your promise of hope to the world. Amen.

Monday, September 15 — Psalm 107:10-16
1 Samuel 5:1-7:1; Luke 24:28-35

With God are strength and wisdom; the deceived and the deceiver are his. Job 12:16

To God whose mercy knows no bounds, 541
we gratefully direct our sounds,
O praise him, alleluia!
Within this space and then beyond
his presence stirs us to respond,
Alleluia!

He makes his sun rise on the evil and on the good, and sends rain on the righteous and on the unrighteous. Matthew 5:45

By your reconciling love 672
ev'ry stumbling-block remove;
each to each unite, endear;
come, and spread your banner here.

God of righteousness, it is easy to point fingers in judgment. But at times we are both the righteous and the unrighteous. Shine your light on what is righteous within us and we will embrace it for your glory. Amen.

Ministers' Covenant Day†

Tuesday, September 16 — Psalm 107:17-22
1 Samuel 7:2-8:22; Luke 24:36-53

Call on me in the day of trouble; I will deliver you, and you shall glorify me. Psalm 50:15

Sing with humble hearts your praises 560
for our Savior's boundless grace;
pay due homage to Christ Jesus,
come with thanks before his face.
Praise him for his death and bleeding,
all our happiness lies there;
praise him for his gracious leading,
praise your faithful Shepherd's care.

Jesus said to the blind man, "What do you want me to do for you?" The blind man said to him, "My teacher, let me see again." Mark 10:51

How good the name of Jesus sounds 487
to all believing ears!
It soothes our sorrows, heals our wounds,
and drives away our fears.
It makes the wounded spirit whole,
and calms the troubled mind;
his manna for each hungry soul,
the lost and weary find.

Teacher, we seek your wisdom to live our lives. Give us eyes to see you while we work and while we play. Amen.

† During a synodal conference in London, Jesus Christ was recognized as chief elder of the Brethren's Church. The day is observed as a covenanting day for servants of the church.

Wednesday, September 17 — Psalm 107:23-32
1 Samuel 9; John 1:1-13

I will give thanks to you, O Lord, for though you were angry with me, your anger turned away, and you comforted me. Isaiah 12:1

Sing praise to God who reigns above, 537
the God of all creation,
the God of pow'r, the God of love,
the God of our salvation.
My soul with comfort rich he fills,
and ev'ry grief he gently stills:
to God all praise and glory!

The grace of our Lord overflowed for me with the faith and love that are in Christ Jesus. 1 Timothy 1:14

O let me hear you speaking 603
in accents clear and still,
above the storms of passion,
the murmurs of self-will.
O speak to reassure me,
to hasten or control;
and speak to make me listen,
O guardian of my soul.

Lord, Jesus Christ, Son of God, have mercy on us. You know the things we require to address the tasks before us. Bless us with your generous hand that we might bless those around us. Amen.

Thursday, September 18 — Psalm 107:33-43
1 Samuel 10; John 1:14-28

The Lord used to speak to Moses face to face, as one speaks to a friend. Exodus 33:11

Be with me, Lord, where'er I go; 733
teach me what you would have me do;
suggest whate'er I think or say;
direct me in the narrow way.

While two of the apostles were talking and discussing, Jesus himself came near and went with them. Luke 24:15

When two friends on Easter day 112br
to Emmaus bent their way,
on that paschal eventide
Christ was walking at their side.
Then their hearts within them glowed
when himself to them he showed,
in the scriptures, as a king
glorified by suffering.

Friend and Teacher, our world needs a wise friend like you. Look at what is happening among your people. Show us how to make a difference. Let the transformation of the world begin with us. Amen.

Friday, September 19 — Psalm 108:1-5
1 Samuel 11,12; John 1:29-42

Samuel said, "(Although) you have done all this evil, far be it from me that I should cease to pray for you." 1 Samuel 12:20,23

Before our Father's throne 680
we pour our ardent prayers;
our fears, our hopes, our aims are one,
our comforts and our cares.

Put yourselves at the service of everyone who works and toils with them... for they refreshed my spirit as well as yours. So give recognition to such persons. 1 Corinthians 16:16,18

Join we all with one accord; 525
praise we all our common Lord;
for we all have heard his voice,
all have made his will our choice.
Join we with the saints of old,
no more strangers in the fold,
one the Shepherd who us sought,
one the flock his blood has bought.

Author of life, you have placed in our lives numerous people who have made significant contributions to our faith journey: family, friends, teachers, even strangers. We ask your blessing upon them. Build them up for their holy work. Amen.

Saturday, September 20 — Psalm 108:6-13
1 Samuel 13; John 1:43-51

The ransomed of the Lord shall return, they shall obtain joy and gladness, and sorrow and sighing shall flee away. Isaiah 51:11

Through all the tumult and the strife, 701
I hear that music ringing.
It sounds and echoes in my soul;
how can I keep from singing?
No storm can shake my inmost calm,
while to that Rock I'm clinging.
Since love is Lord of heaven and earth,
how can I keep from singing?

The eyes of your heart may be enlightened (by God) in order that you may know the hope to which he has called you, the riches of his glorious inheritance in the saints. Ephesians 1:18 (NIV)

How good the name of Jesus sounds 487
to all believing ears!
It soothes our sorrows, heals our wounds,
and drives away our fears.
It makes the wounded spirit whole,
and calms the troubled mind;
his manna for each hungry soul,
the lost and weary find.

How blessed we are, dear Lord. You created us and saw that we were good. You redeemed us and saw that we were holy — all this simply because you love us. Show us how to share your love with someone in our lives today. Amen.

Nineteenth Sunday after Pentecost

Watchword for the Week — For to me, living is Christ and dying is gain. Philippians 1:21

Sunday, September 21 — Jonah 3:10-4:11; Psalm 145:1-8 Philippians 1:21-30; Matthew 20:1-16

I am the Lord, that is my name; my glory I give to no other, nor my praise to idols. Isaiah 42:8

He by his name has sworn, 468
on this we shall depend,
and as on eagles' wings
upborne to heav'n ascend.
There we shall see his face,
his pow'r we shall adore
and sing the wonders of his grace
forevermore.

The scribe said to Jesus, "You are right, Teacher; you have truly said that 'God is one, and besides him there is no other.'" Mark 12:32

The God of Abraham praise, 468
who reigns enthroned above,
the Ancient of eternal days,
the God of love!
The Lord, the great I Am,
by earth and heav'n confessed —
we bow before his holy name
forever blessed.

Yahweh, you are God! You created and set the order of things. You established a covenant and provided a plan for life, both now and eternal. Our job is to love and obey. Protect us from the desire to usurp your authority. Amen.

Monday, September 22 — Psalm 109:1-7
1 Samuel 14:1-40; John 2:1-11

One does not live by bread alone, but by every word that comes from the mouth of the Lord. Deuteronomy 8:3

We would not live by bread alone, 411
but by your word of grace,
in strength of which we travel on
to our abiding place.

As for those who in the present age are rich, command them not to be haughty, or to set their hopes on the uncertainty of riches, but rather on God. 1 Timothy 6:17

Let ev'ry tongue and ev'ry tribe 403
responsive to his call,
to him all majesty ascribe
and crown him Lord of all.

Gracious Lord, we are a wealthy nation. You have given us the responsibility of using our wealth in ways that will glorify you. You ask us to trust you by sharing our wealth with those in need. Remind us that it all belongs to you. Amen.

Tuesday, September 23 — Psalm 109:8-20
1 Samuel 14:41-15:23; John 2:12-25

This is God, our God forever and ever. He will be our guide. Psalm 48:14

Guide me, O my great Redeemer, 790
pilgrim through this barren land.
I am weak, but you are mighty;
hold me with your pow'rful hand.
Bread of heaven, bread of heaven,
feed me now and evermore,
feed me now and evermore.

Christ suffered for sins once for all, the righteous for the unrighteous, in order to bring you to God. 1 Peter 3:18

To him who suffered on the tree 469
our souls, at his soul's price, to gain,
blessing, and praise, and glory be,
"Worthy the Lamb, for he was slain!"

Lord, there are many choices we need to make in our journey of faith. We choose life. We choose you. The choices we face today are merely opportunities to strengthen our faith in you. Amen.

Wednesday, September 24 — Psalm 109:21-31
1 Samuel 15:24-16:13; John 3:1-15

You shall be called by a new name that the mouth of the Lord will give. Isaiah 62:2

God his own shall tend and nourish, 667*
in his holy courts they flourish.
From all evil pow'rs he spares them;
in his mighty arms he bears them.

It is no longer I who live, but it is Christ who lives in me. Galatians 2:20

In you I trust by faith, 488
my Jesus, God and Savior;
on your atoning death
I shall rely forever.
Your suff'rings shall remain
deep on my heart impressed,
O Son of God and man,
till I with you shall rest.

Name us, Lord, and claim us for your own. Have complete authority over us. Call us for your purposes and we will hear you. Do not let our minds or hearts stray from you and we will make this day a living prayer. Amen.

Thursday, September 25 — Psalm 110
1 Samuel 16:14-17:31; John 3:16-26

I have loved you with an everlasting love; I have drawn you with loving-kindness. Jeremiah 31:3 (NIV)

For sinners without merit of their own 325r
which could the burden of great guilt atone,
who no escape from penalty can see,
for such the Lamb of God died on the tree.

Jesus, looking at the man, loved him and said, "You lack one thing; go, sell what you own, and give the money to the poor, and you will have treasure in heaven; then come, follow me." Mark 10:21

How shall I meet my Savior? 60r
How shall I welcome you?
What manner of behavior
is now required of me?
I wait for your salvation;
grant me your Spirit's light;
thus will my preparation
be pleasing in your sight.

Jesus, with love in your eyes you test our faith. You know what we need to change in order to follow you. Embrace us in your love, Lord, so that we might find the courage needed to address the faith we lack. Amen.

Friday, September 26 — Psalm 111
1 Samuel 17:32-58; John 3:27-36

The Lord will fight for you, and you have only to keep still. Exodus 14:14

Neither life nor death shall ever 667*
from the Lord his children sever;
for to them his grace revealing,
he turns sorrow into healing.

We are persecuted, but not forsaken; struck down, but not destroyed. 2 Corinthians 4:9

So come, my Sovereign, enter in; 63r
let new and nobler life begin;
the Holy Spirit guide us on,
until our glorious goal is won.

No matter how great the challenges before us are, dear God, you are greater! Fill us with your Spirit so that peace might be our response when fear threatens to raise its head. Amen.

Saturday, September 27 — Psalm 112
1 Samuel 18:1-19:7; John 4:1-26

O Lord, what do I wait for? My hope is in you. Psalm 39:7

O God, our help in ages past, 461
our hope for years to come,
our shelter from the stormy blast,
and our eternal home!

I know the one in whom I have put my trust, and I am sure that he is able to guard what I have entrusted to him. 2 Timothy 1:12

When peace, like a river, attendeth my way, 754
when sorrows like sea billows roll;
whatever my lot, you have taught me to say,
it is well, it well with my soul.

Savior of the world, our lives are in your hands. We have no doubt that we are safe in you. Lead us to those who are ready to hear your message. Open our mouths and we will speak of your steadfast love and protection. Amen.

Twentieth Sunday after Pentecost

Watchword for the Week — Let the same mind be in you that was in Christ Jesus. Philippians 2:5

Sunday, September 28 — Ezekiel 18:1-4,25-32; Psalm 25:1-9 Philippians 2:1-13; Matthew 21:23-32

This is the day that the Lord has made; let us rejoice and be glad in it. Psalm 118:24

O then with hymns of praise 517
these hallowed courts shall ring;
our voices we will raise
the Three in One to sing,
and thus proclaim in joyful song
both loud and long that glorious name.

The Son of Man is lord even of the Sabbath. Mark 2:28

We dare not trifle now on this, your holy day; 563
in silent awe we bow on this, your holy day.
Check ev'ry wand'ring thought,
and let us all be taught to serve you as we ought
on this, your holy day.

Sabbath Giver, we need to rest in your presence. All week we have been addressing daily concerns. This day is for you. Let your joy direct us as we consider all that we are grateful for. Amen.

Monday, September 29 — Psalm 113
1 Samuel 19:8-20:17; John 4:27-38

God sends his love and his faithfulness. Psalm 57:3 (NIV)

As it was without beginning, 458
so it lasts without an end;
to their children's children ever
shall God's righteousness extend.

Jesus was in the wilderness forty days, tempted by Satan; and he was with the wild beasts; and the angels waited on him. Mark 1:13

And through these days of penitence, 341
and through your Passiontide,
for evermore, in life and death,
O Lord! with us abide.

You were tempted, Lord. We find it hard to imagine that the temptations that challenge us were just as real for you. You are our strength when our passions betray us. We will not be overcome with you by our side. Amen.

Tuesday, September 30 — Psalm 114
1 Samuel 20:18-21:9; John 4:39-42

I will give thanks to you, O Lord, among the peoples; I will sing praises to you among the nations. Psalm 57:9

Praise to the Lord! 530
O, let all that is in me adore him!
All that has life and breath,
come now with praises before him!
Let the amen
sound from his people again.
Gladly forever adore him!

You are a chosen race, a royal priesthood, a holy nation, God's own people, in order that you may proclaim the mighty acts of him who called you out of darkness into his marvelous light. 1 Peter 2:9

Highly favored congregation, 515
loved by Jesus and esteemed,
ne'er forget your destination,
why from this vain world redeemed.

Holy Word, clothe us in holiness. Cause our actions and our words to be holy. That which you have made holy we will not treat as ordinary. Amen.

Wednesday, October 1 — Psalm 115:1-8
1 Samuel 21:10-22:23; John 4:43-54

My salvation and my honor depend on God; he is my mighty rock, my refuge. Psalm 62:7 (NIV)

God is my strong salvation, 769
no enemy I fear;
he hears my supplication,
dispelling all my care;
if he, my head and master,
defend me from above,
what pain or what disaster
can part me from his love?

Like newborn babies, crave pure spiritual milk, so that by it you may grow up in your salvation, now that you have tasted that the Lord is good. 1 Peter 2:2,3 (NIV)

Finish, then, your new creation; 474
pure and spotless let us be;
let us see your great salvation
perfectly restored and free.
Changed from glory into glory,
till in heav'n we take our place,
till we cast our crowns before you,
lost in wonder, love, and praise.

Gracious Savior, we thank you for dying on the cross to save us from our sins. Help us to grow closer to you and to become mature Christians. In your holy name we pray. Amen.

Thursday, October 2 — Psalm 115:9-18
1 Samuel 23; John 5:1-15

The Lord brings the counsel of the nations to nothing; he frustrates the plans of the peoples. Psalm 33:10

We've a story to tell the nations, 621
that shall turn their hearts to the right,
a story of truth and mercy,
a story of peace and light,
a story of peace and light.
For the darkness shall turn to dawning,
and the dawning to noonday bright;
and Christ's great kingdom shall come on earth,
the kingdom of love and light.

God chose what is low and despised in the world, things that are not, to reduce to nothing things that are, so that no one might boast in the presence of God. 1 Corinthians 1:28,29

All things living he does feed; 18br
his full hand supplies their need;
for his mercies aye endure,
ever faithful, ever sure.

Lord, may your will be done among the nations. Prosper our witness all over the world to those who do not yet know you as Lord and Savior. Amen.

Friday, October 3 — Psalm 116:1-7
1 Samuel 24:1-25:17; John 5:16-30

Love truth and peace! Zechariah 8:19

All who love and serve your city, 697*
all who bear its daily stress,
all who cry for peace and justice,
all who curse and all who bless.

Those who do what is true come to the light, so that it may be clearly seen that their deeds have been done in God. John 3:21

We sing to you, O Child Divine; 299
we lift our songs, our candles shine.
Now be your light in us more clear,
reflecting love both far and near.

Heavenly Father, help us to reflect your light and love by our actions. May the light within us shine for the world to see. In the name of Jesus. Amen.

Saturday, October 4 — Psalm 116:8-14
1 Samuel 25:18-44; John 5:31-47

Steadfast love surrounds those who trust in the Lord. Psalm 32:10

If you but trust in God to guide you 712
and place your confidence in him,
you'll find him always there beside you
to give you hope and strength within;
for those who trust God's changeless love
build on the rock that will not move.

Whoever plows should plow in hope and whoever threshes should thresh in hope of a share in the crop. 1 Corinthians 9:10

Revive your work; amid the years 399
our members still employ
on needy souls to sow in tears,
with hope to reap in joy.
Though wide the fields, the lab'rers few,
if you our failing faith renew,
though weak, we as your servants, Lord,
may still fulfill your word.

O Lord, as we put our faith and trust in you, take the seeds we plant and grow them into a rich harvest of souls in your kingdom. Amen.

Twenty-First Sunday after Pentecost

Watchword for the Week — The stone that the builders rejected has become the chief cornerstone. This is the Lord's doing; it is marvelous in our eyes. Psalm 118:22,23

Sunday, October 5 — Isaiah 5:1-7; Psalm 80:7-15
Philippians 3:4b-14; Matthew 21:33-46

It is the Lord your God who has fought for you. Joshua 23:3

Servant of God, well done! 811
Rest from your loved employ;
the battle fought, the victory won,
enter your Master's joy.

A Sabbath rest still remains for the people of God. Hebrews 4:9

O Sabbath rest by Galilee! 739
O calm of hills above,
where Jesus knelt to share with thee
the silence of eternity,
interpreted by love!

Most holy God, as we gather for worship on this Worldwide Communion Sunday, may our hearts be open to the word and sacrament. May we respond in faith and service. In Jesus' name. Amen.

Monday, October 6 — Psalm 116:15-19
1 Samuel 26,27; John 6:1-15

I will satisfy the weary, and all who are faint I will replenish. Jeremiah 31:25

How good the name of Jesus sounds 487
to all believing ears!
It soothes our sorrows, heals our wounds,
and drives away our fears.
It makes the wounded spirit whole,
and calms the troubled mind;
his manna for each hungry soul,
the lost and weary find.

Jesus said, "Come to me, all you that are weary and are carrying heavy burdens, and I will give you rest." Matthew 11:28

Come, you weary, heavy laden, 765
lost and ruined by the fall;
if you tarry till you're better,
you will never come at all.
I will arise and go to Jesus,
he will embrace me in his arms;
in the arms of my dear Savior,
O there are ten thousand charms.

Loving heavenly Father, how comforting it is to know that you carry our burdens on your shoulders. Thank you for giving us rest. Amen.

Tuesday, October 7 — Psalm 117
1 Samuel 28,29; John 6:16-24

You have been my help, and in the shadow of your wings I sing for joy. Psalm 63:7

Christ Jesus lay in death's strong bands, 367
for our offenses given;
but now at God's right hand he stands
and brings us life from heaven:
therefore let us joyful be
and sing God's praises thankfully
with songs of alleluia! Alleluia!

Let us therefore approach the throne of grace with boldness, so that we may receive mercy and find grace to help in time of need. Hebrews 4:16

God of grace and God of glory, 751*
on your people pour your power;
crown your ancient Church's story;
bring its bud to glorious flower.
Grant us wisdom, grant us courage
for the facing of this hour
for the facing of this hour.

Dear God, help us to go about our day with a song in our hearts, giving thanks and praise for your grace and mercy. Amen.

Wednesday, October 8 — Psalm 118:1-9
1 Samuel 30,31; John 6:25-42

The Lord has sent me to comfort all who mourn. Isaiah 61:1,2

Thou the Spring of all my comfort, 772
more than life to me,
whom have I on earth beside thee?
Whom in heav'n but thee?
Savior, Savior, hear my humble cry;
while on others thou art calling;
do not pass me by.

We will be with the Lord forever. Therefore encourage one another with these words. 1 Thessalonians 4:17,18

Rejoice in glorious hope; 372
for Christ, the Judge, shall come
to gather all his saints
to their eternal home.
We soon shall hear the archangel's voice;
the trump of God shall sound, rejoice.

Lord Jesus, we look forward to your glorious second coming when we shall be gathered with the saints who have gone before us and go to our eternal home. Come, Lord Jesus, come. Amen.

Thursday, October 9 — Psalm 118:10-14
2 Samuel 1; John 6:43-51

My eyes are fixed on you, O Sovereign Lord; in you I take refuge — do not give me over to death. Psalm 141:8 (NIV)

Now we bring ourselves to you; 741
cleanse us, Lord, we humbly pray;
undeserving though we be,
draw us closer ev'ry day.
Lord, our refuge, hope, and strength!
Keep, O keep us safe from harm,
shield us through our earthly life
by your everlasting arm.

If for this life only we have hoped in Christ, we are of all people most to be pitied. But in fact Christ has been raised from the dead, the first fruits of those who have died. 1 Corinthians 15:19,20

Jesus Christ is ris'n today, alleluia! 358
Our triumphant holy day, alleluia!
Who did once, upon the cross, alleluia!
Suffer to redeem our loss. Alleluia!

Precious Jesus, because you were raised from the dead, we are raised to new life in you. Through the resurrection, you have conquered sin and death, giving us the hope of eternal life. Thank you Jesus. Amen.

Friday, October 10 — Psalm 118:15-21
2 Samuel 2; John 6:52-59

Can you deceive God, as one person deceives another? Job 13:9

Blessed are they who show their mercy 595
to the guilty and the poor,
for to them, set free from judgment,
shall be opened heaven's door.
Blessed, the sincere and truthful
from the lie's deception free,
for the God of truth and beauty
they in joy will surely see.

Do not be deceived; God is not mocked, for you reap whatever you sow. Galatians 6:7

Father, we praise you; 535*
Jesus, we love you;
Spirit, we thank you,
for these new days;
help us to know, Lord;
help us to grow, Lord;
Help us to sow, Lord,
your love always.

Almighty God, we may deceive ourselves and others, but we cannot deceive you. You know everything we do, both good and bad, and nothing is hidden from your sight. Help us to always sow good seeds, ones that will reap a harvest pleasing to you. Amen.

Saturday, October 11 — Psalm 118:22-29
2 Samuel 3:1-34; John 6:60-71

Do not spurn us, for your name's sake; do not dishonor your glorious throne. Jeremiah 14:21

Born your people to deliver, 262
born a child and yet a king,
born to reign in us forever,
now your gracious kingdom bring.
By your own eternal Spirit
rule in all our hearts alone;
by your all sufficient merit
raise us to your glorious throne.

If we are faithless, he remains faithful. 2 Timothy 2:13

O God, my faithful God, 615
O fountain ever flowing,
without whom nothing is,
all perfect gifts bestowing,
grant me a faithful life,
and give me, Lord, within,
commitment free from strife,
a soul unhurt by sin.

Merciful God, forgive us for the times we have not been faithful to you. Thank you for always remaining faithful to us, even when we don't deserve it. In Jesus' name. Amen.

Twenty-Second Sunday after Pentecost

Watchword for the Week — O Lord, you are my God; I will exalt you, I will praise your name; for you have done wonderful things. Isaiah 25:1

Sunday, October 12 — Isaiah 25:1-9; Psalm 23
Philippians 4:1-9; Matthew 22:1-14

The Lord of hosts is with us; the God of Jacob is our refuge. Psalm 46:7

Lord, your body ne'er forsake, p86
ne'er your congregation leave;
we in you our refuge take,
of your fullness we receive:
ev'ry other help be gone,
you are our support alone;
for on your supreme commands
all the universe depends.

Paul wrote: It is God who makes both us and you stand firm in Christ. 2 Corinthians 1:21 (NIV)

My Jesus, as you will, 534r
O may your will be mine;
into your hand of love
I would my all resign.
Through sorrow or through joy
conduct me as your own,
and help me still to say,
my Lord, your will be done!

Most Holy Lord and God, as we gather for worship on the Lord's Day, may we sing with joy in our hearts and be open to receive the word that is proclaimed. In the name of Jesus, our Savior. Amen.

Monday, October 13 — Psalm 119:1-8
2 Samuel 3:35-5:16; John 7:1-13

Noah did all that God commanded him. Genesis 6:22

Since, O Lord, you have demanded 401*
that our lives your love should show
so we wait to be commanded
forth into your world to go.
Kindle in us love's compassion
so that ev'ry one may see
in our faith and hope the promise
of a new humanity.

The world and its desire are passing away, but those who do the will of God live forever. 1 John 2:17

In all we do, constrained by love, 364
we'll joy to him afford,
and to God's will obedient prove
through Jesus Christ our Lord.
Sing alleluia, and adore
on earth the Lamb once slain,
till we in heav'n shall evermore
exalt his name, Amen.

Father God, all too often we want to go our own way instead of following your way. It is at those times our lives get pretty messed up. So we commit ourselves to be obedient to your will in our lives. In your holy name we pray. Amen.

Tuesday, October 14 — Psalm 119:9-16
2 Samuel 5:17-6:23; John 7:14-24

We are aliens and transients before you, as were all our ancestors; our days on the earth are like a shadow, and there is no hope. 1 Chronicles 29:15

Lift up your standard high! 786
March on in firm array!
As pilgrims through the darkness wend
till dawns the golden day.
Rejoice, rejoice, rejoice, give thanks and sing!

What can be seen is temporary, but what cannot be seen is eternal. 2 Corinthians 4:18

The highest, most holy, 283
light of light eternal,
born of a virgin, a mortal he comes;
Son of the Father
now in flesh appearing!
O come let us adore him, Christ, the Lord.

Eternal God, you have always been and will always be. We look forward to the day when we are called home to you, when we shall live with you forever and ever. In your holy name we pray. Amen.

Wednesday, October 15 — Psalm 119:17-24
2 Samuel 7; John 7:25-44

My people shall be satisfied with my bounty, says the Lord. Jeremiah 31:14

Love is a gift, a present sweet, 536*
love unfailing and complete.
Bonded in love, we are to stand,
guided by the great command.
Love one another, bear no ill,
share of the bounty, do God's will.
Let us by action love profess,
with our deeds as evidence.

God was pleased to have all his fullness dwell in his son. Colossians 1:19 (NIV)

Christ is our Master, Lord, and God, 479
the fullness of the Three in One.
His life, death, righteousness, and blood
our faith's foundation are alone;
his Godhead and his death shall be
our theme to all eternity.

Most bountiful God, we pray for all those who have special needs this day. Grant to them your grace and peace, and may they know that you are with them always. Amen.

Thursday, October 16 — Psalm 119:25-32
2 Samuel 8,9; John 7:45-53

Woe to him who piles up stolen goods and makes himself wealthy by extortion! How long must this go on? Habakkuk 2:6 (NIV)

For sinners without merit of their own 325r
which could the burden of great guilt atone,
who no escape from penalty can see,
for such the Lamb of God died on the tree.

We brought nothing into the world, so that we can take nothing out of it. 1 Timothy 6:7

Blessed are the poor in spirit, 595
claiming nothing as their own,
but as giv'n them by their Father
that his goodness may be shown.
Blessed are they who share the sorrow
of their God's unchanging love;
they shall know his presence with them
and his promised comfort prove.

Loving Father, help us not be too tied to earthly treasures. We must learn to leave all behind when we respond to your call to discipleship. All we will need is you when we leave this earth. Amen.

Friday, October 17 — Psalm 119:33-40
2 Samuel 10,11; John 8:1-11

My flesh and my heart may fail, but God is the strength of my heart and my portion forever. Psalm 73:26

I am Jesus' little lamb; 723
ever glad at heart I am;
for my Shepherd gently guides me,
knows my need and well provides me,
loves me ev'ry day the same,
even calls me by my name.

Blessed be the God and Father of our Lord Jesus Christ, the Father of mercies and the God of all consolation. 2 Corinthians 1:3

My portion is the Lord; 329r
I seek his favor
and in his name and word
confide forever;
the world can never give
so rich a treasure
as in his love to live
and do his pleasure.

Gracious Father, you alone are our strength. Thank you for giving us this strength to deal with the difficulties of life. Thank you for helping us through each day and the trials we face. In the name of Jesus. Amen.

Saturday, October 18 — Psalm 119:41-48
2 Samuel 12; John 8:12-30

Proclaim, give praise, and say, "Save, O Lord, your people." Jeremiah 31:7

Praise the Lord, praise the Lord! 528
He with you deals bounteously.
Highly favored church of Jesus,
he chose you through mercy free
to show forth his matchless praises
and rich fruit, blessed for the Master's use,
to produce, to produce.

Zechariah said, "Blessed be the Lord God of Israel, for he has looked favorably on his people and redeemed them." Luke 1:68

There we to all eternity 543
shall join th'angelic lays
and sing in perfect harmony
to God our Savior's praise;
he has redeemed us by his blood,
and made us kings and priests to God;
for us, for us, the Lamb was slain!
Praise ye the Lord! Amen.

O Lord, our Redeemer, you bought us back from sin and death through your precious blood. Draw us closer into the fellowship of your suffering that we may never take your gift of salvation for granted. Amen.

Twenty-Third Sunday after Pentecost

Watchword for the Week — Sing to the Lord, bless his name; tell of his salvation from day to day. Psalm 96:2

Sunday, October 19 — Isaiah 45:1-7; Psalm 96:1-9,(10-13)
1 Thessalonians 1:1-10; Matthew 22:15-22

It is good that one should wait quietly for the salvation of the Lord. Lamentations 3:26

The springs of salvation from Christ, 616
the Rock, bursting
and flowing throughout all the world's wilderness
bring life and salvation to those who are thirsting
to drink from this spring of salvation by grace;
as streams through the desert refresh the ground
and make land once barren with green abound,
the pow'r of his Spirit, our cold hearts o'erflowing,
renews us for service with lives bright and glowing.

You need endurance, so that when you have done the will of God, you may receive what was promised. Hebrews 10:36

God of church and God of hist'ry, 637*
pour your blessings on your deeds.
Grant endurance for our ventures,
give us strength to serve and lead.
Alleluia! Our Creator,
Christ and Spirit — this our creed.

Almighty God, we thank you for this Sabbath day where we have the opportunity to join with our Christian brothers and sisters in praise and worship of you, our Father, Savior, and Comforter. May our worship this day bring honor and glory to you. Amen.

Monday, October 20 — Psalm 119:49-56
2 Samuel 13:1-33; John 8:31-41

Do not put your trust in princes, in mortals, in whom there is no help. Psalm 146:3

Other refuge have I none; 724
hangs my helpless soul on thee;
leave, ah, leave me not alone,
still support and comfort me.
All my trust on thee is stayed,
all my help from thee I bring;
cover my defenseless head
with the shadow of thy wing.

We have our hope set on the living God. 1 Timothy 4:10

Jesus is my joy, p197
therefore blessed am I;
O, his mercy is unbounded,
all my hope on him is grounded;
Jesus is my joy,
therefore blessed am I.

God of hope, we put our faith and trust in you. Because we have given our hearts and lives to you, we have the hope and assurance of eternal life. Thank you for dying on the cross and saving us from our sins. Amen.

Tuesday, October 21 — Psalm 119:57-64
2 Samuel 13:34-14:33; John 8:42-59

I am with you, says the Lord. Haggai 1:13

Be present with your servants, Lord; 734
we look to you with one accord;
refresh and strengthen us anew,
and bless what in your name we do.

Go into all the world and proclaim the good news to the whole creation. Mark 16:15

O Christians, haste, your mission high fulfilling, 618
to tell to all the world that God is light,
that he who made all nations is not willing
one life should perish, lost in shades of night.
Publish glad tidings, tidings of peace,
tidings of Jesus, redemption, and release.

Dear God, we pray this day for all our missionaries all over the world who are proclaiming the good news of Jesus Christ to those who have never heard it. May you bless their efforts and may many come to know Jesus as Lord and Savior. Amen.

Wednesday, October 22 — Psalm 119:65-72
2 Samuel 15:1-29; John 9:1-12

Your sins have deprived you of good.
Jeremiah 5:25

Hear then, dear Lord Jesus, 746
hear our earnest prayer,
grant your loving mercy,
keep us in your care.
All that is displeasing
unto you, forgive;
more to your name's glory
may we henceforth live.

The good man brings good things out of the good stored up in him, and the evil man brings evil things out of the evil stored up in him.
Matthew 12:35 (NIV)

To you before your passion 342
they sang their hymns of praise;
to you, now high exalted,
our melody we raise.
As you received their praises,
accept the prayers we bring,
for you delight in goodness,
O good and gracious King.

Forgiving Savior, we confess our sins to you, particularly the good that we know to do that we have not done. Forgive our many sins of omission and help us to do better. In Jesus' name we pray. Amen.

Thursday, October 23 — Psalm 119:73-80
2 Samuel 15:30-16:23; John 9:13-34

I will heal their disloyalty; I will love them freely. Hosea 14:4

Thus if we have known him, 273
not ashamed to own him,
nor have spurned him coldly,
but will trust him boldly,
he will then receive us,
heal us, and forgive us.

And as he sat at dinner in Levi's house, many tax collectors and sinners were also sitting with Jesus and his disciples — for there were many who followed him. Mark 2:15

My lasting joy and comfort here 768
is Jesus' death and blood;
I with this passport can appear
before the throne of God.
Admitted to the realms above,
I then shall see the Christ I love,
where countless pardoned sinners meet
adoring at his feet.

Loving Lord, help us to reach out to the sinners and tax collectors of our day, showing the love of Christ to them. Use us as a witness to them that they might come to a saving faith in Jesus Christ. Amen.

Friday, October 24 — Psalm 119:81-88
2 Samuel 17; John 9:35-41

The eyes of the Lord range throughout the entire earth, to strengthen those whose heart is true to him. 2 Chronicles 16:9

He to the lowly soul 584
will still himself impart
and for his dwelling and his throne
will choose the pure in heart.

So make up your minds not to prepare your defense in advance; for I will give you words and a wisdom that none of your opponents will be able to withstand or contradict. Luke 21:14,15

The Church from her dear Master 237r
received the gift divine,
and still that Light she lifteth
o'er all the earth to shine.
It is the golden casket
where gems of truth are stored;
it is the heaven drawn picture
of Christ, the living Word.

Wise and loving Father, give us wisdom that we might always make good decisions in our lives and in the life of the church, always following your call and being obedient to your will. In your holy name we pray. Amen.

Saturday, October 25 — Psalm 119:89-96
2 Samuel 18:1-30; John 10:1-10

In God's hand are the depths of the earth; the heights of the mountains are his also. Psalm 95:4

This is my Father's world, 456
and to my list'ning ears
all nature sings and round me rings
the music of the spheres.
This is my Father's world;
I rest me in the thought
of rocks and trees, of skies and seas —
his hand the wonders wrought.

Jairus begged Jesus repeatedly, "My little daughter is at the point of death. Come and lay your hands on her, so that she may be made well, and live." Mark 5:23

God sent his Son, they called him Jesus, 706
he came to love, heal, and forgive;
he lived and died to buy my pardon,
an empty grave is there to prove my Savior lives.
Because he lives I can face tomorrow,
because he lives all fear is gone;
because I know he holds the future,
and life is worth the living just because he lives.

Merciful and all-powerful God, just as you healed Jairus' daughter, continue to bring miraculous healing to people in our day. Help us to keep the faith that you still perform miracles even today. Amen.

Twenty-Fourth Sunday after Pentecost

Watchword for the Week — You shall be holy, for I the Lord your God am holy. Leviticus 19:2

Sunday, October 26 — Leviticus 19:1-2,15-18; Psalm 1
1 Thessalonians 2:1-8; Matthew 22:34-46

The Lord said to Isaac, "Through your offspring all nations on earth will be blessed." Genesis 26:4 (NIV)

Praise we now the God of nations 637*
who through Israel long ago
called a people in Christ Jesus,
led them on through joy and woe.
Alleluia! Christians faithful,
let our tributes overflow.

Christ has become a servant of the Jews on behalf of God's truth, to confirm the promises made to the patriarchs. Romans 15:8 (NIV)

The everlasting Son p185a
incarnate stoops to be,
takes on himself the servant's form
to set his people free.

Most holy Lord and God, on this first day of the week we gather for worship in honor of your resurrection. As we lift up the cross and suffering you bore on our behalf, may we also celebrate the resurrection and your victory over sin and death. Amen.

Monday, October 27 — Psalm 119:97-104
2 Samuel 18:31-19:30; John 10:11-21

Wondrously show your steadfast love, O savior of those who seek refuge. Psalm 17:7

Are we weak and heavy laden, 743
cumbered with a load of care?
Precious Savior, still our refuge,
take it to the Lord in prayer!
Do your friends despise, forsake you?
Take it to the Lord in prayer!
In his arms he'll take and shield you;
you will find a solace there.

One of the criminals said, "Jesus, remember me when you come into your kingdom." Jesus replied, "Truly I tell you, today you will be with me in Paradise." Luke 23:42,43

Jesus, pitying the sighs 352
of the thief, who near you dies,
promising him paradise:
hear us, holy Jesus.

Heavenly Father, it brings us great comfort to know that when our soul leaves the body we enter into your eternal presence. We look forward to the day when we see you face to face and live in paradise with you forever. Amen.

Tuesday, October 28 — Psalm 119:105-112
2 Samuel 19:31-20:26; John 10:22-33

Praise the Lord! How good it is to sing praises to our God. Psalm 147:1

All praise and thanks to God 533
the Father now be given,
the Son and Spirit blessed,
who reign in highest heaven —
the one eternal God,
whom heav'n and earth adore;
for thus it was, is now,
and shall be evermore.

Speak to one another with psalms, hymns, and spiritual songs. Sing and make music in your heart to the Lord. Ephesians 5:19 (NIV)

Mortals join the mighty chorus, 544
which the morning stars began;
God's own love is reigning o'er us,
joining people hand in hand.
Ever singing, march we onward,
victors in the midst of strife;
joyful music leads us sunward
in the triumph song of life.

Lord, thank you for the rich musical heritage of our beloved Moravian Church. We love to sing the old hymns which express our faith so deeply. May we always be a church that loves to sing. Amen.

Wednesday, October 29 — Psalm 119:113-120
2 Samuel 21; John 10:34-42

The Lord reproves the one he loves, as a father the son in whom he delights. Proverbs 3:12

As a mother looks with favor 659
on the new life in her arms,
searching ev'ry small expression,
sav'ring moments filled with charm,
so God smiles on ev'ry person,
so God takes such keen delight
in the praises that we offer;
we are precious in God's sight.

Peter said to Jesus, "Even though all become deserters, I will not." Jesus said to him, "Truly I tell you, this day, this very night, before the cock crows twice, you will deny me three times." Mark 14:29,30

Christ Jesus knew uncertainty. 337*
Would all forsake, deny, betray?
Would crowds that followed turn away?
Would pow'rs of evil hold their sway?

Dear Jesus, like Peter, we deny you so many times without even realizing it. We don't mean to do it, but we are guilty nonetheless. Forgive us for the times we deny you and we pledge to be more faithful. In your name we pray. Amen.

Thursday, October 30 — Psalm 119:121-128
2 Samuel 22:1-25; John 11:1-16

God make his face to shine upon us — that your way may be known upon earth, your saving power among all nations. Psalm 67:1,2

Stretch forth your hand, our health restore, 267
and make us rise to fall no more;
O let your face upon us shine
and fill the world with love divine.

The grace of the Lord Jesus Christ, the love of God, and the communion of the Holy Spirit be with all of you. 2 Corinthians 13:13

Amazing grace! How sweet the sound 783
that saved a wretch like me!
I once was lost, but now am found,
was blind, but now I see.

Triune God, we thank you for salvation through Jesus Christ, the love and providence of the Father, and the fellowship and presence of the Holy Spirit. Be with us always. Amen.

Reformation Day

Friday, October 31 — Psalm 119:129-136
2 Samuel 22:26-23:17; John 11:17-30

In the midst of the congregation I will praise you. Psalm 22:22

Our God rules on high, almighty to save, 565
and still he is nigh, his presence we have;
the great congregation his triumph shall sing,
ascribing salvation to Jesus, our King.

We are ambassadors for Christ, since God is making his appeal through us; we entreat you on behalf of Christ, be reconciled to God. 2 Corinthians 5:20

Paschal Lamb, by God appointed, 330
all our sins on your were laid;
by almighty love anointed,
you have full atonement made.
All your people are forgiven
through the virtue of your blood;
opened is the gate of heaven;
we are reconciled to God.

Lord and Savior Jesus Christ, you have reconciled us to God through the shedding of your precious blood. Our sins have been atoned for and will not stand against us. We give our hearts and lives to you, O Lord, our Redeemer. Amen.

All Saints Day

Watchword for the Day — Salvation belongs to our God who is seated on the throne, and to the Lamb! Revelation 7:10

Saturday, November 1 — Psalm 119:137-144
2 Samuel 23:18-24:25; John 11:31-44

All Saints Day — Revelation 7:9-17; Psalm 34:1-10,22
1 John 3:1-3; Matthew 5:1-12

They shall live in safety, and no one shall make them afraid. Ezekiel 34:28

God whom we serve, our God can save, p106
can damp the scorching flame,
can build an ark, can smooth the wave,
for such as love his name.

God guaranteed it by an oath, [that] we who have taken refuge might be strongly encouraged to seize the hope set before us. Hebrews 6:17,18

Let us call to mind with joy p108
those who have before us gone,
who obtained the victory
through the blood of Christ alone;
that we all may zealously
imitate their constancy,
till we too the prize receive
and with them in glory live.

Almighty God, Redeemer and Sustainer, we offer you thanks and praise for the holy lives of all your servants — the prophets, apostles, and martyrs — who have shone forth as lights in the world and sacrificed their lives in testimony of their faith. Enable us also to be faithful. Amen.

Twenty-Fifth Sunday after Pentecost

Watchword for the Week — O send out your light and your truth; let them lead me. Psalm 43:3

Sunday, November 2 — Micah 3:5-12; Psalm 43
1 Thessalonians 2:9-13; Matthew 23:1-12

If you do not stand firm in faith, you shall not stand at all. Isaiah 7:9

How firm a foundation, you saints of the Lord, 709
is laid for your faith in his excellent word!
What more can he say than to you he has said,
to you who for refuge to Jesus have fled?

Peter got out of the boat, started walking on the water, and came toward Jesus. But when he noticed the strong wind, he became frightened, and beginning to sink, he cried out, "Lord, save me!" Matthew 14:29,30

The years have all been crowded p13
with tokens of your love,
and many who have sought you
now worship you above.
But we, O Lord, still need you,
our pilgrim feet to stay,
for evil often triumphs as faith to fear gives way.

Shepherd, many things frighten us: sickness, death, conflict, war, poverty, failure. Panic overtakes us. Life overwhelms us. When we feel lost, come to us; when we feel covered in darkness, take us by the hand; when we are filled with fear, assure us of your loving presence. Amen.

Monday, November 3 — Psalm 119:145-152
1 Kings 1:1-27; John 11:45-57

My heart recoils within me; my compassion grows warm and tender. I will not execute my fierce anger; for I am God and no mortal, the Holy One in your midst. Hosea 11:8,9

I heard the voice of Jesus say, 606
"Behold, I freely give
the living water; thirsty one,
stoop down and drink and live."
I came to Jesus, and I drank
of that life-giving stream;
my thirst was quenched, my soul revived,
and now I live in him.

Paul wrote: I give thanks to my God always for you because of the grace of God that has been given you in Christ Jesus. 1 Corinthians 1:4

No condemnation now I dread, 773
for Christ, and all in him, is mine!
Alive in him, my living Head,
and clothed in righteousness divine,
bold I approach the eternal throne
and claim the crown, through Christ, my own.

God of mercy, no matter who we are, we come to you by your grace as one people of faith. We have all needed your cleansing salvation to remove the guilt of sin. Thousand, thousand thanks to thee, dearest Lord forever be. Amen.

Tuesday, November 4 — Psalm 119:153-160
1 Kings 1:28-53; John 12:1-11

May the Lord, who is good, pardon everyone who sets his heart on seeking God. 2 Chronicles 30:18,19 (NIV)

You are the way; to you alone 661
from sin and death we flee;
and those who would the Father seek
your followers must be.
You are the truth; your word alone
true wisdom can impart;
you only can inform the mind
and purify the heart.

A woman whose little daughter had an unclean spirit immediately heard about him, and she came and bowed down at his feet. She begged him to cast the demon out of her daughter. Mark 7:25,26

Gracious Savior, gentle Shepherd, 660
children all are dear to you;
may your loving arms enfold them
in your care their whole life through;
fondly tend and safely keep them
in your mercy strong and true.

Heavenly Father, all the little daughters and young sons in the world are yours. Teach us how to deliver them from the evil of this world. Protect them. Embrace them in your loving arms. Amen.

Wednesday, November 5 — Psalm 119:161-168
1 Kings 2:1-38; John 12:12-19

May God be gracious to us and bless us. Psalm 67:1

Grace and peace from God, our blessed Savior, 444
be with all who love his name;
church of Christ, his service deem a favor,
joyfully his death proclaim,
be prepared for rest or for employment,
from activity derive enjoyment,
serve with zeal and faithfulness,
filled with love his name confess.

We believe that we will be saved through the grace of the Lord Jesus. Acts 15:11

Amazing grace, how sweet the sound 783
that saved a wretch like me!
I once was lost, but now am found,
was blind, but now I see.
'Twas grace that taught my heart to fear
and grace my fears relieved;
how precious did that grace appear
the hour I first believed.

God of infinite mercy, we have forgotten the depths of your love for us. We no longer recall that your grace is given to us freely without consideration of our spiritual condition. But in this moment, we stop and remember, and we are thoroughly amazed by your grace. Amen.

Thursday, November 6 — Psalm 119:169-176
1 Kings 2:39-3:28; John 12:20-36

You shall not hate in your heart anyone of your kin; you shall reprove your neighbor, or you will incur guilt yourself. Leviticus 19:17

Where charity and love prevail, 785*
there God is ever found;
brought here together by Christ's love
by love we thus are bound.

If anyone is detected in a transgression restore such a one in a spirit of gentleness. Galatians 6:1

We now forgive each other's faults 785*
as we our own confess,
that we may love each other well
in Christian gentleness.

Guide and Teacher, you call us to unity, but we are divided by our differences. We avoid awkward subjects we must face together. We talk about each other but not to each other. Give us wisdom and strength to love one another. Amen.

Friday, November 7 — Psalm 120
1 Kings 4:1-28; John 12:37-50

The Lord rises to argue his case; he stands to judge the peoples. Isaiah 3:13

Jesus shall reign where'er the sun 404
does its successive journeys run;
his Kingdom stretch from shore to shore,
till moons shall wax and wane no more.

Love has been perfected among us in this: that we may have boldness on the day of judgment, because as he is, so are we in this world. 1 John 4:17

Make my calling and election, 808
Jesus, ev'ry day more sure;
keep me under your direction,
till I, through almighty pow'r,
unto endless glory raised
in your mansions shall be placed.
When in you I end my race,
weeping shall forever cease.

Holy God, you are righteous, and you judge the earth. Yet, we are not afraid. You are shaping us to be holy like yourself. You are empowering us to love even our enemies. We are thankful for the blessings of your holiness. Amen.

Saturday, November 8 — Psalm 121
1 Kings 4:29-5:18; John 13:1-17

But who can detect their errors? Clear me from hidden faults. Psalm 19:12

Sinners, turn! Why will you die? 311r
God, your Maker, asks you, why?
God, who did your being give,
made you with himself to live;
he the fatal cause demands,
asks the work of his own hands:
why, you thankless creatures, why,
will you cross his love and die?

The Holy Spirit whom God poured out on us richly through Jesus Christ our Savior, so that, having been justified by his grace, we might become heirs according to the hope of eternal life. Titus 3:6,7

Father, now your sinful child 779
through your love is reconciled.
By your pard'ning grace I live;
daily still I cry, forgive.
Lord, forgive me, day by day,
debts I cannot hope to pay,
duties I have left undone,
evils I have failed to shun.

Create in me a clean heart, O God; and renew a right spirit within me. Do not cast me away from your presence, and do not take your Holy Spirit from me. Restore to me the joy of your salvation, and sustain in me a willing spirit. Amen. (Moravian Book of Worship, p. 79)

Twenty-Sixth Sunday after Pentecost

Watchword for the Week — Keep awake therefore, for you know neither the day nor the hour. Matthew 25:13

Sunday, November 9 — Amos 55:18-24; Psalm 70
1 Thessalonians 4:13-18; Matthew 25:1-13

Deliverance belongs to the Lord; may your blessing be on your people! Psalm 3:8

God of grace and God of glory, 751*
on your people pour your power;
crown your ancient Church's story;
bring its bud to glorious flower.
Grant us wisdom, grant us courage
for the facing of this hour,
for the facing of this hour.

Keep alert, stand firm in your faith, be courageous, be strong. 1 Corinthians 16:13

Stand up, stand up for Jesus, 752
stand in his strength alone;
the arm of flesh will fail you,
you dare not trust your own.
Put on the gospel armor,
each piece put on with prayer;
where duty calls, or danger,
be ever faithful there.

God, we pray for your deliverance when we become confused and disheartened. Thank you for strength which is far greater than we thought possible. Thank you for insight when the way seems unclear. We ask that today you walk before us. Amen.

* Used by permission of Elinor Fosdick Downs.

Monday, November 10 — Psalm 122
1 Kings 6; John 13:18-30

Truly the day of the Lord is great; terrible indeed — who can endure it? Yet even now, says the Lord, return to me with all your heart. Joel 2:11,12

Just as I am, without one plea 762
but that thy blood was shed for me,
and that thou bidd'st me come to thee,
O Lamb of God, I come, I come!
Just as I am; thy love unknown
has broken every barrier down;
now to be thine, yea, thine alone,
O Lamb of God, I come, I come!

Find out what pleases the Lord. Ephesians 5:10 (NIV)

My God, I love you, not because 361r
I hope for heaven thereby;
nor yet because, if I love not,
I must forever die.

We eagerly come to you, O Savior. We long to be near you. If we drift away today, call our names. Enable us to hear your voice speaking to us, guiding us. Amen.

Tuesday, November 11 — Psalm 123
1 Kings 7:1-33; John 13:31-38

Happy are all who take refuge in him. Psalm 2:12

Though Satan should buffet, 754
though trials shall come,
let this blessed assurance control,
that Christ has regarded my helpless estate,
and has shed his own blood for my soul.

Lord, to whom can we go? You have the words of eternal life. John 6:68

Lord, your word abideth 240r
and our footsteps guideth;
who its truth believeth
light and joy receiveth.

O Christ, some might suggest that there is another way to go, another way to believe. But we choose to follow you. You have always sustained us in life. As you have been faithful to us, so enable us to remain faithful to you. Amen.

Wednesday, November 12 — Psalm 124
1 Kings 7:34-8:16; John 14:1-14

You shall not be partial to the poor or defer to the great. Leviticus 19:15

We taste you, O you living bread, 385r
and long to feast upon you still;
we drink of you, the fountainhead,
and thirst our souls from you to fill.

Paul wrote to Timothy: I charge you, in the sight of God and Christ Jesus to do nothing out of favoritism. 1 Timothy 5:21 (NIV)

Then shall all shackles fall; the stormy clamor 488r
of wild war music o'er the earth shall cease;
love shall tread out the baleful fire of anger,
and in its ashes plant the tree of peace.

God of all creation, when we meet a stranger today, when we encounter one whose life does not appear to reflect a love for Christ; fill our hearts with your love for that person. Teach us to reach beyond our barriers. Amen.

Chief Elder Festival

Thursday, November 13 — Psalm 125
1 Kings 8:17-53; John 14:15-24

Chief Elder Festival† — Ezekiel 34:11-16,23-24; Psalm 8
Hebrews 4:14-16; John 10:1-10

Arise, shine; for your light has come, and the glory of the Lord has risen upon you. Isaiah 60:1

Morning Star, O cheering sight! 281
Ere thou cams't, how dark earth's night!
Jesus mine, in me shine;
in me shine, Jesus mine;
fill my heart with light divine.

If we walk in the light as he himself is in the light, we have fellowship with one another and the blood of Jesus his Son cleanses us from all sin. 1 John 1:7

Heart with loving heart united, 401*
met to know God's holy will.
Let his love in us ignited
more and more our spirits fill.
He the Head, we are his members;
we reflect the light he is.
He the Master, we disciples,
he is ours and we are his.

Christ, you are the light of the world. You are also the light of the church. Thank you for your presence, your guidance, and your strength. We give you our hearts and our lives to serve only you. Guide our church into your will. Amen.

† On November 13, 1741, announcement was made to the congregations of the Brethren's Church of the Chief Eldership of Jesus Christ.

Friday, November 14 — Psalm 126
1 Kings 8:54-9:19; John 14:25-15:8

When Job's three friends heard of all these troubles that had come upon him... they met together to go and comfort him. They sat with him on the ground seven days and seven nights, and no one spoke a word to him, for they saw that his suffering was very great. Job 2:11,13

Let us each for others care, 672
each another's burden bear,
to your church a pattern give,
showing how believers live.

Each of us should please his neighbor for his good, to build him up. Romans 15:2 (NIV)

What brought us together, what joined our hearts? 675
The pardon which Jesus, our High Priest, imparts;
'tis this which cements the disciples of Christ,
who are into one by the Spirit baptized.

O Savior, thank you for being our comforter, healer, and friend when we suffer. We desire to follow your example by loving our neighbors when they suffer. We ask that you grant to us your wisdom and the strength of your love for this task. Amen.

Saturday, November 15 — Psalm 127
1 Kings 9:20-10:29; John 15:9-17

Lift up your voice like a trumpet! Announce to my people their rebellion. Isaiah 58:1

Out of the deep I cry to you, 317r
my God, with heart's contrition;
bow down your ear in grace to me,
and hear you my petition;
for if in judgment you will try
man's sin and great iniquity,
ah, who can stand before you?

Jesus said, "Those who are ashamed of me and of my words in this adulterous and sinful generation, of them the Son of Man will also be ashamed when he comes." Mark 8:38

Thus if we have known him, 270
not ashamed to own him,
nor have spurned him coldly,
but will trust him boldly,
he will then receive us,
heal us, and forgive us.

Merciful God, we confess that we are like sheep gone astray. We have turned to our own way. Yet, you amaze us with the bounty of your salvation. We will not be ashamed of that; we will sing of your love to our generation. Amen.

Twenty-Seventh Sunday after Pentecost

Watchword for the Week — So teach us, O God, to count our days that we may gain a wise heart. Psalm 90:12

Sunday, November 16 — Zephaniah 1:7, 12-18; Psalm 90:1-8,(9-11),12
1 Thessalonians 5:1-11; Matthew 25:14-30

O give thanks to the Lord, for he is good; for his steadfast love endures forever. Psalm 106:1

Now thank we all our God 533
with heart and hands and voices,
who wondrous things has done,
in whom his world rejoices;
who, from our mother's arms,
has blessed us on our way
with countless gifts of love,
and still is ours today.

Thanks be to God through Jesus Christ our Lord! Romans 7:25

I give you thanks unfeigned, p89
O Jesus, friend in need,
for what your soul sustained
when you for me did bleed.
Grant me to lean unshaken
upon your faithfulness,
till I from earth am taken
to see you face to face.

Every present Spirit, if we wrote a story about our lives, we would find you on every page. You are always there, always loving, always calling us to be faithful as you have been. We can think of no greater thanks than to give you our lives. Amen.

Monday, November 17 — Psalm 128
1 Kings 11:1-25; John 15:18-16:4

I am the first and I am the last; besides me there is no god. Isaiah 44:6

Your majesty, how vast it is, 471
and how immense the glory,
which you, O Jesus, do possess;
the heav'ns proclaim your story;
the legions of angels exalt your great name,
your glory and might are transcendent;
and thousands of thousands your praises proclaim,
upon you gladly dependent.

Holy, holy, holy, the Lord God the Almighty, who was and is and is to come. Revelation 4:8

Holy, holy, holy Lord God almighty! 381
Early in the morning our song shall rise to thee;
holy, holy, holy, merciful and mighty!
God in three persons, blessed Trinity!

Almighty God, Creator of everything spiritual and physical, the One who breathed life into our souls; we worship you this day. We seek you with our minds. We join our voices with all creation in exalting your holy name. Hallelujah to our Savior! Amen.

Tuesday, November 18 — Psalm 129
1 Kings 11:26-12:24; John 16:5-16

The days are surely coming, says the Lord, when I will raise up for David a righteous Branch, and he shall reign as king and deal wisely, and shall execute justice and righteousness in the land. Jeremiah 23:5

Crown him with many crowns, 405
the Lamb upon his throne;
hark, how the heav'nly anthem drowns
all music but its own!
Awake, my soul, and sing
of him who set us free,
and hail him as your matchless King
through all eternity.

The high priest asked him, "Are you the Messiah, the Son of the Blessed One?" Jesus said, "I am." Mark 14:61,62

Hail to the Lord's anointed! 263
Great David's greater Son!
Hail, in the time appointed,
his reign on earth begun!
He comes to break oppression,
to set the captive free,
to take away transgression,
and rule in equity.

Have mercy on us, God! We yearn for justice, but cruelty fills our world. We hear of horrors, and we fear all is lost. Come, Lord Jesus. Deliver us from the evil within us, from the violence in your world, from the darkness of sin. Amen.

Wednesday, November 19 — Psalm 130
1 Kings 12:25-13:22; John 16:17-33

I will give them a heart to know that I am the Lord. Jeremiah 24:7

He is Lord, he is Lord! p80*
He is risen from the dead and he is Lord!
Ev'ry knee shall bow, ev'ry tongue confess
that Jesus Christ is Lord.

In every way you have been enriched in Christ Jesus, in speech and knowledge of every kind. 1 Corinthians 1:5

By your holy word instruct them; 660
fill their minds with heav'nly light;
by your pow'rful grace constrain them
always to approve what's right;
let them know your yoke is easy,
let them prove your burden's light.

They called you teacher when you walked this earth, dear Jesus. Now you call your church to this task. We pray for those who teach in our churches and for those who preach as you lead them. Bless the seeds they plant in our hearts. Amen.

Thursday, November 20 — Psalm 131
1 Kings 13:23-14:20; John 17:1-19

"The Lord is my portion," says my soul, "therefore I will hope in him." Lamentations 3:24

I am trusting you, Lord Jesus, 542r
trusting only you,
trusting you for full salvation,
great and free.

Through Christ you have come to trust in God, who raised him from the dead and gave him glory, so that your faith and hope are set on God. 1 Peter 1:21

Who puts his trust in God most just 537r
has built his house securely;
he who relies on Jesus Christ,
heaven shall be his most surely.

We turn our eyes on you, Christ. By faith we look into your face and receive blessings found nowhere else. But we are sometimes distracted by the waves around us as Peter was. When we look away, take us by the hand and lift us. Amen.

Friday, November 21 — Psalm 132
1 Kings 14:21-15:8; John 17:20-26

Be still, and know that I am God! Psalm 46:10

Be still, my soul: your God will undertake 757
to guide the future, as in ages past.
Your hope, your confidence let nothing shake;
all now mysterious shall be bright at last.
Be still, my soul: the waves and winds still know
the Christ who ruled them while he dwelt below.

Jesus prayed, "Righteous Father, these know that you have sent me. I made your name known to them, and I will make it known, so that the love with which you have loved me may be in them, and I in them." John 17:25,26

Lord of glory, God most high, 744
man exalted to the sky,
with your love my heart now fill;
prompt me to perform your will!
Then your glory I shall see;
blessed for all eternity.

Heavenly Father, we long to know you fully, but we will never understand all that you are. We rejoice that there will never be an end to our discoveries about your glory and power. In this moment, we wait before you — touch us, we pray. Amen.

Saturday, November 22 — Psalm 133
1 Kings 15:9-16:14; John 18:1-11

Woe to those who acquit the guilty for a bribe, but deny justice to the innocent. Isaiah 5:22,23 (NIV)

Then shall all shackles fall; the stormy clamor 488r
of wild war music o'er the earth shall cease;
love shall tread out the baleful fire of anger,
and in its ashes plant the tree of peace.

Whatever is true, whatever is honorable, whatever is just, whatever is pure, whatever is pleasing, whatever is commendable, if there is any excellence and if there is anything worthy of praise, think about these things. Philippians 4:8

May the mind of Christ my Savior 585
live in me from day to day,
by his love and pow'r controlling
all I do and say.
May the love of Jesus fill me
as the waters fill the sea;
him exalting, self abasing —
this is victory.

Forgive us, righteous God, when we cry 'holy, holy, holy' to you and yet allow impurity in our thoughts and actions. We ignore injustice and pretend all is well, when we allow fear to keep us silent. Teach us to be holy as you are. Amen.

Reign of Christ (Christ the King Sunday)

Watchword for the Week — God says, "I will seek the lost, and I will bring back the strayed, and I will bind up the injured, and I will strengthen the weak." Ezekiel 34:16

Sunday, November 23 — Ezekiel 34:11-16,20-24; Psalm 95:1-7a Ephesians 1:15-23; Matthew 25:31-46

Restore to me the joy of your salvation, and sustain in me a willing spirit. Psalm 51:12

O, to grace how great a debtor 782
daily I'm constrained to be!
Let that grace, Lord, like a fetter,
bind my wand'ring heart to thee.
Prone to wander, Lord, I feel it,
prone to leave the God I love,
here's my heart, O take and seal it;
seal it for thy courts above.

The man who was born blind answered, "The man called Jesus made mud, spread it on my eyes, and said to me, 'Go to Siloam and wash.' Then I went and washed and received my sight." John 9:11

Come, faithful Shepherd, bind me 795
with cords of love to thee,
and evermore remind me
that thou hast died for me;
O may the Holy Spirit
set this before my eyes,
that I thy death and merit
above all else may prize.

You have given to each of us stories to tell. They are wonderful stories of your touch on our lives, simple stories of your grace. Today we will praise you for restoring us to wholeness. You are our all in all. Amen.

Monday, November 24 — Psalm 134
1 Kings 16:15-17:24; John 18:12-24

The memory of the righteous is a blessing. Proverbs 10:7

Countless hosts before God's throne, 561r
where the Lamb abideth,
and as God and man his own
to life's fountain guideth,
now possess
perfect bliss,
which to us is wanting
and for which we're panting.

From now on there is reserved for me the crown of righteousness, which the Lord, the righteous judge, will give me on that day, and not only to me but also to all who have longed for his appearing. 2 Timothy 4:8

Ten thousand times then thousand 394
in sparkling raiment bright,
the armies of the ransomed saints
throng up the steeps of light!
'Tis finished, all is finished,
their fight with death and sin.
Fling open wide the golden gates
and let the victors in!

Eternal God, we remember all those who lived their lives faithfully for you. Thank you for the blessings of their witness. We rejoice for them that they now have that crown of righteousness, worshiping around your throne. We also long for your appearing. Come, Lord Jesus. Amen.

Tuesday, November 25 — Psalm 135:1-12
1 Kings 18; John 18:25-40

So Moses and Aaron went to Pharaoh, and said to him, "Thus says the Lord, 'Let my people go, so that they may worship me.'" Exodus 10:3

Lo! The hosts of evil round us 751*
scorn the Christ, assail his ways!
From the fears that long have bound us,
free our hearts to faith and praise.
Grant us wisdom, grant us courage
for the living of these days,
for the living of these days.

Humble yourselves under the mighty hand of God, so that he may exalt you in due time. 1 Peter 5:6

Lead on, O King eternal: 753
we follow, not with fears,
for gladness breaks like morning
where'er your face appears:
your cross is lifted o'er us;
we journey in its light;
the crown awaits the conquest;
lead on, O God of might!

God of all people, you have declared liberty to captives and release to prisoners. We pray for those who are imprisoned and oppressed for their faith. Strengthen them. Makes us one in spirit with them in their endurance. Enable them to persevere. Amen.

* Used by permission of Elinor Fosdick Downs

Wednesday, November 26 — Psalm 135:13-21
1 Kings 19; John 19:1-11

Go, and may the Lord be with you! 1 Samuel 17:37

May the God of hope go with us ev'ry day, 708
filling all our lives with love and joy and peace.
May the God of justice speed us on our way,
bringing light and hope to ev'ry land and race.
Praying, let us work for peace,
singing, share our joy with all.
Working for a world that's new,
faithful when we hear Christ's call.

Paul wrote to Timothy: You then, my child, be strong in the grace that is in Christ Jesus. 2 Timothy 2:1

Peace, perfect peace, in this dark world of sin? 710
The blood of Jesus whispers peace within.

Eternal God, we cherish the lives you have given to us. Yet, major changes we face sometimes make our lives hard. We rest in you when the familiar things vanish, for you are ever present, never changing. We ask for your blessing this day. Amen.

Thursday, November 27 — Psalm 136
1 Kings 20:1-21; John 19:12-24

I praised and honored the one who lives forever. For his sovereignty is an everlasting sovereignty, and his kingdom endures from generation to generation. All the inhabitants of the earth are accounted as nothing. Daniel 4:34,35

Praise the Lord! You heav'ns, adore him, 454
praise him, angels in the height;
sun and moon, rejoice before him;
praise him, all you stars and light.
Praise the Lord! For he has spoken;
worlds his mighty voice obeyed;
laws which never shall be broken
for their guidance he has made.

To the King of the ages, immortal, invisible, the only God, be honor and glory forever and ever. 1 Timothy 1:17

Worship, honor, glory, blessing, 454
Lord, we offer as our gift;
young and old, your praise expressing,
our glad songs to you we lift.
All the saints in heav'n adore you;
we would join their glad acclaim;
as your angels serve before you,
so on earth we praise your name.

We praise you, O God. We acclaim you as Lord. To you all angels, all the powers of heaven, the cherubim and seraphim, sing in endless praise: holy, holy, holy Lord, God of power and might; heaven and earth are full of your glory. Amen.

Friday, November 28 — Psalm 137
1 Kings 20:22-21:16; John 19:25-37

The Lord works vindication and justice for all who are oppressed. Psalm 103:6

Today we all are called to be 696*
disciples of the Lord,
to help to set the captive free,
make plowshare out of sword,
to feed the hungry, quench their thirst,
make love and peace our fast,
to serve the poor and homeless first,
our ease and comfort last.

He has filled the hungry with good things, and sent the rich away empty. Luke 1:53

Open then our hearts and senses 684**
to your Spirit's varied ways.
Overcome our self defenses
so we hear the prayer and praise
which the folk of countless cultures
in new worlds and rhythms raise.

It is hard for us to think about poverty. It is complicated, painful, and tragic; it makes us uncomfortable. Yet, your call to serve the oppressed and the hungry still rings in our ears. Strengthen us to follow you by serving those you love. Amen.

Saturday, November 29 — Psalm 138:1-5
1 Kings 21:17-22:28; John 19:38-20:9

The Lord will be king over the whole earth. On that day there will be one Lord, and his name the only name. Zechariah 14:9 (NIV)

Jesus' name, Jesus' name, 324
source of life and happiness!
In this name true consolation
mourning sinners may possess;
here is found complete salvation.
Blessed Jesus, we your name will praise
all our days, all our days.

The whole multitude of the disciples began to praise God joyfully with a loud voice for all the deeds of power that they had seen, saying, "Blessed is the king who comes in the name of the Lord! Luke 19:37,38

All glory, laud, and honor 342
to you, Redeemer, King,
to whom the lips of children
made sweet hosannas ring.
You are the King of Israel
and David's royal Son,
now in the Lord's name coming,
the king and Blessed One.

Triumphant God, tomorrow we will sing, "Hosanna, blessed is he who comes in the name of the Lord." Prepare our hearts to worship you. Fill us with praise for our Savior! We welcome you into our midst as the Advent season begins. Amen.

First Sunday of Advent

Watchword for the Week — Then they will see 'the Son of Man coming in clouds' with great power and glory. Mark 13:26

Sunday, November 30 — Isaiah 64:1-9; Psalm 80:1-7,17-19
1 Corinthians 1:3-9; Mark 13:24-37

Let your face shine upon your servant; save me in your steadfast love. Psalm 31:16

Jesus makes my heart rejoice, 662
I'm his sheep and know his voice;
he's a Shepherd, kind and gracious,
and his pastures are delicious;
constant love to me he shows,
yea, my very name he knows.

Joyfully give thanks to the Father, who has enabled you to share in the inheritance of the saints in the light. Colossians 1:12

O bless the Lord, my soul! 546
His mercies bear in mind!
Forget not all his benefits!
The Lord to all is kind.

O Savior, as you have joyfully come to us, we gladly open our hearts to you. We draw close to you this day and pray that you would fill us with your Spirit. We dedicate these weeks of Advent to you. Come, Lord Jesus, come. Amen.

Monday, December 1 — Psalm 138:6-8
1 Kings 22:29-53; John 20:10-23

And I sought for anyone among them who would repair the wall and stand in the breach before me on behalf of the land, so that I would not destroy it; but I found no one. Ezekiel 22:30

"Fear not, I am with you; O be not dismayed, 709
for I am your God and will still give you aid;
I'll strengthen you, help you and cause you to stand
upheld by my righteous, omnipotent hand.

Christ Jesus humbled himself and became obedient to the point of death — even death on a cross. Philippians 2:8

Most gracious God and Lord, 488
the world's almighty Savior,
worthy to be adored
by all, both now and ever!
Those souls are blessed indeed
who cling to you in faith,
as you for us were laid
low in the dust of death.

Gracious God, let us stand humble before you as pillars of your faith and obedient to your word, that we may be worthy of your sacrifice. Amen.

Tuesday, December 2 — Psalm 139:1-6
2 Kings 1:1-2:18; John 20:24-31

Let the favor of the Lord our God be upon us, and prosper for us the work of our hands — O prosper the work of our hands! Psalm 90:17

Teach me your patience; share with me 735
a closer, dearer company.
In work that keeps faith sweet and strong,
in trust that triumphs over wrong.

Simon answered, "Master, we have worked all night long but have caught nothing. Yet if you say so, I will let down the nets." Luke 5:5

Long ago apostles heard it 600
by the Galilean lake,
turned from home and work and fam'ly,
leaving all for his dear sake.

O Lord, our Provider, let us listen to you when you tell us what needs to be done. Give us the faith to trust in you. Amen.

Wednesday, December 3 — Psalm 139:7-12
2 Kings 2:19-3:27; John 21:1-14

I stretch out my hands to you; my soul thirsts for you like a parched land. Psalm 143:6

Day by day, at home, away, 723
Jesus is my staff and stay.
When I hunger, Jesus feeds me,
into pleasant pastures leads me;
when I thirst, he bids me go
where the quiet waters flow.

Jesus said, "If anyone is thirsty, let him come to me and drink. Whoever believes in me, as the Scripture has said, streams of living water will flow from within him." John 7:37,38 (NIV)

Trusting his mild staff always, 662
I go in and out in peace;
he will feed me with the treasure
of his grace in richest measure;
when a-thirst to him I cry,
living water he'll supply.

Holy Provider, you have given us all that we need to survive. Let us use these gifts to help others, and to your glory. Amen.

Thursday, December 4 — Psalm 139:13-16
2 Kings 4:1-37; John 21:15-25

All kings will bow down to him and all nations will serve him. Psalm 72:11 (NIV)

As with gladness men of old p190
did the guiding star behold;
as with joy they hailed its light,
leading onward, beaming bright;
so, most gracious Lord, may we
evermore your splendor see.

The wise men were asking, "Where is the child who has been born king of the Jews? For we observed his star at its rising, and have come to pay him homage." Matthew 2:2

All praise to you, eternal Son, p192
whose advent has our freedom won,
whom with the Father we adore
and Holy Spirit, evermore.

Lord Jesus, as we prepare for your coming as the infant son of God, make us ever mindful of the sacrifices you have made on our behalf. Amen.

Friday, December 5 — Psalm 139:17-24
2 Kings 4:38-5:14; Acts 1:1-14

My God sent his angel and shut the lions' mouths so that they would not hurt me. Daniel 6:22

Perfect submission, perfect delight, 714
visions of rapture now burst on my sight.
Angels descending bring from above
echoes of mercy, whispers of love.
This is my story, this is my song,
praising my Savior all the day long.
This is my story, this is my song,
praising my Savior all the day long.

Suddenly an angel of the Lord appeared and a light shone in the cell. He tapped Peter on the side and woke him, saying, "Get up quickly." And the chains fell off his wrists. Acts 12:7

There is a balm in Gilead 500
  to make the wounded whole,
there is a balm in Gilead
  to heal the sin-sick soul.
If you cannot preach like Peter,
  if you cannot pray like Paul,
you can tell the love of Jesus, and say,
  "He died for all."

Savior Lord, we thank you for your saving ways. Help us to have the faith of Daniel and the words of Paul when we pray. Amen.

Saturday, December 6 — Psalm 140:1-5
2 Kings 5:15-6:23; Acts 1:15-26

Amos said, "I am a herdsman, and a dresser of sycamore trees, and the Lord took me from following the flock, and the Lord said to me, 'Go, prophesy to my people Israel.'" Amos 7:14,15

Savior, like a shepherd lead us; 731
much we need your tender care;
In your pleasant pastures feed us,
for our use your folds prepare.
Blessed Jesus, blessed Jesus,
you have bought us; yours we are.
Blessed Jesus, blessed Jesus,
you have bought us; yours we are.

Jesus said to Simon, "Do not be afraid; from now on you will be catching people." When the fishermen had brought their boats to shore, they left everything and followed him. Luke 5:10,11

Take my life that it may be 610
all your purpose Lord, for me.
Take my moments and my days;
let them sing your ceaseless praise,
let them sing your ceaseless praise.

Father, great Fisher of men, we sing your praises and yearn to spread the story of your saving ways. Give us the words to use so that we may bring others to you, and that they may come to know you as we do. Amen.

Second Sunday of Advent

Watchword for the Week — He will feed his flock like a shepherd; he will gather the lambs in his arms, and carry them in his bosom. Isaiah 40:11

Sunday, December 7 — Isaiah 40:1-11; Psalm 85:1-28-13
2 Peter 3:8-15a; Mark 1:1-8

Your eyes beheld my unformed substance. In your book were written all the days that were formed for me, when none of them as yet existed. Psalm 139:16

How shall the young direct their way? 510
What light shall be their perfect guide?
Your word, O Lord, will safely lead
if in its wisdom they confide.

In God we live and move and have our being. Acts 17:28

Proclaim to every people, tongue, and nation 618
that God, in whom they live and move, is love;
tell how he stooped to save his lost creation,
and died on earth that we might live in love.
Publish glad tidings, tidings of peace,
tidings of Jesus, redemption, and release.

Great Shepherd of life, help us to teach our children the ways in which they should go. Let us teach by example, that we may guide them as you have guided us through life. Amen.

Monday, December 8 — Psalm 140:6-13
2 Kings 6:24-7:20; Acts 2:1-13

Help us, O God of our salvation, for the glory of your name; deliver us, and forgive our sins, for your name's sake. Psalm 79:9

God forgives all your transgressions, 458
all diseases gently heals,
God redeems you from destruction,
and with you so kindly deals.

If we confess our sins, he who is faithful and just will forgive us our sins and cleanse us from all unrighteousness. 1 John 1:9

Father, now your sinful child 779
through your love is reconciled
By your pard'ning grace I live;
daily still I cry, forgive.

Forgiving Friend, we know that our sins are forgiven through the sacrifice of your son, our Lord and Savior. Help us to forgive others as we have been forgiven. Amen.

Tuesday, December 9 — Psalm 141:1-4
2 Kings 8; Acts 2:14-28

Take courage, all you people of the land, says the Lord; work, for I am with you. Haggai 2:4

Jesus, Master, whom I serve, p42
though so feebly and so ill;
strengthen hand and heart and nerve,
all your bidding to fulfill,
open now my eyes to see
all the work you have for me.

And whatever you do, in word or deed, do everything in the name of the Lord Jesus, giving thanks to God the Father through him. Colossians 3:17

Praise to the Lord, who will prosper your work 530
and defend you;
surely his goodness and mercy
shall daily attend you.
Ponder anew
what the almighty can do
if with his love he befriend you.

Holy Redeemer, we know that you are always with us. Whatever we do, we do in your holy name and to the glory of God the Father. Amen.

Wednesday, December 10 — Psalm 141:5-10
2 Kings 9; Acts 2:29-47

Come, let us go to entreat the favor of the Lord, and to seek the Lord of hosts; I myself am going. Zechariah 8:21

The ground of my profession 769
is Jesus and his blood;
he gives me the possession
of everlasting good.
To me his Holy Spirit
speaks many a precious word
of rest to one who's seeking
a refuge in the Lord.

They brought to him a deaf man who had an impediment in his speech; and they begged him to lay his hand on him. Mark 7:32

Thou, O Christ, art all I want; 724
more than all in thee I find;
raise the fallen, cheer the faint,
heal the sick and lead the blind.
Just and holy is thy name,
I am all unrighteousness,
false and full of sin I am,
thou art full of truth and grace.

Gracious Lord, in you we find all that we need. You are our redeemer, our healer, our guide, our hope for salvation. We seek you in all that we do. Amen.

Thursday, December 11 — Psalm 142
2 Kings 10; Acts 3:1-10

The God of heaven is the one who will give us success, and we his servants are going to start building. Nehemiah 2:20

Christ is our cornerstone, 517
on him alone we build;
with his true saints alone
the courts of heaven are filled;
on his great love our hopes we place
of present grace and joys above.

Jesus said, "I will show you what someone is like who comes to me, hears my words, and acts on them. That one is like a man building a house, who dug deeply and laid the foundation on rock." Luke 6:47,48

We are God's house of living stones, 512
built for his mighty own habitation;
he fills our hearts, his humble thrones,
granting us life and salvation.
Yet to this place, an earthly frame,
we come with thanks to praise his name;
God grants his people true blessing.

Father, we build our faith upon the rock of your word. Our faith shall never falter because you are the foundation of our lives. May our lives always reflect your word. Amen.

Friday, December 12 — Psalm 143:1-6
2 Kings 11; Acts 3:11-26

Happy are those who live in your house, ever singing your praise. Psalm 84:4

To you our vows with sweet accord, 677
head of your church, we pay;
we and our house will serve you, Lord;
your word we will obey.
Grant us and all our children grace
in word and deed your name to praise,
and in each family, your will
and purpose to fulfill.

Christ says, "In my Father's house there are many dwelling places." John 14:2

The church of Christ, 516
which he has hallowed here
to be his house, is scattered far and near
in north, and south, and east, and west abroad;
and yet in earth and heav'n, thro' Christ, her Lord,
the church is one.

Gracious Lord, we praise you in many languages, and in many places; yet there is only one triune God, the Father, the Son, and the Holy Spirit to whom we pray. Amen.

Saturday, December 13 — Psalm 143:7-12
2 Kings 12,13; Acts 4:1-12

His dominion shall be from sea to sea, and to the ends of the earth. Zechariah 9:10

Bless your maker, all you creatures, 458
ever under God's control;
all throughout his vast dominion
bless the Lord of all, my soul!

The Angel said to Mary, "You will conceive in your womb and bear a son. He will reign over the house of Jacob forever, and of his kingdom there will be no end." Luke 1:31,33

King of kings, yet born of Mary, 271
as of old on earth he stood,
Lord of lords, in human vesture —
in the body and the blood —
he will give to all the faithful
his own self for heav'nly food.

Father of all humanity, we are growing ever more anxious to celebrate again the birth of your son, our savior Jesus Christ. Through him, we will continue to be ever closer to you. Thank you for the saving life of your son. Amen.

Third Sunday of Advent

Watchword for the Week — May the God of peace sanctify you entirely; and may your spirit and soul and body be kept sound and blameless at the coming of our Lord Jesus Christ. 1 Thessalonians 5:23

Sunday, December 14 — Isaiah 61:1-4,8-11; Psalm 126
1 Thessalonians 5:16-24; John 1:6-8,19-28

I know that my Redeemer lives. Job 19:25

Jesus, my Redeemer, lives! p215
I, too, unto life must waken;
he will have me where he is.
Shall my courage then be shaken?
Shall I fear? Or could the Head
rise and leave his members dead?

Jesus is able for all time to save those who approach God through him, since he always lives to make intercession for them. Hebrews 7:25

Alleluia! Heav'nly High Priest, 373
here on earth our help, our stay;
alleluia! Hear the sinful
cry to you from day to day.
Intercessor, Friend of sinners,
earth's Redeemer, hear our plea,
where the songs of all the sinless
sweep across the crystal sea.

Great Intercessor, we pray that you will hear our prayers as we ask for forgiveness for our sins, and we pray that you will guide us to better lives. In the name of our dear Savior, Jesus Christ. Amen.

Monday, December 15 — Psalm 144:1-4
2 Kings 14; Acts 4:13-22

In the place where it was said to them, "You are not my people," it shall be said to them, "Children of the living God." Hosea 1:10

Join hands, disciples of the faith, 523
whate'er your race may be.
All children of the living God
are surely kin to me.

All who are led by the Spirit of God are children of God. Romans 8:14

Move in our midst, O Spirit of God. 489
Go with us down from your holy hill.
Walk with us through the storm and the calm.
Spirit of God, now go with us still.

Friend of all, we know that we are all children of God; no matter what our color, our country, or the language we speak. Bring us all together for the glory of God the Father. Heal our differences and guide us on the path to unity. Amen.

Tuesday, December 16 — Psalm 144:5-8
2 Kings 15; Acts 4:23-37

He was despised and rejected by others; a man of suffering and acquainted with infirmity. Isaiah 53:3

Hail, O once despised Jesus! 330
Hail, O Galilean King!
You have suffered to release us,
hope, salvation, joy to bring.
Hail, O agonizing Savior,
bearer of our sin and shame;
By your merits we find favor;
life is given through your name.

The soldiers clothed him in a purple cloak, and after twisting some thorns into a crown, they put it on him. And they began saluting him, "Hail, King of the Jews!" They struck his head with a reed, spat upon him, and knelt down in homage to him. Mark 15:17-19

To avert from us God's wrath, 416
Jesus suffered in our stead;
by an ignominious death
he a full atonement made;
and by his most precious blood
brought us, sinners, nigh to God.

Holy Father, we can only imagine what it must have been like to give your only son to die for our sins. For this great sacrifice, we give you our thanks and our everlasting love. Amen.

Wednesday, December 17 — Psalm 144:9-15
2 Kings 16:1-17:6; Acts 5:1-11

The Lord declares, "Those who honor me I will honor, and those who despise me shall be treated with contempt." 1 Samuel 2:30

Are we weak and heavy laden, 743
cumbered with a load of care?
Precious Savior, still our refuge,
take it to the Lord in prayer!
Do your friends despise, forsake you?
Take it to the Lord in prayer!
In his arms he'll take and shield you;
you will find a solace there.

Glory to God in the highest heaven, and on earth peace among those whom he favors! Luke 2:14

"All glory be to God on high, 296
and to the earth be peace;
good will henceforth from heav'n to all
begin and never cease,
begin and never cease."

Lord our Father, we bring our heaviest burdens to you in prayer, confident that you will help us to deal with whatever comes our way. To you be the glory forever and ever. Amen.

Thursday, December 18 — Psalm 145:1-7
2 Kings 17:7-41; Acts 5:12-16

Whatever your hand finds to do, do with your might. Ecclesiastes 9:10

The task your wisdom has assigned 638
here let me cheerfully fulfill,
in all my work your presence find
and prove your good and perfect will.

God our Father, who loved us and through grace gave us eternal comfort and good hope, comfort your hearts and strengthen them in every good work and word. 2 Thessalonians 2:16,17

God and man indeed, 473
comfort in all need,
you became a Man of sorrows
to gain life eternal for us
by your precious blood,
Jesus, man and God.

Heavenly Father, comfort our hearts and give us the strength to carry out your will to be a comfort and teacher to those who are longing for your word and guidance. Amen.

Friday, December 19 — Psalm 145:8-16
2 Kings 18; Acts 5:17-40

Thus says the Lord, "If you turn back, I will take you back." Jeremiah 15:19

But examine first your case, 416
whether you be in the faith;
do you long for pard'ning grace?
Is your only hope his death?
Then, how e'er your soul's oppressed,
come, you are a worthy guest.

As you have received Christ Jesus the Lord, continue to live your lives in him. Colossians 2:6

As you, Lord, have lived for others, 648
so may we for others live;
freely have your gifts been granted,
freely may your servants give.
Yours the gold and yours the silver,
yours the wealth of land and sea;
we but stewards of your bounty
held in solemn trust will be.

Holy Father, we pray that we may be worthy guests at your table. We know that through your sacrifice we have been saved, but we must continue to live our lives to your service and glory. Amen.

Saturday, December 20 — Psalm 145:17-21
2 Kings 19:1-28; Acts 5:41-6:7

Justice, and only justice, you shall pursue. Deuteronomy 16:20

His righteous government and power 320
shall over all extend;
on judgment and on justice based,
his reign shall have no end.

I press on toward the goal for the prize of the heavenly call of God in Christ Jesus. Philippians 3:14

You make us rejoice in serving, 622*
giving strength where we had none;
certain tasks had seemed unnerving,
but you've proven you're the one
who gives gifts of love and power,
confidence and self-control.
Fill us now, this very hour;
help us reach your kingdom's goal.

God of justice, grant to us the gifts of your love, faith, power, confidence, and self-control, for it is through these gifts that we will reach your kingdom. In praise and glory. Amen.

Fourth Sunday of Advent

Watchword for the Week — The Mighty One has done great things for me, and holy is his name. Luke 1:49

Sunday, December 21 — 2 Samuel 7:1-11,16; Luke 1:47-55
Romans 16:25-27; Luke 1:26-38

Then Jacob woke from his sleep and said, "Surely the Lord is in this place — and I did not know it!" Genesis 28:16

Be thou my vision, O Lord of my heart; 719
nought be all else to me save that thou art —
thou my best thought, by day or by night,
waking or sleeping, thy presence my light.

Indeed, God is not far from each one of us. Acts 17:27

Jesus, yourself to us reveal. p204
Grant that we may not only feel
some drawings of your grace,
but in communion with you live,
and daily from your death derive
the needful strength to run our race.

God who is everywhere, be with us this day, and every day as we seek to follow you and your teachings. We draw from your strength to live each day in your path, the path to everlasting life. Amen.

Monday, December 22 — Psalm 146:1-7
2 Kings 19:29-20:21; Acts 6:8-7:3

David strengthened himself in the Lord his God. 1 Samuel 30:6

Be present with your servants, Lord; 734
we look to you with one accord;
refresh and strengthen us anew,
and bless what in your name we do.

The Lord is faithful; he will strengthen you and guard you from the evil one. 2 Thessalonians 3:3

See the Lord, your keeper, stand 729
omnipotently near.
Now he holds you by the hand,
and banishes your fear;
shadows with his wings your head,
guards from all impending harms;
round you and beneath are spread
the everlasting arms.

Faithful Friend, be ever near us as we seek to do your will. Strengthen us in faith and in body as we go forth to live our lives to your service. Amen.

Tuesday, December 23 — Psalm 146:8-10
2 Kings 21:1-22:10; Acts 7:4-16

One who rules over people justly, ruling in the fear of God, is like the light of morning, like the sun rising. 2 Samuel 23:3,4

What God's almighty pow'r has made, 537
in mercy he is keeping;
by morning glow or evening shade
his eye is never sleeping.
And where he rules in kingly might,
there all is just and all is right:
to God all praise and glory!

Masters, you know that you also have a Master in heaven. Colossians 4:1

Christ shall bless your going out, 729
shall bless your coming in;
kindly compass you about,
till you are saved from sin.
Like your spotless Master, you,
filled with wisdom, love, and pow'r,
holy, pure, and perfect now,
both now and evermore.

God, you created the sun to shine over all the earth. Let your light lead all your people that their paths may be pleasing to you. Amen.

Wednesday, December 24 — Psalm 147:1-6
2 Kings 22:11-23:20; Acts 7:17-29

Better a patient man than a warrior, a man who controls his temper than one who takes a city. Proverbs 16:32 (NIV)

Spirit of God, burst forth in flame, 491*
searing our conscience, staking your claim.
Burn up the clutter, brand us apart;
warm every recess of my cold heart.
Fill us with Spirit, fill us with joy!
Your life to inherit, your gifts to employ;
your love to embody, great God within,
Spirit of Christ, let that new life begin!

When the fullness of time had come, God sent his Son. Galatians 4:4

God with us, God with us, p191
God made known in human frame;
in his name rejoice with gladness,
since to save the lost he came;
none need sink in hopeless sadness,
for Immanuel is now with is,
God with us, God with us.

Lord, as we now look forward to tomorrow with great anticipation, let us greet our Savior with prayers and song. Let us sing your praises all the day long! Amen.

Nativity of the Lord (Christmas Day)

Watchword for the Day — Jesus is the reflection of God's glory and the exact imprint of God's very being, and he sustains all things by his powerful word. Hebrews 1:3

Thursday, December 25 — Psalm 147:7-14
2 Kings 23:21-24:20; Acts 7:30-43

Nativity of the Lord — Isaiah 52:7-10; Psalm 98
Hebrews 1:1-4,(5-12); John 1:1-14

I will send survivors to the nations, to the coastlands far away that have not heard of my fame or seen my glory; and they shall declare my glory among the nations. Isaiah 66:19

We've a message to give to the nations, 621
that the Lord who's reigning above
has sent us his son to save us,
and show us that God is love.
For the darkness shall turn to dawning,
and the dawning to noon-day bright,
and Christ's great kingdom shall come on earth,
the kingdom of love and light.

The shepherds returned, glorifying and praising God for all they had heard and seen, as it had been told them. Luke 2:20

Come with the gladsome shepherds, 284
quick hast'ning from the fold;
come with the wise men, pouring
incense and myrrh and gold.
Come to him, poor and lowly,
around the cradle throng,
come with your hearts of sunshine,
and sing the angels' song.

Lord Jesus, today we celebrate your birth; your coming to earth as a baby. We worship you and give you the gift of our lives, ever faithful to you until we come to live with you again in our father's kingdom. Amen.

Friday, December 26 — Psalm 147:15-20
2 Kings 25; Acts 7:44-60

Let us go with you, for we have heard that God is with you. Zechariah 8:23

O Holy Spirit, stir us now, 299
inspire our hearts to make this vow:
we will go forth into the night
and share with all your gift of light.

Some men of Cyprus and Cyrene were proclaiming the Lord Jesus. The hand of the Lord was with them, and a great number became believers and turned to the Lord. Acts 11:20,21

Jesus calls us; o'er the tumult 600
of our life's wild, restless sea,
day by day his voice is sounding,
saying, "Christian, follow me."

Gracious Father, we hear you calling to us over all of the distractions of our daily lives and we long to hear what you have to say to us. Help us to silence the earthly din and listen to you. Amen.

Saturday, December 27 — Psalm 148:1-6
1 Chronicles 1:1-37; Acts 8:1-8

A shoot shall come out from the stump of Jesse, and a branch shall grow out of his roots. Isaiah 11:1

How bright appears the Morning Star 278
with mercy beaming from afar;
the host of heav'n rejoices;
O righteous Branch, O Jesse's Rod,
O Son of man and Son of God,
we too will lift our voices.
Jesus, Jesus, holy, holy, yet most lowly
now draw near us;
great Immanuel, kindly hear us.

It is I, Jesus, I am the root and the descendant of David, the bright morning star. Revelation 22:16

Songs of thankfulness and praise, 313
Jesus, Lord, to you we raise,
manifested by the star
to the sages from afar;
branch of royal David's stem
in your birth at Bethlehem;
anthems be to you addressed,
God in flesh made manifest.

Light of our life, our morning star, guide us as you led the wise men so long ago, so that we may worship our Lord and Savior, Jesus Christ. Amen.

First Sunday after Christmas

Watchword for the Week — But when the fullness of time had come, God sent his Son, born of a woman, born under the law, in order to redeem those who were under the law, so that we might receive adoption as children. Galatians 4:4,5

Sunday, December 28 — Isaiah 61:10-62:3; Psalm 148
Galatians 4:4-7; Luke 2:22-40

I live as an alien in the land. Psalm 119:19

Here I find my greatest treasure; 782
hither by the help I've come;
and I hope, by thy good pleasure,
safely to arrive at home.
Jesus sought me when a stranger,
wand'ring from the fold of God;
he, to rescue me from danger,
bought me with his precious blood.

Jesus said, "Foxes have holes, and birds of the air have nests; but the Son of Man has nowhere to lay his head." Matthew 8:20

Jesus, still lead on 799
till our rest be won;
and although the way be cheerless,
we will follow calm and fearless;
guide us by your hand
to the promised land.

Holy Redeemer, we are all strangers in this strange land. Be our guide so that we might find the eternal rest with our heavenly father. Amen.

Monday, December 29 — Psalm 148:7-14
1 Chronicles 1:38-2:17; Acts 8:9-25

There shall once more be heard the voice of mirth and the voice of gladness, the voice of the bridegroom and the voice of the bride, the voices of those who sing, "Give thanks to the Lord of hosts, for the Lord is good, for his steadfast love endures forever!" Jeremiah 33:11

We covenant in church and home p121
this peace to show each other,
to represent your steadfast love
as sister and as brother.
O, may we through each other know
your grace which fails us never,
and find at last our true abode
within your house forever. Amen.

The grace of God has appeared, bringing salvation to all. Titus 2:11

'Twas grace that taught my heart to fear 783
and grace my fears relieved;
how precious did that grace appear
the hour I first believed.

Gracious God, the gift of your dear son, our Lord Jesus Christ, has gladdened our hearts and lifted our spirits for we know that through him, we shall find eternal gladness! Amen.

Tuesday, December 30 — Psalm 149
1 Chronicles 2:18-55; Acts 8:26-40

He is the Lord our God; his judgments are in all the earth. Psalm 105:7

His righteous government and power 320
shall over all extend;
on judgment and on justice based,
his reign shall have no end.

[Let] no one wrong or exploit a brother or sister in this matter, because the Lord is an avenger in all these things. 1 Thessalonians 4:6

O, may we, who mercy need, 352
be like you in heart and deed,
when with wrong our spirits bleed:
hear us, holy Jesus.

Heavenly Father, we trust you to be the judge in all things. Your justice will be served at the day of atonement, when each of us will come to meet you face to face and all will be revealed. Amen.

Wednesday, December 31 — Psalm 150
1 Chronicles 3; Acts 9:1-9

Now if you are unwilling to serve the Lord, choose this day whom you will serve. But as for me and my household, we will serve the Lord. Joshua 24:15

To you our vows with sweet accord, 677
head of your church, we pay;
we and our house will serve you, Lord;
your word we will obey.
Grant us and all our children grace
in word and deed your name to praise,
and in each family, your will
and purpose to fulfill.

To all who received him, who believed in his name, he gave power to become children of God. John 1:12

Then forth they went, with tongues of flame 396
in one blessed theme delighting;
the love of Jesus, and his name,
God's children all uniting.
That love our theme and watchword still;
the law of love may we fulfill —
give love as love we're given.

Lord God, we have made the decision to serve you, and only you. You are our one true god, and we praise and glorify you with every word from our mouths. Amen.

Directory of Moravian Churches in the United States & Canada

Moravian Church in North America
Northern and Southern Provinces

2008

The Moravian Church in North America
1021 Center Street, Bethlehem, PA 18018
459 South Church Street, Winston-Salem, NC 27101

Published by the Interprovincial Board of Communication
Moravian Church in North America

www.moravian.org

(Printed in the U.S.A.)

CONTENTS

ADDRESSES OF CHURCHES

Churches are listed alphabetically by state and then alphabetically by city of physcial location. More information about the Moravian Church in the United States and Canada can be found at www.moravian.org.

NP = Northern Province
SP = Southern Province
CD = Canadian District
ED = Eastern District
WD = Western District

ALBERTA, CANADA (NP, CD):

BRUDERHEIM -
Bruderheim Church
Highway 45
Mail: PO Box 208
Bruderheim AB T0B 0S0
Canada
O: 780.796.3775
F: 780.796.3736
email:
admin.bruderheimmoravian@shaw.ca
www.bruderheimmoravian.org

CALGARY -
Christ Church
600 Acadia Drive SE
Calgary AB T2J 0B8
Canada
O: 403.271.2700
F: 403.271.2810
email: moravian@nucleus.com
www.christmoravian.com

Good Shepherd Community Church
6311 Norfolk Drive NW
Calgary AB T2K 5J8
Canada
O: 403.274.4888
F: 403.451.1556
email:
admin@goodshepherdmoravian.org
www.goodshepherdmoravian.org

EDMONTON -
Edmonton Church
9540 83rd Avenue NW
Edmonton AB T6C 1B9
Canada
O: 780.439.1063
F: 780.439.8168
email:
edmontonmoravian@shaw.ca
www.edmontonmoravian.com

Millwoods Church
2304 38th Street
Edmonton AB T6L 4K9
Canada
O: 780.463.7427
F: 780.461.3058
email: mcchurch@telus.net

Rio Terrace Church
15108 76 Avenue
Edmonton AB T5R 2Z9
Canada
O/F: 780.487.0211
email: rioterracechurch@shaw.ca
www.rioterracemoravianchurch.ca

SHERWOOD PARK -
Good News Church
2 Primrose Boulevard
Sherwood Park AB T8H 1G2
Canada
O: 780.467.0337
F: 780.449.4305
email: goodnewschurch@yahoo.com
www.goodnewschurch.ca

South Edmonton - Heimtal Church
RR 3
South Edmonton AB T6H 4N7
Canada
O: 780.955.7305
email: heimtal@telus.net

CALIFORNIA (NP, WD):
Banning - Morongo Church
11440 Potrero Road
Banning CA 92220
Mail: PO Box 352
Banning CA 92220-0352
O: 951.849.3067
email:
morongomoravian@verizon.net

Downey- Downey Church
10337 Old River School Road
Downey CA 90241
O: 562.927.0718
F: 562.927.0858
email: office@downeymoravian.org
www.downeymoravian.org

DISTRICT OF COLUMBIA (NP, ED):
Washington - Faith Church
405 Riggs Road NE
Washington DC 20011-2515
O: 202.635.9012
F: 202.635.9014
email:
writeus@faithmoravianchurch.org
www.faithmoravianchurch.org

FLORIDA (SP):
Longwood- Rolling Hills Church
1525 State Road 434 W
Longwood FL 32750-3877
O: 407.332.8380
www.rhmoravian.org

Miami- King of Kings Church
1880 NW 183rd Street
Miami FL 33056
O: 305.553.0173

New Hope
6001 SW 127th Avenue
Miami FL 33183-1427
O: 305.273.4047
F: 305.226.0516
email: nhmiami@yahoo.com

Prince of Peace Church
1880 NW 183 Street
Miami FL 33056
O: 305.628.2061
F: 305.625.5365
email: pop@bellsouth.net
www.floridamoravian.org

West Palm Beach - Palm Beach Church
297 27th Street
West Palm Beach FL 33407
O: 561.832.1363
F: 561.832.1363 (call first)

GEORGIA (SP):
Stone Mountain - First Church of Georgia
4950 Hugh Howell Road
Stone Mountain GA 30087
O: 770.491.7250
F: 770.414.5678
email: information@gamoravian.org
www.gamoravian.org

ILLINOIS (NP, WD):

West Salem -
West Salem Church
PO Box 27
West Salem IL 62476-0027
O: 618.456.8532
email: wsmor1@otbnet.com
www.westsalemmoravian.org

INDIANA (NP, WD):

Hope -
Hope Church
202 Main Street
Hope IN 47246
O: 812.546.4641
email:
pastor@hopemoravianchurch.org
www.hopemoravianchurch.org

MARYLAND (NP, ED):

New Carrollton -
Trinity Church
7011 Good Luck Road
New Carrollton MD 20784
O: 301.441.1814

Thurmont -
Graceham Church
8231-A Rocky Ridge Road
Thurmont MD 21788
O: 301.271.2379
F: 301.271.4241
email:
pastorj@gracehammoravian.org
www.gracehammoravian.org

Upper Marlboro -
St. Paul's Church
8505 Heathermore Boulevard
Upper Marlboro MD 20772
O: 301.627.4200
www.spmoravian.org

MICHIGAN (NP, WD):

Daggett -
Daggett Church
102 Old US Highway 41
Daggett MI 49821
O: 906.753.6995

Unionville-
Unionville Church
2711 Cass Street
Unionville MI 48767
O: 989.674.8686
email: moravian@airadv.net

Westland -
Grace Church
31133 Hively Avenue
Westland MI 48185
O/F: 734.721.9290

MINNESOTA (NP, WD):

Altura -
Our Savior's Church
PO Box 161
Altura MN 55910-0161
O: 507.796.5612

Chaska -
Chaska Church
115 E 4th Street
Chaska MN 55318
O: 952.448.4000
F: 952.448.6016
email:
chaskamoravian@embarqmail.com

Maple Grove -
Christ's Community Church
13250 93rd Avenue
Maple Grove MN 55369
O: 763.420.7187
F: 763.420.6232
www.ccc-mg.org

Northfield -
Northfield (Main Street) Church
713 Division Street
Northfield MN 55057
O: 507.645.7566

Saint Charles -
Berea Church
PO Box 402
Saint Charles MN 55972-0402
O: 507.932.3584

Victoria -
Lake Auburn Church
7460 Victoria Drive
PO Box 160
Victoria MN 55386
O: 952.443.2051
email:
lakeauburnchurch@juno.com

Waconia -
Waconia Church
209 E 2nd Street
Waconia MN 55387
O: 952.442.2920
F: 952.442.2972
email: wmoravian@earthlink.net
www.waconiamoravian.com

NEW JERSEY (NP, ED):

Cinnaminson -
Palmyra Church
1921 Cinnaminson Avenue
Cinnaminson NJ 08077
Mail: PO Box 2468
Cinnaminson NJ 08077-2468
O: 856.829.2886

Egg Harbor -
Egg Harbor City Church
235 Boston Avenue
Egg Harbor City NJ 08215
O: 609.965.1920
F: 609.965.5123
www.moravianchurchehc.com

Riverside -
First Church
228 E Washington Street
Riverside NJ 08075-3629
O: 856.461.0132
F: 856.764.7032
email:
riversidemoravian@verizon.net
www.riversidemoravian.org

Union -
Battle Hill Church
777 Liberty Avenue
Union NJ 07083
O: 908.686.5262
email: bhmoravian@verizon.net

NEW YORK (NP, ED):

Bronx -
Tremont Terrace Church
1621 Pilgrim Avenue
Bronx NY 10461
O: 718.829.2156
F: 718.829.0044

Brooklyn -
Fellowship Church (Meeting at Church of the Evangel [U.C.C.])
1950 Bedford Avenue
Brooklyn NY 11225
O: 718.287.7200

John Hus Church
153 Ocean Avenue
Brooklyn NY 11225
O: 718.856.2200
F: 718.856.2201
email:
jhussecretary1@optonline.net

NEW HARTFORD -
Good Shepherd Church
350 Higby Road
New Hartford NY 13413
O: 315.724.9392

NEW YORK -
First Church
154 Lexington Avenue
New York NY 10016
Mail: PO Box 1874
Murray Hill Station
New York NY 10156-0609
O: 212.683.4219
F: 212.683.9734

United Church
200 E 127th Street
New York NY 10035
Mail: PO Box 90
New York NY 10035-0090
O: 212.722.2109
F: 212.987.2818

QUEENS -
Grace Church
178-38 137th Avenue
Springfield Gardens
Queens NY 11434
O: 718.723.2681
F: 718.723.4288
email: gracemoravian@verizon.net

STATEN ISLAND -
Castleton Hill Church
1657 Victory Boulevard
Staten Island NY 10314
O: 718.442.5215 or 718.442.5309
F: 718.442.5211
email: pastor@chmchurch.com
www.moraviansi.com

Great Kills Church
74 Hillside Terrace
Staten Island NY 10308
O: 718.317.7788
F: 718.356.2826
email: GKMoravian@aol.com
www.moraviansi.com

New Dorp Church
2205 Richmond Road
Staten Island NY 10306-2557
O: 718.351.0090
F: 718.351.0290
email:
ndmcthree.moravian@verizon.net
www.newdorpmoravianchurch.com

Vanderbilt Avenue Church
285 Vanderbilt Avenue
Staten Island NY 10304
O: 718.447.2966
www.moraviansi.com

NORTH CAROLINA (SP):
ADVANCE -
Macedonia Church
700 NC Hwy 801 N
Advance NC 27006
O: 336.998.4394
F: 336.940.5317
email: macedonia@yadtel.net
www.macedoniamoravianchurch.org

BETHANIA -
Bethania Church
5545 Main Street
Bethania NC 27010
Mail: PO Box 170
Bethania NC 27010-0170
O: 336.922.1284
F: 336.922.1294
email:
bethaniaoffice@windstream.net
www.bethaniamoravianchurch.org

CHARLOTTE -
Little Church on the Lane
528 Moravian Lane
Charlotte NC 28207
O: 704.334.1381
F: 704.333.2281 (call first)
email: littlechurch@carolina.rr.com
www.littlechurchonthelane.com

Peace Church
4418 Rea Road
Charlotte NC 28226
O: 704.759.9939
F: 704.927.1688
email: general@peacemoravian.com
www.peacemoravian.com

CLEMMONS -
Clemmons Church
Spangenberg Avenue
Clemmons NC 27012
Mail: PO Box 730
Clemmons NC 27012
O: 336.766.6273
F: 336.766.3794
email:
Office@clemmonsmoravian.org
www.clemmonsmoravian.org

DURHAM -
Christ the King Church
4405 Hope Valley Road
Durham NC 27707
O: 919.489.1711
F: 919.419.0032 (call first)
email: office@ckmc-church.org
www.ckmc-church.org

EDEN -
Leaksville Church
712 McConnell Street
Eden NC 27288
Mail: PO Box 35
Eden NC 27289
O: 336.623.9440
email:
leaksvillemoravian@embarqmail.com
www.leaksvillemoravian.org

GREENSBORO -
First Church
304 S Elam Avenue
Greensboro NC 27403
O: 336.272.2196
F: 336.275.7800
email:
office@greensboromoravian.org
www.greensboromoravian.org

HOLLY SPRINGS -
Holly Springs Church
104 Osterville Drive
Holly Springs NC 27540
Mail: PO Box 296
Holly Springs NC 27540
O: 919.363.2138
www.moravianchurch.org

HUNTERSVILLE -
New Beginnings Church
201 Seagle Street
Huntersville NC 28078
Mail: PO Box 2278
Huntersville NC 28070
O: 704.992.2003
F: 704.992.2002
email:
newbeginnings100@bellsouth.net
www.newbeginningsmoravian.org

KERNERSVILLE -
Good Shepherd Church
1474 Kerner Road
Kernersville NC 27284
O: 336.993.6633
F: 336.993.6633 (call first)
email:
secretary@goodshepherdmoravian.com
www.goodshepherdmoravian.com

Kernersville Church
504 S Main Street
Kernersville NC 27284
O: 336.993.3620
F: 336.993.7052
email: kmchurch@embarqmail.com
www.kernersvillemoravian.org

KING -
King Church
228 W Dalton Road
King NC 27021
O: 336.983.2710
F: 336.983.7045 (call first)
email: kmclisa@aol.com
www.kingmoravian.org

LEWISVILLE -
Unity Church
8300 Concord Church Road
Lewisville NC 27023
O: 336.945.3801 or 336.945.3877
email: unitymc@alltel.net
www.unitymoravian.org

LEXINGTON -
Enterprise Church
2733 Enterprise Church Road
Lexington NC 27295-9233
O: 336.764.1281

MAYODAN -
Mayodan Church
S 3rd Avenue and Adams Street
Mayodan NC 27027
Mail: PO Box 245
Mayodan NC 27027-0245
O: 336.548.2645
F: 336.548.2645 (call first)

MT. AIRY -
Grace Church
1401 N Main Street
Mt. Airy NC 27030
O: 336.786.5627
F: 336.786.5627
email:
gracemoravian@earthlink.net
www.gracemoravianchurch.org

NEWTON -
New Hope Church
2897 Sandy Ford Road
Newton NC 28658
O: 828.294.4802
F: 828.294.1237
email: newhopemoravian@aol.com

OAK RIDGE -
Moravia Church
2920 Oak Ridge Road
Oak Ridge NC 27310
O: 336.643.5166
F: 336.643.5166 (call first)

RALEIGH -
Raleigh Church
1816 Ridge Road
Raleigh NC 27607
O: 919.787.4034
F: 919.787.4250
www.raleighmoravian.org

RURAL HALL -
Mizpah Church
3165 Mizpah Church Road
Rural Hall NC 27045
O: 336.924.1661

Rural Hall Church
7939 Broad Street
Rural Hall NC 27045
Mail: PO Box 487
Rural Hall NC 27045-0487
O: 336.969.9488
F: 336.969.1819
email: rhmoravian@msn.com
www.rhmc.org

WALNUT COVE -
Fulp Church
1556 US 311 Highway S
Walnut Cove NC 27052
O: 336.591.7940
email: fulpmoravian@aol.com

WILMINGTON -
Covenant Church
4126 S College Road
Wilmington NC 28412
O: 910.799.9256
F: 910.799.9256 (call first)

WINSTON-SALEM -
Advent Church
1514 W Clemmonsville Road
Winston-Salem NC 27127
O: 336.788.4951
F: 336.788.0739
email: amchurch@triad.rr.com
www.adventmoravian.org

Ardmore Church
2013 W Academy Street
Winston-Salem NC 27103
O: 336.723.3444
F: 336.723.5710
email: officeamc@triad.rr.com
www.ardmoremoravian.org

Bethabara Church
2100 Bethabara Road
Winston-Salem NC 27106
O: 336.924.8789
F: 336.924.8789 (call first)
email: office@bethabara.org
www.bethabara.org

Bethesda Church
740 Bethesda Road
Winston-Salem NC 27103
O: 336.765.1357
F: 336.768.6977

Calvary Church
600 Holly Avenue
Winston-Salem NC 27101
O: 336.722.3703
F: 336.724.1956 (call first)
email:
ncalvarymoravia@triad.rr.com
www.calvarymoravian.org

Christ Church
919 W Academy Street
Winston-Salem NC 27101-5103
O: 336.722.2007
F: 336.722.2004
www.christmoravianchurch.org

Fairview Church
6550 Silas Creek Parkway
Winston-Salem NC 27106
O: 336.768.5629
F: 336.768.5637
email:
fmc@fairviewmoravianchurch.org
www.fairviewmoravianchurch.org

Friedberg Church
2178 Friedberg Church Road
Winston-Salem NC 27127-9073
O: 336.764.1830
F: 336.764.4524
email: info@friedbergmoravian.org
www.friedbergmoravian.org

Friedland Church
2750 Friedland Church Road
Winston-Salem NC 27107
O: 336.788.2652
F: 336.788.0305

Fries Memorial Church
251 N Hawthorne Road NW
Winston-Salem NC 27104
O: 336.722.2847
F: 336.722.2132
email: frieschurch@aol.com

Home Church
529 S Church Street
Winston-Salem NC 27101
O: 336.722.6171
F: 336.723.5085
email:
home1771@homemoravian.org
www.homemoravian.org

Hope Church
2759 Hope Church Road
Winston-Salem NC 27127
O: 336.765.8017
email: pastormerritt@bellsouth.net
www.hopemoravian.org

Hopewell Church
701 Hopewell Church Road
Winston-Salem NC 27127
O: 336.788.2289

Immanuel-New Eden Church
3680 Old Lexington Road
Winston-Salem NC 27127
O: 336.788.1561

Konnoak Hills Church
3401 Konnoak Drive
Winston-Salem NC 27127
O: 336.788.9321
F: 336.785.0211
email: khmc3401@bellsouth.net
www.khmoravian.org

La Iglesia Moravia - Cordero de Dios
(Lamb of God Moravian Church)
2009 Peachtree Street
Winston-Salem NC 27107
O: 336.788.4148

Messiah Church
1401 Peace Haven Road
Winston-Salem NC 27104-1397
O: 336.765.5961
F: 336.659.6642
email: messiah1@bellsouth.net

New Philadelphia Church
4440 Country Club Road
Winston-Salem NC 27104
O: 336.765.2331
O: 336.768.5961
F: 336.765.5536
www.npmc.org

Oak Grove Church
120 Hammock Farm Road
Winston-Salem NC 27105
O: 336.595.8167
email:
oakgrovemoravian@earthlink.net

Olivet Church
2205 Olivet Church Road
Winston-Salem NC 27106
O: 336.924.8063
F: 336.922.9005
email: olivet@alltel.net
www.olivetmoravian.org

Pine Chapel
324 Goldfloss Street
Winston-Salem NC 27127
O: 336.723.7118
email: pinechapel1@juno.com

Providence Church
929 Old Hollow Road
Winston-Salem NC 27105
O: 336.767.8234
F: 336.767.8234

St. Philips Church
3002 Bon Air Avenue
Winston-Salem NC 27105
O: 336.722.3933

Trinity Church
220 E Sprague Street
Winston-Salem NC 27127
O: 336.724.5541 or 336.724.5542
F: 336.724.1246
email: office@trinitymoravian.org
www.trinitymoravian.org

Union Cross Church
4295 High Point Road
Winston-Salem NC 27107
O: 336.769.2411
email: ucmc@bellsouth.net
www.unioncrossmoravian.org

NORTH DAKOTA (NP, WD):

DAVENPORT -
Canaan Church
4465 159 Avenue SE
Davenport ND 58021
O: 701.347.4730

DURBIN -
Goshen Church
4201 153rd Avenue SE
Durbin ND 58059
Mail: PO Box 336
Leonard ND 58052
O: 701.645.2466

FARGO -
Shepherd of the Prairie
6151 25th Street S
Fargo ND 58104
O: 701.235.5711 or 701.645.2466
email: office@shepherdfargo.org
www.shepherdfargo.org

LEONARD -
Bethel Church
State Highway 18
Leonard ND 58052
Mail: PO Box 336
Leonard ND 58052
O: 701.645.2466 or 701.645.2436

OHIO (NP, ED):

DOVER -
First Church
319 Walnut Street
Dover OH 44622
O: 330.364.8831
F: 330.602.6711
email:
pastor@firstmoravianchurch.org
www.firstmoravianchurch.org

DUBLIN -
Church of the Redeemer
3883 Summitview Road
Dublin OH 43016-8426
O: 614.766.5030
or 614.766.5032
www.redeemermoravian.org

GNADENHUTTEN -
Gnadenhutten Church
145 N Walnut Street
Gnadenhutten OH 44629
Mail: PO Box 126
Gnadenhutten OH 44629-0126
O: 740.254.4374
email: gnaden1@tusco.net
http://web.tusco.net/gnadenmoravian

Lewis Center—
The Promise
7465 Crossing Place
Lewis Center OH 43035
O: 740.549.1716
email:
pastor@thepromisechurch.net
www.thepromisechurch.net

New Philadelphia -
Fry's Valley Church
594 Fry's Valley Road SW
New Philadelphia OH 44663-7830
O: 740.254.9373
email: frysvalleymc@yahoo.com

Schoenbrunn Community Church
2200 E High Avenue
New Philadelphia OH 44663
O: 330.339.1940
F: 216.274.9998
email:
Secretary@schoenbrunnmoravian.org
www.schoenbrunnmoravian.org

Sharon Church
4776 Moravian Church Road SE
New Philadelphia OH 44663
Mail: PO Box 385
Tuscarawas OH 44682-0385
O: 740.922.5507
F: 740.922.0895
email: smcohio@tusco.net

Uhrichsville -
First Church
315 N Water Street
Uhrichsville OH 44683
O: 740.922.0886

ONTARIO, Canada (NP, ED):

Toronto -
New Dawn Church
7 Glenora Avenue
Toronto ON M6C 3Y2
Canada
O: 416.656.0473
email:
newdawnmoravian@bellnet.ca

PENNSYLVANIA (NP, ED):

Allentown -
Calvary Church
948 N 21st Street
Allentown PA 18104-3785
O: 610.435.6881
email: calvarym@ptd.net

Midway Manor Church
1201 N Ulster Street
Allentown PA 18109
O: 610.434.8041
email: mmmoravian@enter.net

Bethlehem -
Advent Church
3730 Jacksonville Road
Bethlehem PA 18017
O: 610.866.1402 or 610.868.0477
F: 610.868.0507
email: adventmoravian@verizon.net
www.adventmoravianchurch.com

Central Church
73 W Church Street
Bethlehem PA 18018
O: 610.866.5661 or 610.866.0607
F: 610.866.7256
email:
office@centralmoravianchurch.org
www.centralmoravianchurch.org

College Hill Church
72 W Laurel Street
Bethlehem PA 18018
O: 610.867.8291
F: 610.865.3067
email:
church@collegehillmoravian.org
www.collegehillmoravian.org

East Hills Church
1830 Butztown Road
Bethlehem PA 18017
O: 610.868.6481
F: 610.868.6219
email: easthillsmc@enter.net
www.easthillsmc.org

Edgeboro Church
645 Hamilton Avenue
Bethlehem PA 18017
O: 610.866.8793
F: 610.866.8583
email:
churchoffice@edgeboromoravian.org
www.edgeboromoravian.org

West Side Church
402 Third Avenue
Bethlehem PA 18018
O: 610.865.0256
email: mail@westsidemoravian.org
www.westsidemoravian.org

CANADENSIS -
Canadensis Church
Route 447
Canadensis PA 18325
Mail: PO Box 209
Canadensis PA 18325-0209
O: 570.595.7114

CENTER VALLEY -
Grace Church
5900 Old Bethlehem Pike
Center Valley PA 18034
Mail: PO Box 183
Center Valley PA 18034-0183
O: 610.282.3263
email: gracemoravian@yahoo.com

COOPERSBURG -
Coopersburg Church
234 South Main Street
Coopersburg PA 18036
O: 610.282.1908
email: coopmoravian@aol.com

EASTON -
First Church
225 N 10th Street
Easton PA 18042
O: 610.258.6317
email: eastonmoravian@rcn.com
www.firstmoravianeaston.org

Palmer Township Church
2901 John Street
Easton PA 18045-2544
O: 610.253.2510
F: 610.253.7401
email: pmc@palmermoravian.org

EMMAUS -
Emmaus Church
146 Main Street
Emmaus PA 18049
O: 610.965.6067
F: 610.966.5420
email: emcsecretary@verizon.net
www.emmausmoravian.org

HELLERTOWN -
Mountainview Church
331 Constitution Avenue
Hellertown PA 18055
O: 610.838.9344
email:
mountainviewmoravian@verizon.net

LANCASTER -
Lancaster Church
1460 Eden Road
Lancaster PA 17601
O: 717.397.9722
www.lancastermoravian.com

LEBANON -
Lebanon Church
1115 Birch Road
Lebanon PA 17042-9123
O: 717.273.5864
F: 717.273.0255
email: lebmoravian@nbn.net

LITITZ -
Lititz Church
8 Church Square
Lititz PA 17543
O: 717.626.8515
F: 717.626.8258
www.lititzmoravian.org

NAZARETH -
Nazareth Church
4 South Main Street
Center Square
Nazareth PA 18064
Mail: PO Box 315
Nazareth PA 18064-0315
O: 610.759.3163
F: 610.759.3175
email: nazmoroffice@rcn.com
www.nazarethmoravian.org

Schoeneck Church
316 N Broad Street Extension
Nazareth PA 18064
O: 610.759.0376
F: 610.759.9762
email:
schoeneck@schoeneckmoravian.org

NEWFOUNDLAND -
Newfoundland Church
Route 191
Newfoundland PA 18445
Mail: PO Box 221
Newfoundland PA 18445-0221
O: 570.676.8201

PHILADELPHIA -
Redeemer Church
2950 S 70th Street
Philadelphia PA 19142
O: 215.365.6448
www.redeemerphiladelphia.org

READING -
Reading Church
1116 Perry Street
Reading PA 19604-2005
O: 610.374.0886
email:
readingmoravian@1USA.com
www.readingmoravian.org

YORK -
Covenant Church
901 Cape Horn Road
York PA 17402
O: 717.755.3269
email: covenantpastor@comcast.net
www.covenantmoravianyork.org

First Church
39 N Duke Street
York PA 17401
O: 717.843.2239
F: 717.815.0339
email:
yorkfirstmoravian@verizon.net
www.firstmoravianchurch.worthyofpraise.org

VIRGINIA (SP):

ARARAT -
Willow Hill Church
577 Willow Hill Road
Ararat VA 24053

CANA -
Crooked Oak Church
1641 Bear Trail Rd.
Cana VA 24317

Mt. Bethel Church
127 Mt Bethel Road
Cana VA 24317
O: 276.755.4690
email:
Info@mtbethelmoravianchurch.org
www.mtbethelmoravianchurch.org

WISCONSIN (NP, WD):

APPLETON -
Freedom Church
W3457 Center Valley Road
Appleton WI 54913-8937
O: 920.734.1278
email:
freedommoravianchurch@netzero.com

CAMBRIDGE -
London Church
County Road O
Cambridge WI 53523
Mail: N5610 Hwy O
London WI 53523
O: 608.764.1482

DEFOREST -
Christian Faith Church
805 E Holum Street
DeForest WI 53532
O: 608.846.5876

EPHRAIM -
Ephraim Church
9970 Moravia
Ephraim WI 54211
Mail: PO Box 73
Ephraim WI 54211-0073
O: 920.854.2804
email: emoravian@dcwis.com
www.ephraimmoravian.org

GREEN BAY -
East Side Church
505 E Allouez Avenue
Green Bay WI 54301
O: 920.432.1457
F: 920.432.1507
email: eastmoravian@juno.com
www.gbem.org

West Side Church
1707 S Oneida Street
Green Bay WI 54304
O: 920.499.4433
F: 920.499.9966
www.wsmoraviangb.org

Lake Mills -
Lake Mills Church
301 College Street
Lake Mills WI 53551
O: 920.648.5412
F: 920.648.3669
www.lakemillsmoravianchurch.org

Madison -
Glenwood Church
725 Gilmore Street
Madison WI 53711
O: 608.233.8709
F: 608.233.2595

Lakeview Church
3565 Tulane Avenue
Madison WI 53714
O: 608.249.1973
F: 608.249.1588

Pittsvile -
Veedum Church
County Road E
Pittsville WI 54466
Mail: PO Box 244
Pittsville WI 54466-0244
O: 715.884.6911

Rudolph -
Rudolph Church
1490 Main Street
Rudolph WI 54475
Mail: PO Box 144
Rudolph WI 54475-0144
O: 715.435.3333
email:
rudolphmoravianchurch@g2a.net

Sister Bay -
Sister Bay Church
10924 Old Stage Road
Sister Bay WI 54234
O: 920.854.4080
email: mwellert@dcwis.com

Sturgeon Bay -
Sturgeon Bay Church
323 S 5th Avenue
Sturgeon Bay WI 54235
O: 920.743.6218
F: 920.743.0440
email: sbmc@charterinternet.net

Watertown -
Ebenezer Church
N8071 High Road
Watertown WI 53094
O: 920.206.0222
email: emc1853@juno.com

Watertown Church
510 Cole Street
Watertown WI 53094
O: 920.261.7494
F: 920.206.9030
email:
watertownmoravianchurch@yahoo.com
www.watertownmoravianchurch.org

Wisconsin Rapids -
Kellner Church
Junction of County Hwys U and W
Wisconsin Rapids WI 54494
Mail: 8011 County Highway FF
Wisconsin Rapids WI 54494
O/F: 715.423.2688
email: morekell@wctc.net

Saratoga Church
11131 52nd Street S
Wisconsin Rapids WI 54494
O: 715.325.3081

Wisconsin Rapids Church
310 First Avenue S
Wisconsin Rapids WI 54495-4155
O: 715.423.0180
email: moravian@wctc.net
www.wrmoravian.org

MORAVIAN FELLOWSHIPS

CALIFORNIA:

San Diego Fellowship—
Ginger Kullman, *Coordinator*
411 S Beech Street
Escondido CA 92025
O: 619.745.6633

FLORIDA:

Margate Fellowship—
The Rev. Joe Nicholas
6060 SW 7th Street
Margate FL 33068
O: 305.628.2061
F: 305.625.5365

New Covenant Fellowship—
The Rev. Ofreciano Julias
1621 Quail Drive Bldg 203
W Palm Beach FL 33409
O: 561.615.0912

Meeting Location:
West Palm Beach Moravian
297 27th Street
West Palm Beach FL 33407

Surinam Moravian Fellowship—
Alfred Yorks, *Coordinator*
2433 NW 55th Street
Miami FL 33142
O: 305.401.5479

Meeting location:
Prince of Peace Moravian Church
1880 NW 183 Street
Miami FL 33056
O: 305.628.2061

Sarasota Fellowship—
Wycliffe Diego, *Coordinator*
4921 81st Avenue
Terrace East
Sarasota FL 34243
O: 941.355.8370

Meeting location:
4445 S Lockwood Ridge Road
Sarasota FL 34243

Tampa Fellowship—
Federico Velasquez, *Coordinator*
1912 E Shadowlawn Avenue
Tampa FL 33610
O: 813.476.7969

Meeting Location:
St. Paul Lutheran Church
5103 N Central Avenue
Tampa FL 33610

NORTH CAROLINA:

Morning Star Fellowship-
325 Mt Carmel Road
Asheville NC 28806
Hank Jackson, *Provincial Acolyte*
O: 828.251.2081

Community Fellowship—
Welcome-Arcadia Road
Welcome NC 27374
Mail: PO Box 397
Welcome NC 27374-0397
O: 336.731.8265

Jack Nance, *Coordinator*
3733 Konnoak Drive
Winston-Salem NC 27127
O: 336.784.5252

MORAVIAN FELLOWSHIPS CONTINUED

SOUTH CAROLINA:

Palmetto Fellowship—
Martha Stocks, *Coordinator*
105 Pine Tree Circle
Spartanburg SC 29307
O: 864.582.1442

Meeting location:
Central United Methodist Church
233 N Church Street
Spartanburg SC 29307
O: 864.597.0200

WASHINGTON:

Seattle Fellowship—
Maxine Nienow Simmons
31 Koeppe Drive
Sequim WA 98382
O: 360.683.1140

Richard and Joan Thomas
20904 3rd Avenue S
Des Moines WA 98198
O: 206.824.6411
email: jmtthomas@comcast.net

NEW & EMERGING CHURCHES

CALIFORNIA:

Palo Alto —
Faith Moravian Church
The Rev. Raymond Humphrey
PO Box 4034
Menlo Park CA 94026
O: 650.575.4677

INDIANA:

Indianapolis—
New Hope Community Church
The Rev. Jason Graf
7001 Arlington Avenue
Indianapolis IN 46237
O: 317.881.6204
www.newhopeindy.org

MINNESOTA:

St. Michael —
New Horizons Community Church
The Rev. David Glasser
405 5th Street NW
St. Michael MN 55376
O: 763.497.9024
email: newhorizonstma@aol.com
www.newhorizons-stma.org

ONTARIO, CANADA:

Mississauga—
The Journey Community
The Rev. Christopher T. New
Church Planter
c/o 3820 Allcroft Road
Mississuga ON L5N 6V6
Canada
email: journeychurch@sympatico.ca

Winston Josiah, *Administrator*
c/o 1508 - 3605 Kariya Drive
Mississauga ON L5B 3J4
Canada
O: 905.897.1212

MORAVIAN CHURCH IN NORTH AMERICA PROVINCIAL & DISTRICT OFFICES

The Provincial Elders' Conference - Northern Province

The Rev. David L. Wickmann, President
Office: 1021 Center St., PO Box 1245, Bethlehem, PA 18016-1245
O: 610.867.7566, 800.732.0591
www.mcnp.org

NORTHERN PROVINCE - DISTRICT EXECUTIVE BOARDS

Eastern District

The Rev. Gary M. Straughan, President
1021 Center St., PO Box 1245, Bethlehem, PA 18016-1245
O: 610.865.0302, 800.732.0591, F:610.866.9223
www.mcnp.org/edeb/edeb.htm

Western District

The Rev. James T. Hicks, President
750 Windsor St., Suite 209, PO Box 386, Sun Prairie, WI 53590
O: 800.206.5928, 608.837.0537, F: 608.825.6610
email: WDNewsAndNotes@aol.com
www.moravianwest.org

Canadian District

The Rev. Stephen A. Gohdes, President
600 Acadia Dr. SE, Calgary, Alberta T2J 0B8, Canada
O: 403.271.2700
www.moravian.ca/who.html

The Provincial Elders' Conference - Southern Province

The Rt. Rev. Dr. D. Wayne Burkette, President
Office: 459 S. Church St., Winston-Salem, NC 27101
O: 336.725.5811, 888.725.5811, F: 336.723.1029
www.mcsp.org

PRAYER DAYS AND SPECIAL EMPHASES

The following prayer days or special emphases have been authorized by the Northern Provincial Synod or by the Provincial Elders' Conferences of the Northern and Southern Provinces of the Moravian Church in North America:

Ecumenical Sunday: The last Sunday in January.

For Retired Ministers (optional): The last Sunday in January.

For Moravian Unity Work: The first Sunday in March.

For Board of Evangelism and Homeland Missions (Southern Province): The last Sunday in April.

Moravian Music Sunday: Fifth Sunday of Easter (fourth Sunday after Easter).

For Moravian Retirement Community (Southern Province): The second Sunday in May.

For Outdoor Ministries (Northern Province): The Sunday after Trinity.

For Camps & Conferences (Southern Province): The Sunday after Trinity.

For World Peace and Nuclear Disarmament (Northern Province): The first Sunday in August.

For Public Education and Moravian Educational Institutions (Southern Province): The last Sunday in August.

For Public Education (Northern Province): The last Sunday in August.

For Christian Education: The second Sunday in September.

For Church Development (Northern Province): The third Sunday in September.

For the Church's Ministry to Senior Citizens (Northern Province): The fourth Sunday in September.

For Older Adults (Southern Province): The fourth Sunday in September.

For Children: A Sunday in October.

For World Mission: The second Sunday in October.

For Peace with Justice and Freedom (Northern Province): The third Sunday in October.

Moravian Women's Sunday (Northern Province): The first Sunday in November (date optional).

For the Bible Society: The Sunday before Thanksgiving.

For Moravian College and Theological Seminary (Northern Province): The Sunday on or immediately after November 20.

World AIDS Day: December 1st.

CHURCH CAUSES

Northern Province

Members and friends of the Moravian Church can show continuing interest in its work by making the Church a beneficiary in their will or by making an outright monetary gift. The programs of the Northern Province are administered by the following incorporated boards:

Moravian Church, Northern Province
The Society for Promoting the Gospel
Trustees of the Moravian Larger Life Foundation
The Provincial Women's Board
The Moravian Archives
The Executive Board of the Eastern District of the Moravian Church in America, Northern Province
The Executive Board of the Eastern District of the Moravian Church in America, Northern Province for the Foster Fund
Hope Conference and Renewal Center
Moravian Hall Square Historic District, Inc.
Moravian Hall Square Retirement Community, Inc.
Moravian Manors, Inc.
Moravian Open Door, Inc.
Sperling-Zimmerman Memorial Home
The Executive Board of the Western District of the Moravian Church in America, Northern Province
Marquardt Memorial Manor, Inc.
Moravian Care Ministries, Inc.
Mt. Morris Camp and Conference Center
The Board of Elders of the Canadian District of the Moravian Church in America, Northern Province
Canadian Moravian Foundation
Van Es Camp and Conference Centre
Board of World Mission of the Moravian Church
Moravian Music Foundation, Inc.
Linden Hall Seminary at Lititz, Pennsylvania
Moravian Academy
Moravian College
Moravian Theological Seminary
Interprovincial Board of Communication

Southern Province

The programs of the Southern Province are administered by the following boards and agencies:

The Provincial Elders' Conference
The Board of Evangelism and Homeland Missions*
Mission Society of the Moravian Church, South, Inc.
Board of World Mission of the Moravian Church
Salem Academy and College
The Board of Christian Education*
Laurel Ridge, Moravian Camp, Conference, & Retreat Center*
The Archives*
Salemtowne
The Pension Fund*
Moravian Music Foundation, Inc.
Provincial Women's Board*
Moravian Theological Seminary
Sunnyside Ministry*
Interprovincial Board of Communication

**Not incorporated. Bequests to these boards and agencies should be made for their use to the Moravian Church in America, Southern Province.*

REMITTANCES

Contributions for provincial or general church causes should be sent to the provincial treasurer:

NORTHERN PROVINCE: Controller, 1021 Center Steet, PO Box 1245, Bethlehem, Pennysylvania 18016-1245

SOUTHERN PROVINCE: Treasurer, 459 South Church Street, Winston-Salem, North Carolina 27101

PLANNED GIFTS AND BEQUESTS: For information about estate plans or information about charitable trusts, annuities, and other forms of planned gifts to support one or more of the above ministries or your church, contact Paul McLaughlin, President of Moravian Ministries Foundation at 455 South Church Street, Winston-Salem, North Carolina 27101, phone 888.722.7923.

HISTORICAL NOTES

Organization dates of congregations in the United States and Canada and dates of the worldwide Moravian Church:

JANUARY

1-	1815	Sharon, Tuscarawas, Ohio
	1858	Chaska, Minnesota
	1915	Waconia, Minnesota
	1968	United, New York, New York, merger of New York III and IV
3-	1856	Ordination of John Andrew Buckley, the first Moravian minister of African descent, Antigua, West Indies
	1932	First service of confirmation of Moravians in Honduras
5-	1992	New Hope, Miami, Florida
6-	1963	Church of the Good Shepherd, Utica, New York, continuing three congregations in Utica dating back to 1856
12-	1757	The first Moravian convert baptized on Antigua, West Indies
19-	1964	Rio Terrace, Edmonton, Alberta, Canada
20-	1889	Wisconsin Rapids, Wisconsin
21-	1951	Konnoak Hills, Winston-Salem, North Carolina
28-	1966	Palm Beach, West Palm Beach, Florida
30-	1864	Sturgeon Bay, Wisconsin
31-	1971	St. Paul's, Upper Marlboro, Maryland

FEBRUARY

2-	1891	Bethel, Leonard, North Dakota
	1964	Trinity, New Carrollton, Maryland
3-	1957	Official organization of Morongo Moravian Church, Banning, California; result of Indian mission work begun in 1889
9-	1749	Warwick, now Lititz, Lititz, Pennsylvania
12-	1978	Covenant, Wilmington, North Carolina
	1989	Good Shepherd, Kernersville, North Carolina
13-	1870	Unionville, Michigan
	1983	New Hope, Newton, North Carolina

MARCH

1-	1457	Date observed in commemoration of the founding in Bohemia of the Unitas Fratrum, now known as the Moravian Church
5-	1939	Calvary, Allentown, Pennsylvania

MARCH (Continued)

14- 1849 Arrival of first Moravian missionaries in Bluefields, Nicaragua
1886 Great Kills, Staten Island, New York
1951 Mountainview, Hellertown, Pennsylvania
15- 1925 Grace, Mount Airy, North Carolina
21- 1993 King of Kings, Miami, Florida
23- 1975 First, Stone Mountain, Georgia
24- 1799 The first Moravian converts baptized on Tobago, West Indies
25- 1752 First, York, Pennsylvania
1995 Morning Star, Asheville, North Carolina
27- 1966 John Hus, Brooklyn, New York
28- 1954 Lakeview, Madison, Wisconsin

APRIL

1- 1756 Arrival on Antigua, West Indies, of Samuel Isles, the first Moravian missionary on that island
1888 First, Easton, Pennsylvania
3- 1896 Sister Bay, Wisconsin
4- 1773 Friedberg, Winston-Salem, North Carolina
6- 1851 Olivet, Winston-Salem, North Carolina
7- 1929 Glenwood, Madison, Wisconsin
9- 1917 Veedum, Pittsville, Wisconsin
10- 1949 Palmer Township, Easton, Pennsylvania
1988 Good News, Sherwood Park, Alberta, Canada
11- 1898 Enterprise, Arcadia, North Carolina
13- 1732 The first Easter sunrise service of the Moravians conducted in the Hutberg cemetery at Herrnhut, Germany
1760 Bethania, North Carolina
1859 Egg Harbor City, New Jersey
1885 Windsor, now Christian Faith, DeForest, Wisconsin
21- 1929 Leaksville, Eden, North Carolina
1976 Our Savior's, Altura, Minnesota, merger of Bethany and Hebron
25- 1890 Arrival on Trinidad, West Indies, of Samuel Thaeler and John Holmes to organize Moravian work on that island
27- 1790 Arrival on Tobago, West Indies, of John and Mary Montgomery (parents of hymnwriter James Montgomery) to begin Moravian work on that island

APRIL (Continued)

1852 New York II, now Tremont Terrace, Bronx, New York
1969 Christ, Calgary, Alberta, Canada

MAY

3- 1728 Beginning of Losungen (Daily Texts) in Herrnhut, Germany
1931 Rural Hall, North Carolina
5- 1822 St. Philip's, Winston-Salem, North Carolina
1895 Fairview, Winston-Salem, North Carolina
6- 1860 West Side, Bethlehem, Pennsylvania
1895 Bruderheim, Alberta, Canada
12- 1727 Unanimous adoption of the first statutes, or Brotherly Agreement, by the settlers at Herrnhut, Germany, the first definite step toward reorganization of the Unitas Fratrum
17- 1863 Palmyra, Cinnaminson, New Jersey
18- 1902 Calgary, now Good Shepherd, Calgary, Alberta, Canada
19- 2002 New Beginnings, Huntersville, North Carolina
22- 1966 Redeemer, Philadelphia, Pennsylvania
1983 Christ's Community Church, Maple Grove, Minnesota
24- 1856 Macedonia, Advance, North Carolina
1878 Goshen, Durbin, North Dakota
25- 1844 West Salem, Illinois
1986 Faith Church of the Nation's Capital, Washington, D.C.
26- 1853 Ephraim, Wisconsin
1963 Acceptance of Saratoga Union, Wisconsin Rapids, Wisconsin, as a Moravian congregation

JUNE

1- 1895 Rudolph, Wisconsin
5- 1898 Willow Hill, Ararat, Virginia
6- 1954 Downey, California
9- 1957 East Hills, Bethlehem, Pennsylvania
11- 1857 Fry's Valley, New Philadelphia, Ohio
12- 1905 Edmonton, Alberta, Canada
1943 Fargo, now Shepherd of the Prairie, Fargo, North Dakota
1955 Battle Hill, Union, New Jersey, continuing the Elizabeth, New Jersey, congregation begun in 1866

JUNE (Continued)

14- 1777 Arrival of the first Moravian missionaries on St. Kitts, West Indies

17- 1722 Beginning of the building of Herrnhut, Germany, by the emigrants from Moravia

1830 Hope, Indiana

1853 Ebenezer, Watertown, Wisconsin

18- 1932 Hopewell, Winston-Salem, North Carolina

20- 1884 Arrival of first Moravian missionaries in Bethel, Alaska

21- 1621 The Day of Blood, so called because on that day 27 patriots, most of them members of the Brethren's Church, were executed at Prague, Bohemia

1924 Advent, Winston-Salem, North Carolina

1958 Grace, Westland, Michigan

25- 1742 Central, Bethlehem, Pennsylvania

1747 Nazareth, Pennsylvania

1876 Fries Memorial, Winston-Salem, North Carolina

26- 1988 Fellowship, Brooklyn, New York

27- 1895 Bruderfeld, now Millwoods, Edmonton, Alberta, Canada

29- 1924 Ardmore, Winston-Salem, North Carolina

JULY

6- 1415 Burning at the stake of John Hus, Bohemian martyr and forebear of the Unitas Fratrum

1763 New Dorp, Staten Island, New York

1800 Gnadenhutten, Ohio

14- 1912 Trinity, Winston-Salem, North Carolina

17- 1955 Grace, Center Valley, Pennsylvania

1927 Crooked Oak, Cana, Virginia

26- 1846 New Philadelphia, Winston-Salem, North Carolina

1896 Heimtal, South Edmonton, Alberta, Canada

30- 1747 Emmaus, Pennsylvania

31- 1752 Arrival of first Moravian missionaries in Labrador

AUGUST

13- 1727 Manifestation of the unity of the Spirit, at the Holy Communion service held in the Berthelsdorf, Germany, church; regarded as the spiritual birthday of the Renewed Moravian Church

AUGUST (Continued)

1837	Newfoundland, Pennsylvania
1900	Clemmons, North Carolina
21- 1732	Departure of the first Moravian missionaries from Herrnhut for St. Thomas in the West Indies; the beginning of Moravian missions and of the modern missionary movement of the Protestant church
26- 1780	Hope, Winston-Salem, North Carolina
2001	The Promise, Lewis Center, Ohio
27- 1727	Beginning of the Hourly Intercession
1872	Formation of the Moravian Prayer Union
31- 1873	Castleton Hill, Staten Island, New York

SEPTEMBER

3- 1780	Friedland, Winston-Salem, North Carolina
5- 1869	Northfield, Minnesota
10- 1911	Daggett, Michigan
11- 1854	Watertown, Wisconsin
13- 1893	Union Cross, Winston-Salem, North Carolina
1896	Mizpah, Rural Hall, North Carolina
15- 2003	Holly Springs, North Carolina
16- 1741	Recognition and acceptance of Christ as the Chief Elder of the Moravian Church
1858	Canadensis, Pennsylvania
1984	New Dawn, Toronto, Ontario, Canada
18- 1768	Baptism of the first Moravian convert on Barbados, West Indies
25- 1887	Oak Grove, Winston-Salem, North Carolina
26- 1765	Arrival of John Wood and Andrew Rittsmansberger on Barbados, West Indies, from Herrnhut to begin Moravian work
29- 1946	Midway Manor, Allentown, Pennsylvania

OCTOBER

2- 1807	Beginning of the Moravian Theological Seminary at Nazareth, Pennsylvania, in 1858 transferred to Bethlehem
3- 1762	Schoeneck, Nazareth, Pennsylvania
1896	Moravia, Summerfield, North Carolina
4- 1953	Raleigh, North Carolina

OCTOBER (Continued)

5- 1908 First, Greensboro, North Carolina
1924 King, North Carolina
6- 1889 London, Cambridge, Wisconsin
7- 2002 Immanuel-New Eden, merger of Immanuel (1912) and New Eden (1923)
8- 1758 Graceham, Thurmont, Maryland
1967 Rolling Hills, Longwood, Florida
10- 1885 Moving into the first house in Bethel, Alaska, by missionaries John Kilbuck and William Weinland
12- 1851 East Side, Green Bay, Wisconsin
17- 2004 Cordero de Dios, Winston-Salem, North Carolina
18- 1889 Stapleton, now Vanderbilt Avenue, Staten Island, New York
20- 1985 Church of the Redeemer, Dublin, Ohio
22- 1899 Bethesda, Winston-Salem, North Carolina
23- 1881 Canaan, Davenport, North Dakota
24- 1874 First, Uhrichsville, Ohio
25- 1896 Christ, Winston-Salem, North Carolina
1914 Edgeboro, Bethlehem, Pennsylvania
31- 1858 Lake Auburn, Victoria, Minnesota

NOVEMBER

7- 1920 The Little Church on the Lane, Charlotte, North Carolina
9- 1980 Grace, Queens, New York
10- 1867 Kernersville, North Carolina
11- 1893 Fulp, Walnut Cove, North Carolina
12- 1909 Kellner, Wisconsin Rapids, Wisconsin
13- 1741 Formal announcement to the congregations of the Moravian Church of the immediate Headship of the Lord Jesus Christ in his church on earth
1771 Home, Winston-Salem, North Carolina
1893 Calvary, Winston-Salem, North Carolina
1965 Covenant, York, Pennsylvania, merger of Bethany and Olivet
14- 1779 Baptism of the first Moravian convert on St. Kitts, West Indies
16- 1924 Pine Chapel, Winston-Salem, North Carolina
1980 Unity, Lewisville, North Carolina

NOVEMBER (Continued)

17- 1753 Arrival of the first Moravians from Bethlehem, Pennsylvania, on the Wachovia Tract in North Carolina to establish a settlement; observed as the anniversary of Bethabara, the first congregation of the Southern Province

1850 Fort Howard, now West Side, Green Bay, Wisconsin

18- 1930 Beginning of Moravian work in Honduras by George Heath in Cauquira

1951 Messiah, Winston-Salem, North Carolina

21- 1880 Providence, Winston-Salem, North Carolina

24- 1963 Park Road, Charlotte, North Carolina, name Peace adopted in 1999

1991 Christ the King, Durham, North Carolina

25- 1852 Mt. Bethel, Cana, Virginia

29- 1896 Mayodan, North Carolina

30- 1746 Lancaster, Pennsylvania

1986 Prince of Peace, Miami, Florida

DECEMBER

4- 1874 Berea, St. Charles, Minnesota

9- 1883 Coopersburg, Pennsylvania

11- 1887 College Hill, Bethlehem, Pennsylvania

13- 1732 Arrival of Leonard Dober and David Nitschmann, the first foreign missionaries of the Moravian Church, on St. Thomas, West Indies

16- 1877 Fries Memorial, Winston-Salem, North Carolina

17- 1914 Reading, Pennsylvania

19- 1747 Lebanon, Pennsylvania

21- 1856 Lake Mills, Wisconsin

22- 1866 Freedom, Appleton, Wisconsin

25- 1862 First, South Bethlehem, Pennsylvania, now Advent, Bethlehem, Pennsylvania

27- 1748 First, New York, New York

1842 First, Dover, Ohio

31- 1865 First, Riverside, New Jersey

1947 Schoenbrunn, New Philadelphia, Ohio

2008

JANUARY

S	M	T	W	T	F	S
		1	2	3	4	5
6	7	8	9	10	11	12
13	14	15	16	17	18	19
20	21	22	23	24	25	26
27	28	29	30	31		

FEBRUARY

S	M	T	W	T	F	S
					1	2
3	4	5	6	7	8	9
10	11	12	13	14	15	16
17	18	19	20	21	22	23
24	25	26	27	28	29	

MARCH

S	M	T	W	T	F	S
						1
2	3	4	5	6	7	8
9	10	11	12	13	14	15
16	17	18	19	20	21	22
23	24	25	26	27	28	29
30	31					

APRIL

S	M	T	W	T	F	S
		1	2	3	4	5
6	7	8	9	10	11	12
13	14	15	16	17	18	19
20	21	22	23	24	25	26
27	28	29	30			

MAY

S	M	T	W	T	F	S
				1	2	3
4	5	6	7	8	9	10
11	12	13	14	15	16	17
18	19	20	21	22	23	24
25	26	27	28	29	30	31

JUNE

S	M	T	W	T	F	S
1	2	3	4	5	6	7
8	9	10	11	12	13	14
15	16	17	18	19	20	21
22	23	24	25	26	27	28
29	30					

JULY

S	M	T	W	T	F	S
		1	2	3	4	5
6	7	8	9	10	11	12
13	14	15	16	17	18	19
20	21	22	23	24	25	26
27	28	29	30	31		

AUGUST

S	M	T	W	T	F	S
					1	2
3	4	5	6	7	8	9
10	11	12	13	14	15	16
17	18	19	20	21	22	23
24	25	26	27	28	29	30
31						

SEPTEMBER

S	M	T	W	T	F	S
	1	2	3	4	5	6
7	8	9	10	11	12	13
14	15	16	17	18	19	20
21	22	23	24	25	26	27
28	29	30				

OCTOBER

S	M	T	W	T	F	S
			1	2	3	4
5	6	7	8	9	10	11
12	13	14	15	16	17	18
19	20	21	22	23	24	25
26	27	28	29	30	31	

NOVEMBER

S	M	T	W	T	F	S
						1
2	3	4	5	6	7	8
9	10	11	12	13	14	15
16	17	18	19	20	21	22
23	24	25	26	27	28	29
30						

DECEMBER

S	M	T	W	T	F	S
	1	2	3	4	5	6
7	8	9	10	11	12	13
14	15	16	17	18	19	20
21	22	23	24	25	26	27
28	29	30	31			

2009

JANUARY

S	M	T	W	T	F	S
…	…	…	…	1	2	3
4	5	6	7	8	9	10
11	12	13	14	15	16	17
18	19	20	21	22	23	24
25	26	27	28	29	30	31
…	…	…	…	…	…	…

FEBRUARY

S	M	T	W	T	F	S
1	2	3	4	5	6	7
8	9	10	11	12	13	14
15	16	17	18	19	20	21
22	23	24	25	26	27	28
…	…	…	…	…	…	…
…	…	…	…	…	…	…

MARCH

S	M	T	W	T	F	S
1	2	3	4	5	6	7
8	9	10	11	12	13	14
15	16	17	18	19	20	21
22	23	24	25	26	27	28
29	30	31	…	…	…	…
…	…	…	…	…	…	…

APRIL

S	M	T	W	T	F	S
…	…	…	1	2	3	4
5	6	7	8	9	10	11
12	13	14	15	16	17	18
19	20	21	22	23	24	25
26	27	28	29	30	…	…
…	…	…	…	…	…	…

MAY

S	M	T	W	T	F	S
…	…	…	…	…	1	2
3	4	5	6	7	8	9
10	11	12	13	14	15	16
17	18	19	20	21	22	23
24	25	26	27	28	29	30
31	…	…	…	…	…	…

JUNE

S	M	T	W	T	F	S
…	1	2	3	4	5	6
7	8	9	10	11	12	13
14	15	16	17	18	19	20
21	22	23	24	25	26	27
28	29	30	…	…	…	…
…	…	…	…	…	…	…

JULY

S	M	T	W	T	F	S
…	…	…	1	2	3	4
5	6	7	8	9	10	11
12	13	14	15	16	17	18
19	20	21	22	23	24	25
26	27	28	29	30	31	…
…	…	…	…	…	…	…

AUGUST

S	M	T	W	T	F	S
…	…	…	…	…	…	1
2	3	4	5	6	7	8
9	10	11	12	13	14	15
16	17	18	19	20	21	22
23	24	25	26	27	28	29
30	31	…	…	…	…	…

SEPTEMBER

S	M	T	W	T	F	S
…	…	1	2	3	4	5
6	7	8	9	10	11	12
13	14	15	16	17	18	19
20	21	22	23	24	25	26
27	28	29	30	…	…	…
…	…	…	…	…	…	…

OCTOBER

S	M	T	W	T	F	S
…	…	…	…	1	2	3
4	5	6	7	8	9	10
11	12	13	14	15	16	17
18	19	20	21	22	23	24
25	26	27	28	29	30	31
…	…	…	…	…	…	…

NOVEMBER

S	M	T	W	T	F	S
1	2	3	4	5	6	7
8	9	10	11	12	13	14
15	16	17	18	19	20	21
22	23	24	25	26	27	28
29	30	…	…	…	…	…
…	…	…	…	…	…	…

DECEMBER

S	M	T	W	T	F	S
…	…	1	2	3	4	5
6	7	8	9	10	11	12
13	14	15	16	17	18	19
20	21	22	23	24	25	26
27	28	29	30	31	…	…
…	…	…	…	…	…	…